Cutted Chicken
in Shanghai

To: Jan Zahrly,
with thanks for your
work in the Peace Corps.

Sharon Winters

祝好.

温丽霞

7 Jan 2014

Cutted Chicken in Shanghai

Sharon Winters

To Marsha Keener, who said, "Being human isn't about being perfect."

To Russell Baker, who wrote my favorite book—*Growing Up.*

"The limits of my language mean the limits of my world."
—Ludwig Wittgenstein

"If you talk to a man in a language he understands, that goes to his head. If you talk to him in his own language, that goes to his heart."
—Nelson Mandela

Acknowledgments

To fellow Mensans, G. Gordon Graham, Joanne Soper, and Bob Meadows, thank you for volunteering to proofread my manuscript and for catching what I missed. This book is a better book because of you, and Gordon, thank you for thinking of the perfect title for this book. To my Chinese friend, Stella, we loved having you visit us here in the States, and I am grateful for your sacrifice of some shopping time to check my Chinese for accuracy. Any remaining errors or confusions are my fault.

To all of my Chinese friends, thank you for becoming part of my life and for teaching me about food, fun, friendship, language, pearls, and the use of chopsticks. I have not forgotten any of you, which means that wherever I go, you are with me. To all of my friends who have ever shared time with me—a minute or many years—you are the colors that have added brilliance to my life, which otherwise would be in black and white.

To those of you who trusted me to use your photos and real names without asking me what I was going to say about you in my book or what photos I planned to use, thank you for your trust and for adding much to the fun I had in Shanghai.

A commendation, however, goes to Martin, who not only allowed me to use his name and photos but gave me complete freedom to write this book without ever asking me what stories I was going to tell about him.

CONTENTS

PREFACE

Sometimes I am a storyteller, and the tales my listeners enjoy the most are real-life stories. Some of their favorite tales are about the years I lived in Shanghai, China, from 1997 until 1999. When my listeners requested real-life stories in the form of a book, especially about my life in Shanghai, the time had come for me to write *Cutted Chicken in Shanghai*.

I kept a journal while I lived in Shanghai and have used this narrative to create a mythical window into the life I lived there. I threw this window open and watched once again the happenings that made me laugh or wonder. I even leaned out this window and yelled hello and *nihao* to the people who have crossed my path, and they waved back to me.

To read *Cutted Chicken in Shanghai* is to sit with me on this window ledge and look out at the landscape of the Middle Kingdom. I can point out where I lived, and the things I did, and the people—they are the most interesting of all.

When my American friends ask me about China, a few stories cannot tell the tale. But perhaps this book can describe my life in Shanghai and the difficult, inspiring, and funny experiences I had, which I now pass on with this book.

In order to give the reader a sense of what it is like to speak and read Mandarin, I have included some pinyin, Chinese characters, and translations of Chinese into English. Pinyin is the phonetic spelling of Chinese characters using the Roman alphabet, and I have left off the tone marks for the most part. The italicized sentences in quotation marks are translations of spoken Chinese into English.

When I was president of New Mexico Mensa, I wrote a column as well as stories for the organizational newsletter, *The New Mensican*, and this book includes some of these stories. Writing contributions made to the *MENSA BULLETIN: The Magazine of American MENSA* and *The Rodent Reader Quarterly* have also been included.

INTRODUCTION

I heard on the radio that the State Department sends English speakers to an intensive language school for six months to learn to read, write, and speak French, but thirty five months to learn Mandarin. This was not good news. The company my husband Martin worked for transferred us to Shanghai, China. Mandarin is China's national language.

To prepare for living in Shanghai, I studied Mandarin at the University of New Mexico. The professor who taught my Chinese class said I knew enough Chinese to manage in China. Really?

Martin and I stayed at a hotel in Shanghai for two weeks. We saw the apartment where we would live, and I got a sense of what life might be like in Shanghai. The Metro is a grocery, clothing, and housewares store. One day, I hailed a cab and told the driver in Mandarin, *"I want to go to the Metro. The address is 80 Gudai Lu."* He took me to a bowling alley. As a result, I knew I would be studying Chinese again once we moved to Shanghai. Speaking Mandarin and reading some Chinese would be necessary for my adjustment to living in Shanghai.

The monthly rent on our Shanghai apartment was forty-three hundred dollars for two bedrooms, two bathrooms, and a kitchen with no dishwasher, no garbage disposal, no oven, no drawers, no counter space, or anything that I would call a refrigerator. The kitchen, however, did have cabinets, two sinks with running water, and four working gas burners. This twenty-eight-floor apartment-hotel building had guards at the front door, an indoor Olympic-sized swimming pool, three restaurants, and a hair salon. Half of the building was apartments, and the other half was hotel rooms.

Once we moved into our apartment, the company gave me three thousand dollars to spend on equipping the kitchen, and to my surprise, this was not too much money. I bought shelving, dishes, containers, utensils, knives, chopsticks, pots, pans, and more. For kitchen appliances, I bought a microwave, slow cooker, coffee pot, food processor, egg beaters, egg poacher, blender, juicer, and a tiny oven that looked like a child's toy. With a ten-inch-wide oven rack, there would be no Thanksgiving turkey. I didn't take any of my kitchen appliances to China because the voltage in China was 220.

While the English name for this building where we would be living is The Supreme Tower, the Chinese name is Ming Cheng Hua Yuan, which means *Bright City Flower Garden*. I came to call it The Tower. In China, there is seldom a correlation between English and Chinese names for restaurants, shops, apartment buildings, and hotels.

The Tower is located in an area of Shanghai called Pudong. The Huangpu River divides the city of Shanghai into an east side and a west side. The east side is Pudong, and the west side is Puxi. From 1978 until 1992, Deng Xiaoping, one of the Chinese leaders at the time, greatly influenced the modernization of China. He designated Pudong, which was farmland before 1990, to be the catalyst for China's new economic growth in finance, free trade, and high-tech manufacturing. In Pudong, there is an area called the Free Trade Zone, and located within this zone is the high-tech manufacturing plant where Martin worked.

When Martin and I returned to the States from our two-week visit to Shanghai, packers for an international shipping company came to our house. They packed fifteen hundred pounds of food and household goods into one large shipping container. Only food that was itemized on The Martin Food List was placed in this container. The Martin Food List is the list of food Martin considers to be edible, and Chinese food has been banished and barred from this list, and yes, we were moving to China.

Among the food items the shippers packed were fifty cans of tuna, fifty cans of chili with no beans, and fifty pounds of dry pinto beans. The most essential food items the shippers packed were Martin's favorite cookies. The shippers also packed ten books of Bugs Bunny stamps and ten Warner Brothers Studio cartoon character mugs. The stamps and mugs would be gifts for our new Chinese friends, although we didn't know who they were yet. We wanted gifts that could only be purchased in the States.

Also included in this shipment were fifty cans of Dinty Moore Stew, which Martin mistakenly calls Demi Moore Stew. Martin's first language is Spanish, and sometimes he mishears a word in English and pronounces it his own way. Martin mentioned to his friends at work that he was moving to Shanghai and taking fifty cans of Demi Moore Stew. A few days before we left the States, Martin's friends gave him a care package. Several boxes of cookies were inside the box along with a can of Dinty Moore Stew with a retyped label over the can that read, "Demi Moore Stew." When Martin makes a mistake in English, he says, "English isn't my first language!"

Sometimes Martin conjugates English words in order to say precisely what he means. My favorite "Martin word" is entangemental—tangent and entanglement. Martin and I were having dinner with some friends when he said, "This is an entangemental situation." Martin knew what he was talking about. The rest of us, however, had never heard this word before, and we were all college graduates with extensive vocabularies. We finally determined that this word came from the *Martin's Modern New English Dictionary*: Entangemental, *adj.* something that will neither involve nor intrigue someone. [1995, *Amer.*]

However, the occasional difficulty Martin had with mispronouncing and conjugating English words no one ever heard of before was nothing compared to the abysmal difficulty Martin had with Mandarin. This language deserves its reputation as one of the five most challenging languages.

Once we were living in Shanghai, Martin worked at least sixty hours every week, and it was up to me to figure out how to do whatever needed to be done at home. I enrolled at Fudan University in Shanghai and intensively studied Mandarin from September 1997 until May 1998. The company paid for all of my Chinese lessons and textbooks starting with the lessons I took at the University of New Mexico.

THE MANDARIN LANGUAGE

My greatest challenge while living in Shanghai was the language. The Mandarin and Wu dialects are two of the seven major dialects in China. The Shanghainese dialect is a subdialect of the Wu dialect and is spoken by many people living in Shanghai. While most people living in Shanghai speak Mandarin as well as Shanghainese, many older people in Shanghai only speak Shanghainese.

One of the problems with having seven major dialects is that people from different regions of China speak Mandarin accented with the major dialect of their region. Also, sounds that accent the native dialect of a region are often tacked onto Mandarin words.

The Beijing accent tacks on the sound of "er" to many Mandarin words. One such word is *na*, which becomes *nar*, and means either *there* or *where* depending on the tone that is used. In Shanghai, people say *nali* instead of *nar*. With the Beijing accent, *yi dian*, which means *a little*, becomes *yi dianr*, and *zheli*, which means *here*, becomes *zher*. In Shanghai, I said *nali*, *zheli*, and *yi dian*, unless I was in Beijing, and then I said *nar* and *zher* and *yi dianr* even though *yi dianr* sounded quirky to me.

The Beijing accent was not used at Fudan University in Shanghai, which was where I studied Chinese. Shanghai people think Beijing people don't know how to speak Mandarin, and vice versa.

On my first trip to Beijing, I quickly learned that the Mandarin spoken in Beijing is different from the Mandarin spoken in Shanghai. For example, when the people in Beijing pronounce words beginning with an "r," such as *ren*, which means *person*, they make this sound by flattening both sides of the tongue against the top teeth, curling up the tip of their tongue without touching the palate, and puckering their lips. For people in Shanghai, this is too much effort, which is why Beijing people say Shanghai people have lazy tongues. I quickly picked up this lazy-tongue accent.

A syllable is a sound, such as *ma*, and Chinese characters are the written forms of these syllables. Chinese is the most difficult writing system in the world, but fortunately only about four thousand out of forty thousand characters are commonly used. Thank you very much. Although each Chinese dialect sounds totally different, all dialects share the same written language. When Chinese people are unsure of what another person has said, they use their index finger to write invisible Chinese characters in the palm of their hand.

Another common practice in China is counting from one to ten on one hand. Counting like this is quite handy when bargaining for a low-cost item.

Mandarin has over one hundred measure words that are problematic. Every noun is assigned one or more of these measure words. The trick is to know which measure words go with each noun and when to use which measure word for that noun. The closest equivalent to a measure word in English is a word like "team" as in a team of horses or "pair" as in a pair of pants. Using a noun without a measure word is not always an option.

Adding to the difficulty of learning Mandarin are the tones, which are the inflections of the voice used with a syllable. The purpose of a tone is to differentiate the meaning of same-sounding syllables. For example, the syllable of *mā* with the first tone means *mother*, *má* with the second tone means *hemp*, *mǎ* with the third tone means *horse*, and *mà* with the fourth tone means *abuse*. There are approximately four hundred syllables, and for the curious, there is a pinyin chart that lists all of the syllables written in pinyin. This chart can be found on the World Wide Web.

According to professors of Chinese at Fudan University, Mandarin has seven tones. I learned to speak Mandarin using the seven tones, which are the four basic tones, two half-tones, and a neutral tone. However, every Mandarin textbook I have seen only lists four tones plus a neutral tone. A neutral tone is not really a tone at all but a lack of a tone, but it is still called a tone. Textbook Mandarin is accented with the dialect spoken in the region of China where Beijing is located. Beijing Mandarin is the standard by which the Mandarin language is judged.

For now, this should be enough to give the reader an idea of how Mandarin is different from English without explaining when to change an original tone to another tone or when to use half-tones or anything about Chinese grammar, word order, vocabulary, compound characters, and other aspects of the language.

TELEVISION

When Martin and I moved to Shanghai, The Tower had three English channels on cable television: *Star TV*, *Wow Wow*, and *CNN*. An American soap opera, *The Bold and the Beautiful*, was on *Star TV*. The episodes of this soap opera shown in Shanghai were aired two years earlier in the States, but since I had never watched this soap opera before moving to Shanghai, it was all new to me. *The Bold and the Beautiful* became my favorite English program. In the evenings, sometimes Martin and I watched *The Simpsons* and *The Wonder Years*. These programs were also new to me, as well as *World Wide Wrestling*, which featured a woman named China.

There were French, Italian, and Spanish channels, as well as five Chinese channels. Most Chinese television programs had Chinese characters at the bottom of the screen. I learned a lot of Mandarin by watching Chinese television. One Chinese program was David Wu's *Learn English*, and he spoke English with an American midwestern accent. His method of teaching English was to write English words, Chinese characters, and American slang on a whiteboard. He was funny and intelligent, and he had more than his share of good looks. This was my favorite Chinese program.

A HISTORY OF MODERN CHINA IN FOUR PARAGRAPHS

My first exposure to China was as a graduate student in humanities at the University of Texas, where I studied Chinese history and literature. According to Chinese history, the People's Republic of China was established October 1, 1949. In 1958, Mao Zedong began the Great Leap Forward, followed by the Cultural Revolution in 1966 that lasted until Mao's death in 1976.

During the Cultural Revolution, young people who should have been in school became Mao's revolutionaries in the Red Guard. These young men and women went to the streets to carry out the idealisms found in Mao's *Little Red Book*. Copies of Mao's book in English and Chinese are still for sale in China. With revolutionary fervor, the Red Guard tried to stamp out old ideas, old culture, and old customs. Academicians and professionals were sent to labor camps in order to rid China of social stratification and to promote Marxist egalitarianism between men and women. Millions of people worked in labor camps with little food and no medical care.

The government rationed food and other necessities of life because almost everything was in short supply. What each family could buy depended on the number of people in a household. For example, if there were three people in a family, they could only buy 0.5 kg of eggs, 1 kg of pork, 1 fish, 1 meter of cloth, and so on every month. Perhaps as many as seventy million people died during the Great Leap Forward and the Cultural Revolution.

When I lived in Shanghai, reminders of China's tragic past were there, but signs of an economic boom surrounded me. Fifteen percent of the world's construction cranes were in Shanghai, and skyscrapers were everywhere. While China's politics are communistic, the Chinese people I knew were socialistic-capitalists.

FRIENDS AND DRIVERS

Because a car accident in Shanghai could cost a company millions of dollars, the company Martin worked for assigned drivers to all US employees and their spouses. Martin and I had two different drivers while we lived in Shanghai. Yang was our driver during the first three months that we lived in Shanghai, and he knew four English words, which were "yes, no, English," and "home." He did, however, learn a few English words from me such as "oops" and "holy cow." Jin was our driver for the rest of our time in China, and he learned more useful English from me such as, "You are SOL."

Speaking Mandarin and having some knowledge of China's history and culture helped me to adjust to living in Shanghai, but this paled in comparison to what my Beijing and Shanghai friends did for me, especially Jin and Stella. Jin drove me around Shanghai and elsewhere, and helped me in countless ways. Stella worked at The Tower and became my closest friend. Jin and Stella were my soft places to land and friends who held out their hands to me, no matter what. Jin and I have kept in touch, and I look forward to seeing him again the next time I am in Shanghai. My friendship with Stella continues to this day.

As I write this, when I look over at my kitchen table, Stella is sitting there looking at her iPad. The walls of our home are vibrating with Shanghainese, Mandarin, Spanish, English, and laughter. Stella is enjoying shopping here in the States in the same way that I enjoyed shopping in China.

When I look over at the table again, there is someone else sitting with Stella. No, it isn't her husband Qian, although he will join us soon. This person does, however, look a lot like Qian. His English name is Jerry. He is five years old and calls me Auntie Sharon. He is Stella's son, and they are staying with us for three months.

Jerry is learning to speak English, which is his third language. Last night, his mother told him, "Jerry, go wash your face and hands."

When dinner was on the table, Stella said, "Jerry, did you wash your face and hands?"

Jerry said, "Oops. I'm so busted."

SHANGHAI JOURNAL

June 24, 1997: Arrival in Shanghai

The flight from Albuquerque, New Mexico, to Shanghai takes a total of twenty-nine hours, with a seven-hour layover in Japan. Around midnight, our jet lands at the Shanghai Hongqiao International Airport. Yang, our driver, is waiting for us outside the PRC Customs Area. There are hundreds of people at the airport who are talking and shouting in Chinese and even walking in a Chinese way. I can hardly understand what people are saying. I feel deep regret that my Mandarin is rudimentary. The muggy Shanghai air blasts us as we walk to Yang's van.

Around two o'clock in the morning, we arrive at our Shanghai apartment, and Yang helps Martin carry our luggage to the master bedroom. The only closet in this apartment is a four-foot-wide armoire. As I begin unpacking my suitcases, I say, "Marty, where are you going to put your clothes?"

June 27, 1997: Meeting Stella

A lot of people in China have an English name as well as a Chinese name. I met one of the managers at The Tower today, and her English name is Stella. She is cheerful, intelligent, and funny, and she speaks a little English.

July 2, 1997: Whaaaaaa!

In my kitchen, there is a four-foot-high white box trying to be a refrigerator. Last night, I made *frijoles* for Martin with a pound of pinto beans. I put the leftover beans in a glass bowl and placed this bowl in the white box. Around eight o'clock last night, I heard a crash.

This morning, when I open the white box, I see that the dish of beans has fallen through the glass shelf of the "refrigerator." I phone Stella and say, *"Stella, I have a problem. Could you come upstairs?"*

When Stella sees the broken shelf, she says, *"Whaaaaaa! How did this happen?" "Whaaaaaa!"* is a Chinese expression of excitement.

I point to the dish of *frijoles* as it sadly sits at the bottom, covered with glass shards, and say, *"Big dish. Little refrigerator."*

Stella will get us a real refrigerator.

July 4, 1997: Mr. Follower

Martin and I need to buy groceries, and Yang drives us to the Metro. As I take a grocery cart at the front door, I notice that a Chinese man has started to follow us as Martin and I go up and down the aisles. As we find the items we need, we place them in our basket, and this guy, Mr. Follower, is right behind us. Then, as I am wheeling our grocery cart down the canned goods aisle, a Chinese woman leans over my cart and sticks her head in my basket. She gawks at the food in our cart, and then she looks at me with a baffled look. I am as baffled by her reaction as she is by my groceries.

Chinese bakery shops don't make tortillas, and until Martin has a business trip back to the States and can stock up on tortillas, he will have to find some bread that he might like. I push our grocery cart *behind* Martin because this is the only way I can keep track of him—outside of putting a GPS ankle bracelet on him. Martin likes to wander off in a grocery store, and sometimes I spend more time looking for him than shopping.

When Martin and I find the bakery section, Mr. Follower is still tagging along. Martin takes a loaf of bread off the shelf and examines the Chinese characters on the wrapper as if he is checking the grams of carbohydrates on the label. I don't bother to tell him that he is holding the bread upside down. Martin nods to himself, purses his lips, and puts the loaf in our cart. Is Martin ready to leave the store now?—No.

Martin returns to the bread section and crosses his arms. Mr. Follower steps up to the bread shelf and takes down the same bread Martin has just put in our cart. Martin uncrosses his arms, takes the loaf of bread out of our basket, and puts it back on the shelf. Mr. Follower also puts his loaf of bread back on the shelf.

Martin stands with one hand poised on his chin and then walks over to the shelves with dinner rolls. He selects a package and examines the rolls, front and back and front and back and . . . I think I am about to go mad right here, right now. Can he not make up his mind? Decide and go forth. Isn't that the battle cry of men and their motto?

Martin puts the rolls back and selects another package of rolls. The second package of rolls looks just like the first package of rolls, and then he does the twirling thing again. I watch the rolls as Martin turns them over and over and over until he finally puts them in our basket. Thank you. Can we go now?

When Mr. Follower takes a package of the same rolls, Martin takes the rolls out of our cart, puts them back on the shelf, takes down a loaf of bread, and puts the loaf of bread in our basket. Mr. Follower puts his rolls back and takes the same kind of bread off the shelf that Martin has just put in our cart.

Now, I am hovering over the basket, waiting and ready for Martin to make his move. Martin starts to reach into our cart, but before he can even touch the most recently favored selection, I snap up the loaf of bread and say, "Marty, come on! This could go on all day."

July 6, 1997: Two Important Words

This morning, at the Shanghai Expatriate Association meeting, I receive a lot of useful information from the other expatriate wives. I especially enjoy talking with Marie, who is from Switzerland. Some of the women in this group play mah-jongg every Friday, and this sounds like fun.

There are many McDonald's and KFC restaurants here. Yang taught me how to say McDonald's, *Màidāngláo*, and Kentucky Fried Chicken, *Kěn Dé Jī*. Because hamburgers and KFC chicken are on The Martin Food List, I will teach these important words to Martin.

Tonight at dinner, Martin told me that the Chinese people he works with call him the man-with-the-fake-beard. For Martin's coworkers, Martin is the first man they have ever seen up close who has thick facial hair. Before meeting Martin, their only exposure to a man with a beard has been in the movies, and if it is on the screen, then it is not real. Since Chinese men can't grow beards, the Chinese people who work with Martin can only conclude that Martin glues his beard on every morning.

July 7, 1997: A Fake Beard

When Stella comes up to our apartment this morning, she says, "Today, I do not want to work. Would you help me with my English?" She has several English workbooks with her and has done some of the exercises. I am glad to correct her work for her.

When she is standing by our front door and ready to go back downstairs, I say, *"At the company where Martin works, people say that he is wearing a fake beard. Do you think so too?"*

"Oh yes," she says. *"That is a fake beard."*

This evening, as Martin and I are about to sit down to dinner, Stella comes up to our apartment. She has ordered an all-in-one washer-dryer for us and wants to know when this appliance can be delivered to our apartment.

I take this opportunity to show her that Martin's beard is not a fake one. She watches closely as I gently tug on Martin's beard, and I say, *"See, this is a real beard."*

Stella looks even closer as she yanks on his beard and says, *"Whaaaaaa! Very good glue."*

July 8, 1997: A Kilo?

Yang took me to the Metro this morning. I wanted to buy a coffeepot along with a few groceries. Snake powder, pickled baby alligators, pigeon meat, groceries, household goods, and appliances can be found at the Metro. While neither Martin nor I drink coffee, other people might want coffee when they come over to our apartment.

In the appliance aisle, as I try to figure out which coffeepot is the best one to buy, three Chinese women appear next to me. Their eyes follow my every move. Yang stands next to me, too. He does this when he wants me to hurry.

When I take down the first coffeepot, the Chinese women comment and point to the coffeepot in my hands. I put this automatic coffeepot back up. When I take down a second one, their conversation becomes even more enthusiastic. I don't like this coffeepot, either. When I take down the third coffeepot, their conversation becomes loud and highly animated. The third coffeepot is what I need, and when I put this coffeepot in my cart, I hear, *"Whaaaaaa!"* as they each seize a coffeepot like mine. I am a selection committee of one.

I need some eggs but have forgotten how to say this word in Chinese. My dictionary is in Yang's van, so I say, *"Yang, I need,"* and I imitate the clucking sounds of a chicken. Yang takes me to the egg section.

I also want to get some white wine for cooking. I see some bottles of clear liquid stacked up in the middle of an aisle. I look at the label written in Chinese. *"Yang, can I drink this?"*

"No. No. No," he says as he points to a mosquito bite on his arm. Oh, this is medicine. Then I see some bottles of imported wine, but the bottles are too tall for my "refrigerator" with the Napoleon complex.

There are some bottles at the end of an aisle that are just the right size. I am Goldilocks as I point to the little bottles. *"Yang, can I drink this?"*

Yang has a mischievous look on his face as he picks up the bottle and points to the number "48" in the middle of a jumble of Chinese characters. Forty-eight proof! No thanks.

At the Metro, I buy fruits and vegetables but no meat because it doesn't look appetizing. Yang and I go to the Portman Hotel. The meat shop at this hotel imports its meat from Australia, and I want to buy a pound of ground beef.

Inside the meat shop, there is a long glass case. In front of what looks like ground beef, there is a sign taped to the glass that reads 120 yuan per kilo, which is about ten dollars for a kilo. A kilo? I have to learn the metric system, too. *Whaaaaaa!* Not only do I not know the Mandarin word for kilo, I don't even know if I *want* a kilo of meat. Or maybe I want two kilos of ground beef.

No one at the meat shop speaks English, but I hear a Western woman speaking Mandarin as she stands at the meat case. As someone waits on this woman, another man comes over to me and asks me what I want. I hold my hand out to this fluent-in-Mandarin woman as I say, *"I want what she wants."*

With two kilos of ground beef and two kilos of steaks, I look like I am dragging two bowling balls back to the van, but at least Martin will have something for dinner that is on The Martin Food List.

July 11, 1997: Former Fluffies

Martin is in Beijing, and this morning, when he calls to give me his flight number, he says that he misses me and that I am his number one wife.

I say, "Marty, I am your *only* wife."

This afternoon, an all-in-one washer-dryer is delivered to our apartment. I study the directions for this washer-dryer written in Chinese. There are no illustrations. *Whaaaaaa!* I cannot understand this. I phone Stella. *"Could you come up? I have a problem."*

When Stella comes up, I hand her the booklet and point the way to the washer-dryer and say, *"How do I use this?"*

Stella looks at the instructions for a few minutes. *"Whaaaaaa! I cannot understand this,"* she says as she sets the directions down and turns knobs and pushes buttons. I write down what she tells me to do. After she leaves, I put some bath towels in the all-in-one washer-dryer.

Martin is home by five o'clock, and we have dinner. When he retreats to his home office, I remember the towels I washed. When I take the towels out of the washer dryer, they make ripping sounds as I tug them away from the dryer's drum. These former fluffies are now stiff circles. I take one of the towels to Martin's office.

When he looks at the purple work of art, he says, "What's that?"

"This is a bath towel. I should tell Stella we need a separate dryer."

"You don't need a separate dryer," he says. "You can manage," and he turns back to his work. Martin is so easygoing that nothing bothers him—except when he makes a mistake in English

I leave his office and put the towel in *his* bathroom. The towel hooks nicely over *his* towel bar, and the top half of the stiff circle reaches out into the bathroom like a claw. Tonight, Martin can manage while I use our last fluffy towel for my shower.

July 12, 1997: Martin Is Right

Stella came up to our apartment this morning to tell me that Martin called her quite early this morning. He asked her (or begged her?) to please let him know when a separate dryer could be delivered.

As usual, Martin is right. I can manage, and I didn't even have to make a phone call.

July 13, 1997: Terrifying Shanghai Traffic

It helps to feel lucky before jaywalking across Shanghai streets.

At City Supermarket, the closest parking spot Yang can find is a block away and on the *opposite* side of the street from the market. This means I have to hoof it across a street congested with cars, trucks, bicycles, and rogue motorcyclists oblivious to the rules of the road.

Yang stands with me at the curb, directly across from the market. Drivers are blasting their horns. Rascally truckers, in gigantic rigs, look like evil munchkins as they hunch over their steering wheels. They cut off smaller vehicles and lumber into any lane they want. I am terrified. Even my heart is white with fear.

In a walking-weaving-jogging manner, Yang jaywalks across this road. When he reaches the other side of the street, only then does he notice that I am frozen to the curb. He jaywalks back to where I stand and grabs my hand. I squeeze my eyes shut as he hauls me across the street.

July 20, 1997: Jade Buddha Temple

Amy is a Chinese national who also works at the company. She is the only other Buddhist I know in Shanghai. Today, Amy and I went to the Jade Buddha Temple in Shanghai.

Yang drives as Amy gives directions. There are Bodhisattvas as well as Buddhas at the Jade Buddha Temple. A representation of my favorite Bodhisattva, Guanyin, the goddess of mercy and compassion, is in this temple. Chinese people say that when Guanyin died, her body did not deteriorate for a thousand years. Yang says she is a man. Amy and I say she is a woman. The Jade Buddha Temple has the largest white jade Buddha in the world.

In the courtyard of this temple, there is a four-foot-high square brick structure with water in it. Amy and I stop to watch a Buddhist ceremony. As the monks light candles and place them on the water in this structure, a captivating Chinese woman, wearing high heels and a red, flowing silk dress, saunters through the courtyard. The ceremony stops while the monks stand still and gaze at her.

July 24, 1997: How Much You Pay?

Chinese people frequently ask me how much I have paid for something. I find this annoying. A couple of weekends ago, Martin and I were in a park in Shanghai, and I am wearing an opera-length necklace. A Chinese woman, who is a stranger to me, takes my necklace in her hand and says, *"How much you pay?"*

I no longer say how much I have paid for something because Chinese people *always* say, *"Whaaaaaa! You pay too much."*

Vendors often charge foreigners more than locals, and this is annoying, too. I often don't know how much I should pay for something. Sometimes I give Yang money and ask him to buy what I need.

The smoke alarm in the apartment keeps going off, and there is no smoke. Stella will have someone fix the alarm.

July 27, 1997: A New Name

Bonnie is a Chinese administrator who works at the company, and tonight, we had dinner at the Hard Rock Café. Because my name is hard for Chinese people to pronounce, she suggested three Chinese names for me.

When I return home, two of the managers at The Tower, Kevin and David, are in my apartment trying to figure out how to turn off the smoke alarm. They finally figure it out, and before they go back downstairs, I ask them to choose my Chinese name. They both choose Wen Li Xia. The meaning of this name is warm and beautiful dawn.

July 28, 1997: Calling Home

There is a fourteen-hour difference between China and New Mexico. When it is nighttime in Shanghai, it is daytime in the States. When I want to figure out what time it is in the States, I flip night with day and add two hours to whatever time it is in Shanghai. Then I know what time it is in the States.

When I call my mother tonight, she is out shopping, but I talk with my stepfather. I call him Dad. He says he is fine, and that he loves me. I want to make more phone calls, but at two dollars a minute, this would be expensive.

Last month's phone bill was over ten thousand dollars because of Martin's teleconferences with company employees in the States. Martin and I pay for nonbusiness phone calls.

July 29, 1997: I Will Do My Best

Stella is at my door. "Sharon, today I do not want to work. Let's speak English." As part of our conversation, she tells me that her first birthday is the day she is born, and her second birthday is one year later.

She also tells me that Chinese people are not sensitive about how old they are or how much money they make, which explains why Chinese people sometimes ask me about Martin's salary.

I ask Stella why Chinese people tell me that they will do their best, and then they don't do anything.

Stella laughs and says "I will do my best means, *Are you crazy. I'm not going to do that.*"

I will be using this sentence.

August 1, 1997: The Sacred Drivers' Room

At one of the Shanghai Expatriate Association meetings, someone told me about Magnums—ice cream bars imported from Europe and coated with a thick layer of Belgian milk chocolate over vanilla bean ice cream. These are supposed to be the best ice cream bars in Shanghai. Could Magnums be that delectable?

Yesterday, I bought two Magnums at a kiosk near The Tower. I bought one for Martin and one for me. After I had eaten my Magnum ice cream bar, I looked on The Martin Food List . . . Magnums are not on this list. So, I had to eat Martin's Magnum ice cream bar, too, before he came home.

The kitchens in The Tower are un-American. The architect for this building is a Japanese man. He has designed the kitchen to be the smallest room in every apartment. There are no ovens or dishwashers in any of the apartments at The Tower. Also, a real refrigerator will not fit into any of these kitchens. Some apartments can fit a refrigerator in the small utility room behind the kitchen, but some apartments don't have a utility room.

I want this architect to take a class called, "Cooking in a Closet 101." In the alternative, if he doesn't want to take this class, then his architect's license should restrict him to designing buildings where only *men* will work and live—like prisons.

A large refrigerator has arrived this morning and been placed in the utility room where it will now be a companion to my washer *and* dryer. When I tell Martin that I want an oven, kitchen counter space, and kitchen drawers, he quickly makes arrangements for us to move to another apartment in The Tower. While the kitchen in this new apartment is the same skinny galley kitchen I have now, it is a few feet longer, which will give me two drawers and counter space but no oven.

This new apartment also has floor-to-ceiling windows in all of the rooms. Three bedrooms and three bathrooms are on the second floor. One bedroom and one bathroom are downstairs, along with the kitchen-utility room and living-dining area. Martin said that Amy could give me more information about the move to the new apartment.

Every Friday morning, women from the Shanghai Expatriate Association play mah-jongg. Today, at eight o'clock, Yang took me to Long Bai, which is an apartment complex with a community room. This room has six square tables, and each table can accommodate the required four mah-jongg players.

This is the first time I have ever played mah-jongg, and I lose my first game. When I have to give the winner a lot of my chips, I say, "I'll have to go home early if I run out of chips." No one says anything. Then, when I win the next three games in a row and almost clean everyone out, I say, "Now I don't have to go home early."

One woman at my table laughs as she says, "Yes you do and don't come back."

When Yang picks me up after mah-jongg, he has business cards from two furniture stores. I greatly appreciate these cards because they make shopping easy for me. When I show Yang a business card, he knows exactly where I want to go.

I need groceries, and Yang and I go over to City Supermarket. The closest parking spot Yang can find is, again, *across* the street from the market, and I say, "Holy cow!"

Yang grabs my hand and says, "Holy cow!" as he pulls me off the curb. I squeeze my eyes shut, and weaving-jogging and jaywalking, he drags me across the hazardous road. Yang is picking up useful words from me.

Inside City Supermarket, I buy potatoes and onions for two yuan each, eggs for one yuan each, and a can of baked beans for thirty-two yuan. Right now, one yuan is worth about twelve cents, or conversely, one US dollar is worth a little more than eight yuan. Because I won't be home for a few hours, I can't buy any Magnum ice cream bars at the market.

After shopping at City Supermarket, Yang and I go to the Metro where I am not allowed to carry a purse into the shopping area of the store. But before I leave my purse at the check-in station, I take one thousand yuan out to buy food. In exchange for my handbag, someone gives me a ticket with a number on it.

At the checkout lane, I realize I am short one hundred yuan and say, "Oops."

Yang says, "Oops," and hands me one hundred yuan. When I am going out the door of the Metro, the check-in clerk returns my purse to me, and I repay Yang.

After the Metro, Yang drives over to the factory because I want to talk with Amy about the move to the new apartment. The cost of this new apartment will be sixty-three hundred dollars a month—just for some additional counter space and two kitchen drawers. This price does include the furniture rental, the two extra wardrobe closets for my clothes, and one closet for Martin's clothes. Martin can manage with one closet. That's what I told him.

Paul is Martin's manager, and he is the only man I know who likes to shop. While I am talking with Amy, Paul comes by and says that he has found a terrific place to buy furniture. Since this recommendation comes from Paul, I should investigate this furniture store. Paul writes on a sticky note the words "furniture shop" and hands the note to me. Paul says that his driver Ming knows the name and location of the shop and that Ming is in the drivers' room. This is the room where drivers congregate when they aren't working, and they can talk, read, sleep, or play cards.

After Amy and I finish our conversation, Paul walks with me to the drivers' room so I won't get lost in the building. He leaves me at the doorway where I see about twelve men. When I walk over the threshold of this doorway, the room goes silent, except for one guy who is snoring.

"Is Ming here?" I say. Ming is sleeping on two chairs put together, and someone pokes him to wake him up.

When Yang sees me, he walks over to me. I say to Yang, *"I want to ask Ming something."* I hold Paul's sticky note in my hand. I am going to give this piece of paper to Ming so he can write down the name and address of the furniture store. I set my purse on a table next to me because I need both hands to thumb through my Chinese dictionary to find the measure word for "furniture shop." If I don't use the correct measure word, I will sound like a numskull.

Ming soon stands next to Yang, and his eyes are twinkling with amusement. I can't find the measure word for "furniture shop." I close my Chinese dictionary and set it next to my purse. The word *jiā* means *home* and is also a measure word for some of the things found in a home. I decide to go with *jiā*, 家. *Bǎoluó*, 保罗, is Paul's Chinese name, and I say to Yang, *"Ming knows the furniture shop Paul likes." "Míng zhīdào Bǎoluó xǐhuān de nà jiā jiājù diàn."* "明知道保罗喜欢的那家家具店。"

What happens next surprises me. Yang takes Paul's sticky note from me, slams it down on my dictionary, and says, "No English."

I have no idea what he is trying to tell me. Am I on sacred territory? First out of the room is Ming who grabs my purse and slings it over his shoulder. I am next out of the room as Yang takes me by my elbow, picks up my dictionary, and escorts me out of The Sacred Drivers' Room. Ming and I stand in the hallway while Yang turns back into the room and says something to the other drivers I can't understand. Echoes of their jovial laughter follow us as we walk down the hallway.

We find Amy who asks Ming for the name and location of the store, and Ming gives Yang the information. Yang's cell phone rings, and Martin is ready to go home.

Yang is driving us home, and while he is stopped at a stoplight, a young biker bumps his bicycle into his van. Yang throws his hand out the window, shakes his fist, and yells at the biker. Yang also has a comment or two about the biker's mother.

August 2, 1997: A New Kitchen

My new kitchen with a floor-to-ceiling window and a view

We now live on the top two floors of The Tower—the twenty-seventh and twenty-eighth floors. The smoke alarm has already gone off in this new apartment, and I'm not even cooking. Every time this happens, maintenance comes up and turns it off.

At least this kitchen has two drawers and counter space. From this kitchen window, I can see the Bund and the Huangpu River. Today is a misty, dreary, Shanghai day. As I am fixing dinner, I can hear foghorns from ships on the Huangpu River.

My washer was moved to our new apartment, and now there is a puddle of water on the floor. I called management and asked to have someone come up to fix the leaking pipe.

Modern Shanghai housing

An example of older Shanghai apartment housing.

Shortly after I hang up, I hear a Chinese person knocking on our door. I know this is a Chinese person because I hear someone knocking . . . knocking . . . knocking on the door with only a one-second pause between knocks. This is The Chinese Knock, which continues until the door is opened.

When I open the door, one of the managers comes in and looks at the leaking pipe. Yup. It's leaking. He says someone will fix it before nine o'clock tomorrow morning.

August 3, 1997: Ribbons of Rain

At Babaiban, the largest department store in Asia, I bought a little baking oven and an electric juicer. When Martin was in the States on business, he bought tortillas and cookies that came home with him. With tortillas available, and a little oven with a ten-inch-wide rack, I made three bacon, egg, and cheese burritos and a twice-baked potato for Martin's breakfast. When he sat down at the table, I placed a large glass of freshly squeezed orange juice by his plate. I don't feel like eating.

Martin is leaving for Singapore today, and he needs clean shirts for his trip, but with the pipe to my washer leaking water, I can't wash clothes. This morning, around ten o'clock, I phoned downstairs to management again. No one knows anything about a leaking pipe, but I soon hear The Chinese Knock. When I open the door, there is a fix-it person with tools strapped to his body, and he fixes the leaking pipe.

Martin packed cookies and clean shirts in his suitcase. I gave Martin a note for Yang that said, 星期二, 太太, 9:00, "Tuesday, wife, nine o'clock." At noon, Yang took Martin to the airport.

Too bad I didn't indicate nine o'clock in the morning on my note. Oh well. I don't have Yang's phone number, and I'm too tired to figure out how to let him know. Monday, I don't want to do anything. I want to rest and curl up with my book, *Mind Hunters*, which is about an FBI guy, and it is written in English, thank you very much. Adjusting to life in Shanghai is a daily effort, and sometimes I don't feel like making the effort, so I don't. I stay home, do what I want, and I don't study Chinese.

Martin is gone now. The television is turned off, and the apartment is quiet. I hope Martin's plane has had a safe takeoff. I am leaning against my kitchen window as I write in my journal. I haven't eaten anything all day.

I can hear foghorns from ships on the Huangpu River. When I look out my kitchen window, I can't see the Bund. Gigantic white ribbons of rain are spiraling from the sky, and cold, fat drops of water are slamming against my window. They want to come in. The foghorns are sad, and the weather matches my mood. My stomach feels awful.

August 4, 1997: The Blond Side of Heather

When Martin called me from Singapore tonight, he said that the company has changed his work status to permanent Shanghai employee. This means we will be living in Shanghai for two to three years instead of eleven months, and that Yang can no longer be our driver. Permanent employees are assigned to drivers with cars. Yang drives a van. I don't want to change drivers.

Jakie as a puppy with Heather

When Martin asks me what I want in a permanent driver, I tell him I want someone who can help me with my Chinese homework, and someone who likes to shop. Before Martin hangs up, he reminds me that I am his number one wife, and I say, "Marty, I am *still* your *only* wife."

Tonight I called my youngest son, T-Bone, and left a message on his cell phone. Then I phoned my daughter Heather who said she broke her ankle doing something blonde—even though she is a brunette.

This is my favorite story about Heather. Because Martin has more patience with Heather than I do, he volunteered to take her to the mall to buy a dress for her prom. After finding a store they liked, Heather picked out several dresses to try on, and Martin asked a clerk to unlock a dressing room for her. Heather said that the guy who unlocked the door for her was cute.

The cute clerk told Heather not to shut the door when she came out of the dressing room or it would lock again. Heather wanted to show Martin a dress she liked, and when she came out of the dressing room, she let the door slam shut.

Martin found the clerk again and asked to have the door unlocked for a second time. Heather found another dress she wanted to show Martin, and when she came out of the dressing room, she let the door slam shut again.

The clerk heard the slam, unlocked the door for the third time, and stood by Martin. When Heather let the dressing room door slam shut for a fourth time, Martin turned to the clerk and said, "If she were a blonde, this would all make sense."

August 5, 1997: No Alarm Clock

Paul lives on the opposite end of The Tower from us, and I have been happy to help him during the past few weeks to get a real refrigerator, a washer-dryer, and five-gallon jugs of drinking water.

Paul just phoned and said, "Sharon, would it be OK if I stopped by tomorrow morning? You're up by six thirty, right?"

"Oh yes, I'll be up by then."

Six thirty? I'm not even alive at six thirty. Do I have an alarm clock? I don't think so.

August 6, 1997: No Passport, Either

This morning, Paul hands me a bill of lading and says, "Would you handle this for me? My shipment should arrive this afternoon, and when it's here, they'll call you from downstairs. By the way, I canceled most of Martin's trips, so he'll be in Shanghai most of the time."

"I owe you, Paul."

"No, now we're even."

As Paul walks out the door, I say, "Don't work too hard."

"I always work too hard," he says.

After lunch, a customs agent calls me from the airport. He says that once he has Paul's passport, he can release his shipment. After the box is released, then a transportation company can bring it to The Tower. None of this can be done, however, without Paul's passport, which I don't have.

August 8, 1997: Purse Inspection

The smoke alarm goes off a couple of times a week. Yesterday Stella sent up a repairman to fix the smoke alarm and a door on a credenza. The credenza is fixed, but the smoke alarm is still not working correctly.

The company is sponsoring a dinner for twenty employees and their spouses. The dinner will be held at the Oriental Pearl Radio and TV Tower, which is located across the river from the Bund. The tower is Shanghai's most famous landmark, and the restaurant is in the large revolving ball at the top of the tower. As the restaurant revolves high over Shanghai, diners have a panoramic view.

This evening, Martin returned from Singapore. Yang picked him up at the airport, and Martin's first stop, before coming home, was at McDonald's. Martin had to get a hamburger. After that, Yang picked me up at the apartment and took Martin and me to the TV Tower.

The Oriental Pearl Radio and TV Tower

When we arrive at the tower, we wait in line for an elevator to take us to the restaurant, which is at the top of the TV Tower. Yang takes my purse and goes ahead of us. When Martin and I exit the elevator, Yang is there. For reasons unknown to us, guards inspect all briefcases and purses before they can be taken into the restaurant. The two thousand yuan in my purse is still there when Yang returns my handbag to me.

I am carrying some awards in my hand for Martin to present at this dinner, and a guard stops me as I start to walk into the restaurant. The awards are sheets of paper, but the guard will not let me take them into the restaurant. Yang steps up to the guard and says something to him in Shanghainese. Seconds later, the guard motions to me, and I enter the restaurant with the awards.

Paul's wife, Nelli, is here visiting from the States. When I met her after the dinner, I told her I would love to go shopping with her. Shopping in the States is a chore, but in Shanghai shopping is fun. There are thousands of unique items to see and a lot of bargains. Not a single shopping trip is ever the same.

August 10, 1997: BOOM!

The Shanghai sky is clear and bright, and today is Sunday—just a quiet day at home for us. Martin is watching *CNN* in the living room.

I am in the kitchen fixing lunch when I feel powerful vibrations under my feet. Is The Tower going to collapse?

Martin runs into the kitchen and grabs me as thunderous, rumbling sounds begin. This is the sound of a hundred bass voices humming. I feel Martin's comforting breath on my neck, and he has his arms around my back and waist. The voices get louder and louder, and Martin's grip gets tighter. "Marty, what's happening?"

"I don't know, but if we're going to die, I want us to die together."

The humming quickens into a deafening high-pitched screech of shrill women's voices that ends in a thunderous BOOM!

August 11, 1997: No One Knows

When I go into the kitchen this morning, on the tiled wall behind the sink, there is an eighteen-inch vertical crack. No one we talk to knows what had caused the vibrations or sounds.

August 16, 1997: A Wedding and a Gunfight

As Martin and I walk through a nearby Shanghai park, we see a smiling Chinese bride flouncing in a white billowy dress as a photographer takes pictures. Instead of a veil, she is wearing a large red bow in her hair. I silently wish her much happiness and few troubles.

In modern China, many Chinese women have Western weddings and wear white dresses, unlike traditional Chinese brides who wear *qipaos*. With slits up the sides and a mandarin collar, a *qipao* is red for good luck rather than white, which is the color of death and a ghost.

Martin and I wore blue jeans on our wedding day. We were married on a Friday, which was a good day to be married because the courthouse was open, and we were finished with our classes for the week. Saturday we had enough money to go out to lunch to celebrate our marriage. We took our backgammon game with us and played one game while we waited for our meal.

As Martin and I watch the newlywed couple, I say, "Marty, should we have had a wedding?"

"We didn't have money for a wedding," he says, "and even if we did, would we be happier now? What did it cost us to get married?"

"We bought gold wedding bands on sale for ninety dollars and paid a court clerk six dollars and fifty cents." I watch the bride in the park and remember our wedding day.

I was attending St. Mary's Law School, and Martin was finishing his degree at the University of Texas. For almost a year, we put off getting married because, for me, getting married meant that my scholarships, grant, and law school loan would be cut in half. But if we didn't get married, I risked losing custody of my children because I was living with someone who wasn't my husband, and Texas was in the Bible Belt.

We didn't want anyone to know we were living together, especially my former husband. Every morning, Martin stood outside our apartment and knocked on the door, and T-Bone would answer the door. It would appear as if Martin was living somewhere else.

Our plan was working well until I heard T-Bone throwing up in the bathroom in the middle of the night. "Marty, get up," I said. "T-Bone is sick." I don't do well when someone is upchucking.

Martin put on his jeans and, bare-chested and barefooted, padded into the bathroom and said, "Hey, buddy, what's the matter?" Martin held T-Bone's head as he continued to toss his cookies.

When T-Bone was feeling better, Martin walked him back to his room. As he tucked T-Bone back into bed, T-Bone said, "Martin, what are you doing here?" By the next morning, T-Bone seemed to have forgotten he was sick, and that Martin miraculously appeared when he needed him.

On the following Sunday, my former husband would be picking up my children. Saturday night, before my children went to sleep, I reminded them of *The Rule* when I said, "Don't knock on this bedroom door unless there's a fire." There was no lock on our bedroom door, and I didn't want them to knock so hard on the door that it would open. My three children slept while Martin and I studied late into the night.

The next morning, there was a knock on our bedroom door, and I said, "There better be a fire!"

A deep voice spoke. "There's no fire. It's your ex-husband."

Holy cow! We leaped out of bed. I ran for my robe while Martin ran into my closet, even though his clothes were in a closet on the other side of the room. The only thing in *my* closet that would fit him was a Little Red Riding Hood cape I wore for Halloween.

After that little episode, I said, "Marty, we have to get married," and the next day we bought wedding bands. We told no one about our plan to be married in a few days. On the following Friday, we went to the courthouse and paid the county clerk $6.50, which was the loose change we had between us. The clerk glared at us over the top of her glasses now and then as she counted the pennies. Martin and I swore to her that we were not cousins, she sanctioned our marriage with an official stamp, and we were out of there.

Martin and I hurried to the car. We wanted to tell Martin's mother, Margarita, the happy news. Martin drove to the barrio in San Antonio where his mother lived, and when we were two blocks away from her house, we heard the blaring horns of fire trucks.

When we were one block away from Margarita's house, we heard rounds of gunfire. Martin slowly pulled up to a stop sign and left the motor running. He touched my shoulder. "Honey, get down." I slouched down in the bucket seat of Martin's baby-blue 1973 Mustang.

In the barrio, gang affiliations are identified by the colors of bandanas and how they are worn. A young man was wearing one red bandana around his head and one red bandana around his leg, and he ran screaming down the street. *"Cuidado, cuidado! Tienen pistolas. Tienen pistolas! Cuidado!"* "Watch out, watch out! They have guns. They have guns! Watch out!" The man's arms flailed as he tore down the street. The blast of the fire engine horns stopped.

"Marty, what are you going to do?"

"I'm going to sit here at this stop sign and wait for the gunfire to stop. Just stay down."

Black smoke darkened the sky and rolled down the street. After a few minutes, the gunshots stopped, and Martin turned the car into the clearing smoke. Sixty feet from Margarita's house, fire trucks were pouring water onto a burning car.

A few days later we found out that Jorge was sleeping with Pablo's wife, and Pablo didn't like that, so Pablo set Jorge's car on fire. When Jorge saw his car on fire, he didn't like that, so he pulled out his .357 Magnum and aimed his gun at Pablo. Pablo didn't like that, so Pablo took out his gun, too. They fired their pistols several times and did their best to kill each other, but their bullets flew into the sky and the ground. The police never came to the scene, and the neighbors didn't like that.

Martin and his mother always spoke Spanish, and when we went into Margarita's house, Martin said, *"Mama, we're married."* Martin frequently kidded his mother, and she didn't believe him until he showed her his gold wedding band as he said, *"Look. Here's my ring."*

"Oh, did a priest marry you? When did this happen?"

"Just now, Mama. A county clerk married us at the courthouse a little while ago."

Margarita embraced us as she said, *"But a priest didn't marry you. You must come into the living room. I will give you both a blessing."* Martin was the first of Margarita's eight children to be married. Martin and I knelt down on the living room floor, and Margarita gave us her blessing and God's blessing. All was now right with the world.

Martin's brothers, Jesse and Eddy, and his sisters, Angie and Mary Ann, came into the living room. Jesse liked to tease me, and he said, "Oh, Sharon . . . you married Martin. I am sorry for you, but thank you for marrying him."

August 19, 1997: Yang's Photo

I tell Martin that I don't want to get another driver, and Martin says, "Oh, my honey, everything will be OK."

Today is Saturday. Yang wants to take us to see Yu Yuan, which is a large, famous park in Shanghai. At the park, there is a photographer who is taking pictures with a Polaroid camera. I ask Yang if the three of us can get our picture taken together, and he objects. No problem. In the same way that Yang hauls me across a street, I pull Yang into the picture with us.

I pay the photographer to take two photos of the three of us, and I give one of the pictures to Yang who gazes at the photo before tucking it into his shirt pocket. Martin has work to do, and Yang takes us back to The Tower.

Just after Martin and I finish our lunch, Nelli calls. She wants to know if I want to go shopping with her. I hang up the phone and say, "Good-bye, Marty," and I run out the door.

Yang takes us to the flea market on Dong Tai Lu, and we find many things we like. I purchase a square teapot and three 1940s posters. One poster is an advertisement for cigars. There are women on this poster wearing alluring and flimsy white gowns. They surround Buddha who is in a state of bliss as he meditates.

The two other posters feature Asian women. One poster is of a woman sitting in a boat with a parasol. (A copy of this poster can be seen on one of the living room sets for the television series, *Friends*.) The other poster is of a woman sitting in a chair with a Pekingese dog at her feet and a Victorian floor lamp in the background.

I also buy a stone Chinese chop—also called a Chinese seal—that has a bald man with a bulging forehead coming through the top of the stone. This is the Chinese deity Shoulao, the god of long life. He is often seen with a peach, which is the symbol of immortality.

My best buy is a pair of bronze *Fo* dogs for three hundred dollars. *Fo*, which is pronounced foo, means Buddha, and dogs of *Fo* are Dogs of Buddha. While they are called dogs, they are actually lions and are usually depicted with curly manes and the tufted tail of a lion. Even though they are lions, I call them dogs. These dogs are important symbols in Buddhism and are believed to have protective powers and the capacity to scare away evil. They are often seen in front of sacred buildings by the front gate and in front of Buddhist temples.

These dogs of Buddha usually come in pairs. One *Fo* dog guards the right side, and the other *Fo* dog guards the left. Sometimes *Fo* dogs are mirrored pairs like the pair I bought, and sometimes one is male, and the other is female. This is the balance often seen in Chinese art—what is on the right, must be on the left. Many things come in pairs. The male is sometimes seen with a ball of yarn under his foot, and there is a myth that the male can produce milk from his paws. The female is often seen with her cub.

I also buy an antique wooden makeup box. When the top is lifted up, a mirror unfolds out. A butterfly latch closes this box. The butterfly is a symbol of joy and a happily married woman.

Nelli doesn't speak any Chinese, so Yang helps her to bargain for an antique plate. The seller shouts at Nelli and throws his hand toward her as he says, *"What? Would you also take the shirt off my back for nothing?"*

Nelli asks me what he has said, and when I tell her, she throws her hand toward his shirt and says, "Sure. It's a nice shirt." Nelli purchases the plate made in the 1800s for less than one hundred yuan—less than twelve dollars.

Nelli and I go into a shop that sells fresh flowers. I show her how Chinese people count from one to ten on one hand so that she can make an offer for some flowers she wants to buy. Nelli uses the hand sign for ten yuan to make an offer to the flower shop owner. He doesn't like her price, so Nelli speaks to him in Portuguese, and I say, "Nelli, he doesn't understand Portuguese."

Nellie says, "Well, I have to say something," and she continues to speak to him in Portuguese until he finally throws up his hands and accepts her offer.

Because I know Yang doesn't like to shop, I keep asking him if he wants to go home. He keeps saying no, until finally when I ask him, he says, *"OK, OK. Let's return home."* Nelli says we got him to say uncle.

Yang is exhausted from shopping, but we are energized. Yang was going to take me furniture shopping today, but he begged off and promised to take me tomorrow.

On the way back to The Tower, I tell Nelli that I have spent about four hundred dollars, and she says, "That's a good start."

A typhoon has landed on Shanghai this evening, and our cable television is out. Living on the top two floors of The Tower, Martin and I feel a personal connection with the force of this typhoon. Rain water is seeping under our floor-to-ceiling windows. A young woman from housekeeping brought a stack of towels to our apartment, rolled up each towel, and placed one at the bottom of every window.

August 20, 1997: A Typhoon

This morning, the rain is still coming down, and I take two umbrellas with me to go furniture shopping. One umbrella is for Yang.

At the furniture store Paul likes, I find a desk with two drawers and blond carved wood for about two hundred dollars. I will use this desk for my Buddhist altar. Because Yang has removed the third seat from his van, there is plenty of room for the desk in the back of his van. When we return to The Tower, one of the guards helps Yang take the desk upstairs, which they place facing east. Yang says this is the perfect placement because the desk is facing a Buddhist temple.

After delivering the desk, Yang takes me to an art gallery and framing shop to have my posters framed. As I am paying for my frames at the back of the gallery, I notice an oil painting of an Asian woman. Her short black hair frames her lovely face in profile, and with her nude back to the viewer, she holds a colorful scarf just below her waist. I ask about the price of the painting, and the gallery owner says it is

950 yuan. I offer 750 yuan, which is accepted. The frame has the look of rosewood. The frame alone in the States would cost more than two hundred dollars. The painting is unsigned.

Yang is curious as to why I bought the painting of the nude, and I say, *"Martin will like this painting."* As I stand in the shop, even before I have this painting home, I know I will hang it on the wall of the stairwell where Martin will see it every time he goes upstairs to his office.

When we step out of the framing shop, gusty winds tug hard on our umbrellas, and when the wind tries to steal my umbrella out of my grasp, I say, *"I'm afraid."*

Yang helps me into the backseat of his van, and once he is seated behind the wheel, he says, *"In America, you have typhoons, right?"*

"Not typhoons," I say. *"We have tornadoes and hurricanes."* Rain pounds on the roof of the van, and wind whistles over the windows.

As Yang drives over the cable bridge of the Huangpu River, a tempestuous wind pushes his van sideways, and Yang says, *"Typhoon!"* Then he throws his hand toward the wind and says, *"A typhoon is no problem for me. Yang is a good driver."*

I lean forward and tap Yang on the shoulder. *"Right, right. Yang is a good driver, but is Yang a good swimmer too?"*

There are twenty times more cars than parking spots in Shanghai, and Yang often has trouble finding a parking spot. Yang pulls up to the front of the flea market on Dong Tai Lu, and before he drives off to find a place to park, I say, *"Yang, if you want to eat while I shop, you can catch up with me later. OK?"*

Yang says, *"OK, OK."* This OK, OK, however, does not mean OK. He means that he appreciates my consideration. How do I know?

Halfway down the out-of-doors alleyway of the flea market, when I look to my side, Yang is next to me. He is smiling as he holds his umbrella. He has found a parking spot. It is a good day, and we are happy.

Only a determined shopper shops during a typhoon, and I have become a determined shopper. The rain has no respect for our umbrellas, and we are both getting soaked.

I have made my purchases, and I am ready to go home until I look in a shop window. I see an antique Tibetan prayer mala, strung with beads made from carnelian, which is a gemstone that aligns with passion, creativity, and abundance. The tassel attached to the Buddha bead represents the lotus flower—the universal symbol of enlightenment. The lotus grows from mud, the material life into which we are all born, and travels through the waters of experience. When the lotus blossom breaks through the water, it flowers and remains above the water in a pristine state and basks in the sunlight of enlightenment.

I want to buy this prayer mala, and I walk into the shop. As I am looking at the beads, Yang says, *"These prayer beads are no good. Don't buy them."*

The shop owner and I are bewildered. *"Why not buy these?"* I say. Yang doesn't answer me. I drop my question because I have a rule—I never argue with a Chinese person. Why argue if I can't win? I leave the shop with Yang who suddenly turns back into the shop and says something to the shop owner. When Yang is again next to me, I say, *"OK, OK. Let's return home."* I am ready to go home and dry off.

As Yang and I walk back to the van, I catch a glimpse of myself in a shop window. Wind and rain have made my blond hair stand out in frizzy curls. When I am settled in the backseat of the van, Yang turns around and looks at me. I give him my best witch cackle and say, *"I am a witch."*

Yang lets out a hearty laugh and says, *"I am a witch, too,"* and he cackles like a witch.

I say, *"Yang . . . that is very good."* Maybe even better than my cackle.

I never know what Yang is going to say or do, but he can say the same thing about me. I tell Yang I want to go home. Then I change my mind and ask Yang to take me back to the framing shop because I want to get something framed that I have just purchased.

At the framing shop, after I pay for the frame and matting I want, I only have two hundred yuan left. I look at Yang and say, *"No more money. No more shopping."*

Yang's face glows with the look of hope, and he says, *"Do you want to return home?"*

"No, Yang. I want to go to the Portman. The ATM at the Portman will give me more money." But when I smile, he knows I am teasing him. Yang drives back to The Tower with a beatific smile on his face.

When Martin comes home, he moans about the desk, but he loves the painting of the nude. He also likes the bronze Buddha dogs I bought while shopping with Nelli.

The cable television is still out because of the typhoon, and I can't watch my favorite program. Last week on *The Bold and the Beautiful*, one of the lead characters was taken from her lover. She was taken to a land far, far away. Now she is a captive in a castle, and ladies-in-waiting wait on her—hand and foot. Who stole her away? A prince who loves her, of course. But she doesn't know that, of course.

So, whatever happened to her today? Holy cow! Did the prince win her heart? Did her lover finally find her? And then, if her lover finally found her, did the prince and the lover duel to the death? But if her lover didn't find her, is she pining away and slowly dying of a broken heart? Or did the prince crown her as his princess and take her off into the sunset where they will live happily ever after? (When people ride off into the sunset, do they live in a house?) Or did the writers ruin everything? They always ruin everything because they can't stand for anyone to be happy.

August 21, 1997: Yang's Last Day as Our Driver

Today is Yang's last day as our driver. Tomorrow morning we will have a new driver. I will miss Yang, but Martin and I are glad Yang will be staying with the company as a driver.

Inside a notecard for Yang, I write, *"Martin and I will miss you. Thank you for being an excellent driver for us."* On the front of the notecard, I have painted a Bodhi tree, which is the kind of tree under which Buddha is said to have become enlightened. The Bodhi tree is known as the Tree of Intelligence or the Tree of Meditation. I put 888 yuan inside the card because eight is the luckiest number in China. I put the card and money in a red envelope. Red is for good fortune.

Around noon, Yang drives Nelli and me to one of her favorite hot pot restaurants. At lunch, I mention to Nelli that I can feel the springs in my mattress. Nelli says that when she goes back to the States, she will buy egg-crate foam for me and bring it back with her when she returns to Shanghai. After lunch, Yang takes Nelli back to The Tower, and Yang and I spend the rest of the afternoon shopping until it is time to pick up Martin.

Shortly before five o'clock, Yang and I walk into the factory and go to the office section. Martin is not at his desk, so Yang takes me to Jenny's desk and then leaves for The Sacred Drivers' Room. Jenny is one of the Chinese bilingual administrators, and just as I am asking Jenny how to present Yang's gift to him, Yang reappears. Jenny tells him that Martin and I want to give him a gift.

Yang sees the red envelope in my hand and says, "No, no, no."

I ask Jenny to tell Yang that Martin and I want to express our appreciation with a gift. When Jenny passes on what I have said, his protest gets even louder. People in the office start to gather around us. I look at Jenny for a suggestion, and she shrugs her shoulders. An even bigger audience begins to gather.

Jenny looks at Yang and says, *"She is upset that you won't be her driver. Take the gift."*

Yang touches my arm and says *"Don't be upset,"* but he doesn't take the envelope.

Time for plan B. I hold the envelope in both hands, which is the correct way to offer something, and I extend my arms straight out. I then bow from my waist. As I look at the floor, I can see the toes of Yang's shoes, and his feet don't move. I am not going to stand up until Yang takes the gift.

Now Yang has a dilemma. He doesn't want to take the envelope, but he can't walk away from me. I am the wife of his boss. Checkmate. Yang does not, however, take the envelope. No problem.

Time for plan C. I learned from Stella that when a Chinese person says *qiu qiu ni,* which means *I beg you,* this request is almost impossible for a Chinese person to refuse. Still in my bowed position, I say, *"Qiu qiu ni,"* and the envelope is whipped out of my hands. Everyone laughs, including Yang.

Yang thanks me and takes me over to Martin's desk and then goes back to The Sacred Drivers' Room. Almost as soon as I sit in Martin's chair, Martin appears and is ready to go home. As we walk to the front of the building, we see Yang talking with someone.

Once Martin and I are in the van, Yang says, *"I told your new driver about your schedules."* He most likely also told him I am terrified of crossing streets; that I like to shop, even during typhoons; and that I am a Buddhist and like to go to the Jade Buddha Temple. Martin and I are delighted to see Yang smiling.

Yang drives us home for the last time and helps Martin carry my packages upstairs. Yang motions good-bye to Martin, and I walk with Yang to the door. He shakes my hand and then pats my right hand with his left hand. He walks a few steps down the hallway, and I say, "Yang." When he turns around, I put my hands together and bow to him. Yang returns my bow, and we say, *"Zaijian."* "See you again."

August 22, 1997: Our New Driver

This morning, our apartment intercom phone rings, and I answer. The downstairs guard says, *"Your new driver would like to meet you and your husband. Could you both come downstairs?"*

We go downstairs to The Tower's parking lot, where our new driver stands by his car. Speaking in Mandarin, he says his name is Jin. He tells me that after he drops Martin off at work, he will come back and take me shopping. He points across the street and says he lives with his wife and daughter on the fifth floor of one of the centrally located buildings. He seems kind and easygoing, and he speaks Mandarin with a gentle Shanghai accent.

The buildings Jin points to have neither elevators nor lighted stairwells, which is typical for government housing. At night, people must feel their way to their apartments as they walk up dark stairwells. This is one reason why Martin and I carry flashlights with us everywhere. I keep my flashlight in my survival kit, which also has a Chinese dictionary, American and Chinese money, two credit cards, a package of tissues, and lipstick. Sometimes I even have a chocolate candy bar in my kit, but those darn things keep disappearing.

Jin and his family live in one of those nearby buildings.

I have memorized the phone number for the American embassy, our apartment, and Martin's company, and if I get lost, I have money, lipstick, tissues, and maybe something to munch on while I make a phone call. If I call Martin's company, I know how to say in Chinese, *"I would like to speak to Martin. You know him. He is the guy with the fake beard."*

A couple of weeks ago, Yang and I went to Fudan University. I wanted to register for my Chinese class. At Fudan's administrative office, instead of being able to register for my class, I was given a piece of paper with poorly written instructions in English. The instructions told me to make my check payable to some person, whose name was on the instructions and then deposit my check into this guy's account at the Bank of China. Why can't I write a check payable to Fudan University? The tuition for my Chinese class is almost two thousand dollars.

When Jin returns to The Tower to pick me up, I tell him I would like to go to the Bank of China. When we arrive at the bank, I present my check to a bank teller behind bars. The teller hands my check back to me and says, *"The bank does not have an account for the person whose name is on your check."*

A Chinese woman behind me in line speaks with a British accent when she says, "Perhaps I may help you." Her English is flawless.

"Perhaps you can," I say as I give her the instructions from Fudan University along with my check.

She looks at my check and reads the instructions. When she hands the check and instructions back to me, she says, "This does not seem right to me. May I suggest you give your check directly to someone at Fudan on the first day of class?" She tells Jin in Shanghainese what she has suggested to me, and Jin and I thank her.

Jin asks me what I want to do next, and I say, *"I would like to get something to eat. I want to shop all afternoon. I don't want to go home just because I'm hungry."*

Customarily, the one who pays for the meal is the one who also orders. Jin drives to a Chinese restaurant, and once we are seated at a table, with menus in our hands, I say, *"Jin, I will buy our lunch, but I can't read this menu. If I must order, I will just point to three dishes on the menu, so you should order. OK?"*

I'm not sure what we ate, but lunch was scrumptious, and with full tummies, we were ready to go to a flea market and then grocery shopping. Jin knows where I like to buy groceries because Yang has had The Talk with him. After shopping all afternoon, Jin seems jubilant. Our last stop is to pick up Martin.

At the factory, Martin only has one more thing to do, and then he will be ready to leave for home. I tell Jin I want to wait in his car. I don't want to wait in the office. The only place for me to sit is at Martin's desk or someone's empty desk, which feels invasive to me. I certainly am not going to be allowed to sit in The Sacred Drivers' Room. As Jin is walking with me to his car, he tells me it isn't a good idea for me to be outside by myself, and he says he will wait with me.

While we are waiting for Martin, I take out a piece of paper and two pencils and make a grid of one hundred dots with ten dots across and ten dots down. We take turns connecting two dots until one of us makes a box. Then the person who completes this box is entitled to a consecutive turn. We initial each box we have completed, and the person who has completed the most boxes wins the game. We play this dot-to-box game a few times, and then I take out a deck of cards I purchased this afternoon and teach Jin how to play a game called go fish.

The Chinese talk about "losing-face." I'm not sure what this is all about, but to be on the safe side, I let Jin win the first two games of go fish. Then something occurs to me. I won all of the dot-to-box games. Did he let me win, so I wouldn't lose face?

August 23, 1997: Ma Bell

I have found Chinese people to be frugal and slow to buy something new. Our smoke alarm goes off a couple of times a week, but never when there is any smoke. This smoke alarm doesn't work correctly, and no one has ever been able to fix it, although men from The Tower's maintenance crew have tried many times.

Now, when the smoke alarm goes off, someone from The Tower's maintenance crew comes up to our apartment and just turns off the smoke alarm. By turning off the smoke alarm instead of buying a new one, the Tower's maintenance crew is being frugal and slow to buy something new. How long does a smoke alarm not have to work right before they buy a new one?

On the other side of the ocean, Americans are not as frugal as Chinese people or as slow to buy something new. Even if something works, if it's old, Americans want new.

For our junior year in college, my roommate Jane and I moved out of the dorm and into an apartment. This apartment was built before 1888, and it was haunted by two ghosts.

One ghost enjoyed slamming down the oven door and then rattling the oven rack before putting it back in crooked. This ghost could not remember to close the oven door. To turn on the light in the kitchen, I had to pass the oven. More than a few times, I smacked my shins on that oven door when I went into the kitchen at night to get a glass of water. I heard that ghost laughing at me a couple of times. The laughing made me madder than hurting my shins.

The hallway to this apartment was as long as a bowling alley. The other ghost delighted in knocking and drumming on the plaster walls of the hallway in a boustrophedonic pattern. Fortunately, this ghost and I went to sleep at about the same time.

Even though Jane and I had to share this apartment with two ghosts, it wasn't the dorm, and we could do what we wanted. Jane, however, found something so offensive in our apartment that she had to do something about it.

An old black rotary-dial phone from the 1940s assaulted her sense of aesthetics like a zit between her eyes on prom night. Jane wanted one of those new push-button phones, and she called Ma Bell and said, "We just moved in here . . . and we have a rotary-dial phone, and we would like a new phone . . . one with the push buttons and all."

The man who answered this call for Ma Bell probably hadn't had a date in ten years and was still living with his mother. "Is something wrong with the phone?" he said. "Because if the phone works! There is no reason! To replace . . . a perfectly . . . good . . . phone!"

Jane shouted in the phone, "Hello? . . . Hello?" and then she pounded the receiver on the old wood floor. "Hello? This phone isn't working. Hello? Hello?" Jane hung up, and a new push-button phone was soon installed.

August 29, 1997: The Glommer

When I answer The Chinese Knock, Stella is at our door with flowers and a small birthday cake. These are gifts for me from everyone who works at The Tower.

The Bund (which rhymes with fund) by the Huangpu River

The Peace Hotel is part of an area in Shanghai called the Bund or the Riviera of Asia, where European-style buildings line the Huangpu River. To celebrate my birthday, I want to go to the Jazz Club, which is located on the first floor of the Peace Hotel.

Jin takes us to the Bund. We walk into the Jazz Club, and it looks like an American night club, except that almost everyone is Chinese. Five Chinese guys are playing popular American music from the 1940s and 1950s, and fans of this music are dancing the jitterbug and the swing. The dancers are Chinese couples with captivating dance routines.

After enjoying the music at the Jazz Club for an hour, I want to stroll along the Bund and see the Huangpu River at night. But when we step outside the hotel, a Chinese guy gloms onto us and keeps saying, "Wan buy T-shirr?"

We duck back into the Peace Hotel, and when we come outside again, he is waiting for us. To get away from him, we step into a shop where a woman grabs me and tries to force me to try on a wool coat she wants me to buy. Martin steps between us and takes me back outside, where we walk up and down the main street of the Bund as the chattering glommer follows us. Finally, Jin finds us, and the glommer scurries off.

When Martin and I come home from the Bund, we eat the birthday cake Stella brought up to us this morning. The cake is just enough for two people. Tonight, when I pull the covers back on our bed, there is something by my pillow. It is a birthday card in English from Martin.

August 30, 1997: A Texas Hooker

Around lunch time, Jin takes us over to Malone's American Café—which is owned by Canadians. After we have lunch at the café, Jin drives us to the Portman Hotel. Martin and I go to the basement of this hotel to get money from the Automatic Teller Machine, and a couple of Chinese hookers are loitering around the ATM. Hookers are everywhere—even in tiny Texas towns.

While married to my former husband and raising three children, ages four, three, and almost two, I lived on a ranch in Texas. To keep track of my children, I sewed three different sizes of bells on elastic and slipped these bells around their ankles. The smallest bells went on my youngest child, T-Bone, and the largest bells went on my oldest child, Mikie. Heather was my middle child. Three different sounds. Three different kids. I knew where they were, and if the bells were silent for too long, someone was in trouble or about to get into trouble.

Mikie, T-Bone, and Heather sitting on a small tractor

One day, when my washer broke down, I took my children and their alter egos to the Laundromat. Mikie's alter ego was a stuffed and fuzzy owl. Heather had a blanket, and T-Bone had a little pillow.

In this dusty and isolated cow town of 2,162 residents, there were 40,963 heads of cattle, 120,012 chickens, one paved road, one shoe store, one grocery store, and six feed stores. There was one Laundromat next door to the only pool hall in the town.

I was loading three washers when two fired-up women came storming into the Laundromat. With steam coming out of their noses and ears, one of them said, "I knew that pool hall was gonna be nothin' but trouble. That hooker has made it her gall-darn office."

Mikie shouted loud enough to rattle the tin roof. "Mom, what's a hooker?"

I put two fingers to my temple, which helped me to think as I said, "A hooker . . . is a woman who does trick shots at the pool hall, and her best trick shot is called the hook shot." I was pleased with myself for giving such a clever answer and thrilled that he believed me. Thirty seconds later, I no longer heard the sound of large bells. I left my two remaining children in the care of the two fuming women and ran next door to the pool hall.

With his back to me as he held on to his owl by the neck, Mikie stood next to the only woman in the pool hall. She had languorous legs under a shorter-than-short black leather skirt. Her feet balanced gracefully on stiletto heels. Her see-through blouse was distracting the other pool players as they gazed at her . . . in a state of meditation . . . waiting for her to make her shot . . . not caring who won or lost.

As I blasted through the door, I realized that the men in the pool hall never would have let anything happen to Mikie who was standing by our resident hooker and looking up at her with admiration as she slowly . . . skillfully . . . leaned into her shot.

The sound of balls clicking was the only sound heard before I said, "Mikie . . . What are you doing?"

The men nodded a greeting to me. I nodded a quick greeting to the men and grabbed Mikie's hand. As I hurried him toward the door, his little feet, for brief moments, levitated off the floor, and one wing of his owl flapped like a flag. "Mikie," I said, "you never should have left."

Loud enough to rattle the tin roof again, Mikie said, "But Mom . . . she said I could watch her do tricks." Thunderous laughter was heard all over town.

August 31, 1997: That No-Good Prayer Mala

Princess Diana has died this morning. I am sitting in the living room watching *CNN* with Martin when we hear The Chinese Knock. Martin opens the door. "Honey, Yang is here."

Yang comes over to me and bows as he holds out a box with both hands. *"Open this now,"* he says. The box is wrapped in colorful paper, and Yang begins to pull the paper off to show me how to unwrap this gift. *"Open, open,"* he says, and I finish pulling off the paper.

I lift the lid off this box and gently pull out a heavy Tibetan prayer mala with carnelian beads, strung on red string. These are the extraordinary beads I saw in the flea market shop on Dong Tai Lu that Yang said were no good. These extraordinary beads are now beyond extraordinary because Yang has given them to me.

I hold the mala in both hands and admire the 108 maroon-orange beads. Each bead represents one of the 108 paths to enlightenment. In the middle of the mala is a little red tassel. This is the open heart of compassion, creativity, and passion—the red lotus flower of enlightenment—tied at the bottom of the Buddha bead. *"Yang, thank you, thank you. These are beautiful. You knew I wanted these."*

Yang shakes off my thanks with his hand. *"Look, look. There's more,"* he says.

Beneath a layer of tissue paper is a statue. I pull it out and say, *"Guanyin and a Buddha dog. Yang, thank you. Oh, you know how much I like Guanyin and Buddha dogs."* I hold up the ten-inch statue and admire Guanyin as she stands in the heart of a lotus flower, the place of enlightenment, and pours her mercy onto the world. Her little guardian Buddha dog sits at her feet. *"Yang, thank you for thinking of me on my birthday."*

Yang again shakes off my thanks and says, *"Don't be so polite,"* which is the Chinese way of saying "you are welcome." Yang turns to leave.

I walk with Yang to the door, and as he takes a few steps down the hall, I say, *"Yang."* When he turns to face me, I say, *"Much thanks,"* and I put my hands together and bow to him. Yang mirrors my gesture and smiles at me with that marvelous smile that he has.

September 1, 1997: An Electrifying Woman

The city of Shanghai has over fourteen million people, around eleven million bicycles, and no trees. The summer months are hot and muggy, and in a city without trees, a sea of concrete makes the heat worse. Sometimes, because of the heat, Shanghai women wear pajamas while shopping and dining in restaurants. Some women even wear short babydoll pajamas when they are out and about in Shanghai.

Many of the sidewalks in Shanghai are made of twelve-inch square blocks of concrete with a four-point pattern on them, like a flower with four petals. Sidewalks are usually six to twelve feet wide to accommodate bicycles as well as people on foot. Along the Huangpu River, the walkway is about eighteen feet wide. Because these blocks of concrete shift and are not level, some of the footpaths are like undulating shallow terraces.

Martin and I need an electrical converter. I know how to say "electrical," but I don't know how to say "converter," and none of my dictionaries has this word. *"Jin, I want to go to a shop,"* I say. *"This shop has many electrical things. Do you know where this kind of shop is located?"* Whether Jin drives to Pudong or Puxi, I don't know, but he parks the car, and we walk with care down a buckling sidewalk.

As we are walking to the electric shop, we see a gorgeous young woman walking toward us. She is wearing fire-engine-red silk pajamas with large white polka dots. Her long shiny hair swings behind her. Wearing stiletto heels, she gracefully struts over the broken pavement and sways with a hip-bumping movement that would throw my back out of whack if I tried to walk like that. Her face is the perfection of Asian beauty.

Jin halts in the middle of the sidewalk and gazes at her as she and her clicking heels saunter by us. When Jin starts walking again, he sees me smiling and says, *"Electric."*

Is he talking about the shop?

September 2, 1997: Meeting a Chinese Uncle

Before the turn of the millennium, in Shanghai and elsewhere in China, calling a woman *xiao jie* or Little Sister was the polite way to address a woman when her name was not known. Now, however, addressing a woman as *xiao jie* is an insult because someone who is *xiao jie* is a prostitute. Currently, the polite way to address a woman when her name is not known is to say something like, *"Excuse me. May I bother you? I have a quick question."*

The word *taitai* means *Mrs.* or *wife* and has been and still is a respectful way to address a married woman.

As Jin and I are running errands, he says, *"Today is my daughter's birthday."*

"Oh, let's stop somewhere. I want to get her a card."

Jin looks at me sternly and says, *"Don't want."*

OK. No problem.

Back at my apartment once again, I put one hundred yuan in a coffee mug with the face of a Warner Brothers Studio cartoon character. I wrap this mug in paper and put a bow on top. I write the birthday message inside the note card in English since Jin's daughter is studying English in school. On the front of the note card is a watercolor and India ink painting I have done of Jennifer. She is a cat that has passed on to wherever marvelous cats go.

I know Jin lives across the street in one of the centrally located buildings, but in which building does he live? I need help. I go downstairs to The Tower's main office and ask Stella if she can help me to deliver the gift. "It would be my pleasure to help you," she says.

Stella takes my hand as we cross the street, and I point to a five-story building where Jin's family might live. We walk up four flights of stairs and knock on every door on the fifth floor. No one answers at any of the apartments.

We start walking back down the stairs, and on the third floor landing, a squeaking door opens. In a white tank-top undershirt, a gray-haired Uncle steps up to the doorway and bows. *"What are you doing here?"* he says. Suspenders hold up his baggy Mao Zedong military pants.

Every building has an Uncle who is the eyes and ears of the building. The Uncle is charged with knowing everyone's business. Like a military adjunct, he reports any problems in his building to the governmental housing complex.

Stella explains to Uncle. *"Someone who lives here is this woman's driver. She has a birthday gift for his daughter. Do you know a Mr. Jin?"*

Uncle shakes his head. *"I don't know anyone who is called Jin in this building. You should go to the governmental office, located in the center, only one story."* Uncle bows to us. He steps backward into his flat and waves his hand as he says, *"Good-bye. Good-bye."*

Stella and I go to the central office and walk up to an open door. There are no lights on in the building. My eyes soon adjust to the darkness as I peer into the room with abundant empty desks. Rows and stacks of faded green tomes clutter the room.

There are three women in the room, and melodious giggles punctuate their chatter. Stella and I stand in the doorway and wait for an invitation to enter. Finally, one of the women notices us and says, *"Whaaaaaa! Hello, hello. May I help you?"*

Stella says, *"Little Sister, hello. My friend here wants to give someone's daughter a birthday present. Her father's name is Jin. Maybe you know him?"*

Little Sister stands in front of us. *"Please come in, come in. Of course, I will try to help you. By what name is this person called?"* In China, there are only about one hundred family names, so a complete name is more helpful.

Stella doesn't know Jin's full name, and I say, *"Little Sister, hello,"* and I give her Jin's full name with the correct tones.

When she hears me speak Chinese, she is momentarily surprised, and then she says, *"I will look in this community book for Mr. Jin."* She pulls down a dusty cloth-covered volume from a high shelf. *"I will have a quick look in this book. Hmmm ..."* Little Sister begins flipping through pages with names and other information written in Chinese on every line. *"Mr. Jin is in what profession?"*

Stella says, *"He is her driver."*

"Really? Hmmm ..." She looks in several other books. *"There is a man named Jin, but he works for the People's Police. Mr. Jin works for what company?"* I give her the name of the transportation company for which Jin works, and she says, *"I will call over to Mr. Jin's building. Perhaps Uncle can clear up this matter."* She dials a number on a black rotary-dial

phone from the 1940s. As I hear the click . . . click . . . click . . . of the dial, I remember the phone my college roommate, Jane, and I had, but it's broken now.

Little Sister speaks in Shanghainese to someone on the other end. When she hangs up the phone, she says, *"Uncle knows about Mr. Jin's job change, so everything is OK. He said Mr. Jin's wife is at home. She will come down to meet you."* Stella and I thank Little Sister.

Jin's wife, Wu, soon appears in the doorway. She looks beautiful in a cotton summer dress. She is wearing a gold pendant around her neck. Her short black hair frames her pretty face. I give Wu her daughter's gift and say, *"Wu taitai, I'm happy to meet you. You look beautiful."*

Wu shakes off the compliment. *"Thank you for the gift. Please come up to my home, OK?"*

I don't want to trouble Wu or to make any social blunders. *"Oh, I couldn't,"* I say.

Wu says, *"It would be a pleasure to have you come up to my home."*

I say, *"I don't want to bother you. I am sure you have many things to do today."*

And then Wu invites us to come up to her home for a third time. If I refuse this third invitation, this will be not only ungracious of me but rude as well.

I say, *"We would enjoy visiting your home. We can stay for a few minutes."*

Jin's wife takes us to the fifth floor of one of the centrally located buildings. Wu will not let me take off my shoes, although Stella and Wu leave their shoes by the door.

This apartment is about five hundred square foot and has a daybed on the far wall with a partition pulled to one side. A full-size bed is by the front door. Above the bed, Jin and Wu's wedding photo looks out at us. Over my left shoulder by the doorframe, there is a medallion on the wall. This must be the medallion Jin says that he touches every night when he comes home to his family.

Jin's wife apologizes for the messiness. I don't see any mess, but even if I did, it would not have mattered. *"Wu taitai, your home is lovely. You're a good wife."*

Wu laughs nervously and points to three chairs by the only table in the room. She asks us if we would like a little something to drink, and we both decline. No matter. Wu goes out the door of the apartment.

As Stella and I wait for Wu to return, I look around the room, which has a rich, dark, wood floor. There is a ten-foot-long armoire against one wall with mirrors on the doors. Jin has talked about this armoire. He purchased it when Wu and he married. The armoire is made from rosewood, which is the most prized wood in China.

The bed by the front door has a grass mat over a wood box, and I say, *"Stella, how can anyone sleep on a wood box? Why the grass mat?"*

Stella tells me that wood boxes are sturdy for sleeping, and grass mats keep people cool during hot Shanghai summers. The one-room apartment has an air conditioner, television, and one large window.

Wu returns with an orange kind of drink in two glasses and sets them down in front of us. I want to drink enough to show Wu my appreciation for her hospitality but not so much that she will refill my glass. Perhaps Jin has told her that I don't drink coffee or tea. I don't eat rice, either, so my eating and drinking habits must seem strange to her.

Wu asks me if I would like to see her family photos. When I say I would like that very much, out comes a large photo album. Family relationships are specific in China. In Mandarin, for example, the older brother is called *gege,* and the younger brother is called *didi. Meimei* is the younger sister, and *jiejie* is the older sister. Father's father is *yeye,* and father's mother is *nainai.* One's father's sister is called *guma,* and the husband of one's father's sister is called *gufu.* The wife of one's father's older brother is *bomu.*

However, when Chinese people talk about a cousin-in-law of the sister-in-law on the father's side, things get complicated. I don't know this word and most Chinese people don't know it, either. The list is endless, but "mother" and "father" are easy—*mama* and *baba* or *muqin* and *fuqin.*

Ta, however, can mean *he, she,* or *it,* so sometimes I don't know if a Chinese person is talking about a man, woman, girl, boy, animal, or gift. Mandarin is specific except when it isn't.

Wu sets the heavy book on the table with a thump and goes through each photo. She tells us the who's who of the family on both sides.

When I drink about a third of my drink, Wu takes my glass and goes out the door. Now I have my answer. I should drink less than a third if I don't want my glass to be filled back up again. When she returns, my glass is full again, and she sets the glass down in front of me. She continues to turn the pages of the photo book. When she comes to a picture of Jin in his military uniform, holding a rifle, I say, *"Jin is handsome."*

Wu shrugs off the compliment and says, *"Jin isn't handsome."*

Then she turns to the photo of Jin in his People's Police uniform. Jin looks serious. *"Another handsome photo of Jin,"* I say. Wu laughs off my compliment. Then she proudly shows me pictures of her daughter.

When Wu comes to the end of the pictures, I say, *"Wu taitai, I have enjoyed seeing the photos. We should go now. Thank you for inviting me to your home. Thank you also for the drink."* The three of us stand up. Stella and Wu put their shoes back on, and we walk down the four flights of stairs.

At the curb, Wu takes my right hand. Stella takes my left, and they walk me across the busy street. Jin must have told Wu that crossing Shanghai streets frightens me. When we are at the door of The Tower, Wu says, *"Thank you for my daughter's gift. Please come back and visit me."*

I say, *"Yes, I will visit you again. I hope you will come to my home."*

Wu agrees to visit me, and Stella and I watch Wu until she is on the other side of the road.

At dinner, I tell Martin about the pictures of Jin in his military and People's Police uniform. When Martin finishes his dinner, he takes a flashlight and looks around the apartment for electronic bugs. He says that someone from the company will come up tomorrow and check for bugs with special equipment. (No bugs were ever found.)

September 3, 1997: A Pretty Daughter

Martin and I hear The Chinese Knock, and it is Jin with his daughter. When he introduces his daughter, he says, *"Son or daughter, it doesn't matter."*

I say, *"Your daughter is pretty."*

Jin says, *"Oh no. She is fat. She must eat less. She has brought you and Martin a gift."*

Jin's daughter is shy and will only speak to me in Chinese as she says, *"Thank you for the birthday present. This is for your new home."* In the package is a pink tray and matching pink rug for the bathroom, and there are Cartier tags on both items. Jin and his daughter are observing the custom of reciprocity with gift giving.

September 4, 1997: What Time?

When Jin and I are running errands, he asks me if I will help him learn to speak English. I ask him what he wants to learn first, and he says, *"When Martin tells me what time he wants to go home, I don't always understand what he is saying."*

Jin helps me carry groceries upstairs. I invite Jin to sit at the dining room table and say, "Jin, do you want coffee or a soft drink?"

He says, "No coffee." OK, this means he wants a soft drink.

I step into the utility room and stand in front of the refrigerator as I say, *"Jin, do you want ice?"*

"No ice. Too cold."

I look around the corner of the kitchen where Jin is sitting at the dining room table, and I say, *"Jin, do you want a glass?"* He shakes his head no.

I take his drink to the table and set it down by his right hand, but he doesn't pop the top. Does he want something else? Just to see what will happen, I pull the ring on the top of the can. When I put it back by his hand, he takes a sip of the drink. OK. So, if I am offering something to someone, I need to open it, too. I can do that.

I turn on a tape recorder because I want him to have a recording of his lesson. I draw a clock on a piece of paper and say, *"If Martin says o'clock, he is talking about hours."* Jin already knows how to count from one to twelve in English, and I tell him, *"First, Martin will say the hour, then he will give you another number, unless he says o'clock."*

I write out the numbers by fives and teach him how to say these numbers. Jin practices several times saying the numbers by fives, and then I take a real clock to give him some practice. Jin catches on quickly. I send him home with a tape recorder and the tape of his lesson.

At dinner, I tell Martin that when he wants to tell Jin anything about time, he should say something like, "Jin, four fifteen, home," rather than, "Jin, a quarter after four, home." Martin has some learning to do, too.

September 5, 1997: A Naughty Smoke Alarm

When I come into The Tower this afternoon, David, one of the managers, tells me that someone has come up to our apartment to turn off our smoke alarm. I ask him how anyone knows when a smoke or fire alarm is going off, and he says, "A bell rings in a room on the first floor, but if an alarm goes off in the evening, sometimes the alarm system isn't monitored."

September 6, 1997: Shopping for Rugs

Our apartment is beginning to look like a real home, but it needs more color. This means shopping. The blond wood floors in the living room and dining room of our apartment are bare, and two large carpets would be perfect for these rooms.

Jin and I go to Babaiban's rug department, where I see an eight-by-ten-foot area rug that I like. This thick red wool carpet has a multicolored border and a mandala in the center that is blue, white, green, and pink. Several salespeople hover around us. Because almost everything is negotiable, I ask Jin to negotiate a better price for me, and I point to the rug I want. *"Jin, I would like two of these carpets."* I hand Jin my calculator and walk away. He doesn't need my help.

Jin looks at one of the salespeople and says, *"How much for this red rug?"* After that, I am too far away to hear what everyone is saying, but it sounds like everyone is shouting.

Jin comes over to me and says they only have the one rug and don't want to order another one. I tell Jin I need two identical rugs. Loud enough for them to hear, Jin says, *"Taitai, let's leave. What you want, they don't have."*

"OK, OK," one of the salespeople shouts. *"We will get another one. The price for two rugs is four thousand yuan."*

We walk back over to where the salespeople are standing, and Jin says, *"Two rugs, thirty-two hundred yuan."* After a rapid-fire negotiation, most of which I can't follow, Jin uses my calculator to convert the price from yuan to dollars and says, *"Two rugs. Four hundred American dollars. Is this OK?"* I nod as Jin hands my calculator back to me.

As we are leaving the rug shop, Jin looks worried and says, *"Martin will say, 'Jin, you are bad. You spend too much money.'"*

Jin and I stop at a supermarket on the way home, and Jin helps me carry groceries up to the apartment. Martin is at home, and I say, "Marty, Jin helped me to buy two area rugs for four hundred dollars."

Martin is clueless about the cost of thick wool carpets in the States, and he says, "Why do we need rugs? There is nothing wrong with these floors. Tell Jin not to take you shopping anymore."

"Jin," I say, *"Martin said to tell you, 'Thank you for getting such a good price on those rugs.' He also says he wants me to shop every day and buy whatever I want."*

Jin speaks to Martin in English as he waves good-bye and says, "OK, OK. No problem. Bye-bye."

September 7, 1997: A Beautiful Woman

Tomorrow is the Moon Festival, which is a huge deal here in China, and The Tower will be giving a party for the residents. Stella will be the hostess.

When Martin comes home tonight, Stella is at our apartment. She wants Martin to listen to her Moon Festival speech. She wants me to listen to her speech tomorrow night along with everyone else.

After Stella has practiced her speech several times, Martin calls me into the living room. "Honey, do you have a black belt Stella could borrow?" Stella is wearing a straight black jumper with a white blouse. Her dress hangs on her as if it doesn't know what to do.

Martin follows me upstairs while Stella waits downstairs. I open a drawer with my belts and pull out one. "Would this belt look good on Stella?"

Martin takes the belt from my hand and says, "Stella is a wreck. She is afraid you won't be proud of her English. Is there something you can say to help her?"

"Marty, you can tell her how pretty she looks. *Piaoliang* means *pretty.*"

I pull out my jewelry drawer and find a koi fish brooch. Stella is wearing no jewelry around her beautiful face. I show Martin the brooch and say, "Koi fish symbolize prosperity and good luck." The black enamel koi fish has gold fins and a diamond-like gem for an eye, and I say, "When Chinese people see real koi fish in a pond, they throw coins to the fish because good fortune comes to those who toss the coins."

Stella

When we come back downstairs, Stella is standing where we have left her. She is twisting from side to side and playing with her fingers. Martin approaches her with the belt and puts it around her waist. "Stella, see if this fits."

Stella fastens the belt, which shows off her petite waist. "Oh . . . so beautiful," she says.

I step forward and pin the fish to the shoulder of her jumper. *"Stella, this beautiful fish will bring good luck to a beautiful woman. You have no worries."*

I nudged Martin who says, *"Piaoliang."*

September 12, 1997: Moon Festival Party

This afternoon, I hear The Chinese Knock, and when I open the door, Stella is there. She is holding a bamboo plant with three stalks and says, *"Here is a gift for you and Martin from The Tower. This gift is given on the Moon Festival."* The stalks represent happiness, wealth, and long life.

"Stella, thank you. We will enjoy this."

"Don't be so polite," she says. *"Will you and Martin be at the party tonight? I am so nervous. Be in front so I can see you. You will do this for me?"* Stella is about to cry.

I put my arms around her and give her a hug. *"Stella, your English is good. Don't worry. The fish will bring good luck to you."*

Stella hugs me back. *"I am so nervous."* She is smiling when she leaves.

As soon as Martin gets home, he eats some dinner since he won't be eating any of the Chinese food at the party. Just as Martin sets his plate on the kitchen counter, we hear The Chinese Knock. Stella is at the door wearing her black jumper and belt with the good-luck koi fish brooch pinned to her shoulder. I invite her into our living room. The eye of the fish winks as she walks, and she says, "Will you and Martin be going downstairs to the party now? I am so nervous."

Martin says, "Stella . . . *piaoliang.* Don't worry. If you make a mistake, I will make a face like this," and Martin pinches up his face and looks like a lovesick grouper. Stella laughs, and then she makes a face like a cross-eyed lovesick grouper.

Stella points to the brooch. "This fish is beautiful. I know it will bring good luck to me."

Martin and I nod in agreement, and then Martin points toward the door. "Go now *piaoliang*. I have to wash my hair, take a bath, and go shopping for new pants."

Stella says, *"Whaaaaaa!* Martin, you will miss the party. *Sharon, make him go downstairs."*

"Stella," I say, *"he is teasing you. We will come down now."*

Stella puts her hand over her heart. "Martin, you scared me. *Sharon, make Martin go to the Moon Festival."*

I assure her that we will be going downstairs shortly. Martin and I hug her and send her on her way.

In the party room, there is a large buffet table with moon cakes, duck soup, slices of duck meat, cold cuts and bread, sushi, finger sandwiches with ham and tomato slices, sausages wrapped with bacon, cold chicken, and little cheesecakes for dessert. Duck is always eaten during the Moon Festival.

Martin walks over to the buffet table. "Honey, what are these green things?" Martin's cookie radar is on, and he thinks these are cookies.

I pick up one and take a bite and say, "You wouldn't like it." I put some lunch meat on some bread and make a sandwich for him to nibble on. I taste one of the moon cakes, and they aren't sweet. Chinese pastries and desserts are low on the glycemic scale. A Dunkin' Donut fan couldn't get a buzz eating a baker's dozen.

A man from France is standing by himself, and I walk over to him. Speaking French, I introduce myself. Then I remember that the "F" in France does not stand for "Friendly." I excuse myself and go over to a man from Germany who speaks English, which is good because I can only count from one to ten in German as well as say yes, no, good luck, and you are a blockhead.

There are several Japanese men attending. I don't hear them speaking English, and I only know three Japanese words—*hai, hara-kiri,* and *kamikaze.*

Stella taps on a glass. She is ready to give her speech, and she says, "Welcome to our celebration of the Moon Festival. We have many things for you to eat. Tonight, for those of you who do not know about the Moon Festival, I would like to tell the story.

"More than one thousand years ago, there was a beautiful woman whose name was Chang E. The archer Hou Yi was in love with her. Chang E and Hou Yi are Chinese deities." Stella tells us how the earth became surrounded by ten suns, and Hou Yi shot nine of them down and saved the earth from burning. As a reward, he was given the pill of immortality, but Chang E took the pill instead, which also enabled her to fly. She flew to the moon where she still lives today.

And then Stella says, "When we look at the moon, we can see the shadow of the rabbit that also lives there. Chang E wanted Hou Yi to become immortal too, and she commanded the rabbit to produce the pill of immortality for Hou Yi. The rabbit is still trying to make the pill. The next time you see the moon full and bright, this means Hou Yi is visiting Chang E. So in honor of Chang E and Hou Yi, the lunar gods, the Chinese make moon cakes."

Stella tells the story well, but she doesn't explain how the mortal Hou Yi has been able to visit Chang E for hundreds of years. Oh well. Chinese lore doesn't know everything, and as it is with stories about gods, not everything needs to be explained nor can it be explained.

September 13, 1997: Shopping with Paul

Paul has asked me to go furniture shopping with him, and Paul's driver, Ming, takes us to several shops. Ming is patient and has no trouble understanding my Chinese. When Paul has questions about some of the furniture he wants to buy, I am able to ask questions for him and interpret the answers. I am still amazed that Paul likes to shop.

After about four hours of looking at furniture, I am tired. Paul, however, would have kept going except that I begged for mercy.

Ming takes us back to The Tower, and Paul says to Ming, "You are an officer and a gentleman."

Ming looks worried as he asks me, *"What did Paul call me?"*

"Paul said you're an extremely good person."

Ming nods to Paul as he says, *"Xiexie."* "Thank you."

September 141997: Red Rugs

When I hear The Chinese Knock, I open the door, and two Chinese men are standing in front of me. *"Taitai, hello. We want to know if you're home. We have your rugs. Can we bring them to you?"*

I look outside my apartment door and don't see any rugs. *"Yes, yes. You may bring the rugs."*

"Good, good. We will walk back to Babaiban to get your rugs."

They could have given me a call to see if I was at home. Maybe they didn't have my phone number.

An hour or so later, the two men return with my area rugs, which weigh over one hundred pounds each. They have carried these rugs, rolled up, over their shoulders for the three blocks from Babaiban.

When they come in, they take off their shoes, roll out the rugs, and whip them around like dinner napkins. The rugs are placed where I want them. One carpet is placed under the dining room table, and the other carpet is placed in the living room.

I take two soft drinks from my refrigerator, open the cans, and pass the drinks to them, which they accept. *"The rugs look good where you have placed them for me,"* I say. I hold forty yuan in my hands for each of them, and they refuse to take it, perhaps because I didn't put the money in envelopes.

I stand in front of the door and block their exit. When they have their shoes back on I say, *"If you won't take this, then you may not leave."*

They look at each other, and the man who does the talking for the two of them shrugs his shoulders and says, *"OK, OK. Thank you, thank you."*

I say, *"Don't be so polite."*

September 15, 1997: A Dozen Roses

Today is my first day at Fudan University. Fourteen Western women are in my Chinese class. Down the hall from our classroom, there is another Chinese class, which is only for Japanese women who already know how to write many Chinese characters. None of them speaks English. Our class will meet five days a week, from nine o'clock until noon.

Speaking in Mandarin, our professor, Ms. Chang, asks us to tell her our names. If we have a Chinese name, she only wants us to tell her that name. When it's my turn, I say, *"My name is Wen Li Xia."*

Professor Chang says, *"Very good. Please come up to the blackboard. Write your name."*

I say, *"Sorry, I don't know how to write Wen Li Xia."*

After class, Jin is waiting for me, and I say, *"Jin, I have a problem."* Jin looks concerned. *"Taitai has what problem?"*

"Professor Chang said to me, 'Write your Chinese name.' I don't know how to write Wen Li Xia."

"Taitai has no problem. Jin can teach you how to write your Chinese name." I love this about men. They live to solve problems.

Jin reaches toward his pocket and says, *"Martin's secretary gave me this note."* He pulls out a piece of paper and reads something written in Chinese. *"Martin wants bacon for dinner. He also wants cookies to take with him to Japan."* After dinner, Martin will be leaving for Japan. Jin puts the note back in his pocket and says, *"Jin looked in City Supermarket. They have no bacon. Taitai, do you want to go to the Portman Hotel?"*

"Sure, sure, the Portman has good bacon."

Jin and I go to the hotel where I buy a half of a kilo of bacon at the Australian meat shop. Then we go to Babaiban, which has cookies Martin likes and Magnum ice cream bars I like.

After Jin helps me carry groceries upstairs, he shows me how to write my Chinese name. He is a patient teacher, and I practice writing my name until Jin says, *"Very good. Tomorrow, taitai can write her name for the professor."*

I go to the kitchen, cut the wrappers off two Magnum ice cream bars, and pass a bar to Jin without asking him if he wants one. *"Thank you, Jin, for helping me to write my name."*

He says, *"Don't be so polite. Now Jin and taitai are happy. Tomorrow, the professor will be happy, too. Martin has bacon and cookies. Everyone is happy."*

When we finish our ice cream bars, Jin explains my homework assignment to me, and we make a plan. Every morning, once Jin is parked in front of Fudan University, I will pass my homework to him, and he will show me what is wrong with my work. Then I will dash into the classroom, correct my work, and my homework will be perfect. Perhaps this is more like a plot than a plan. This isn't cheating, is it? Whatever it is, I am giddy with the anticipation of perfection. After Jin has finished his ice cream bar, he leaves to pick up Martin at the factory.

Martin comes home early, has dinner, packs cookies in his luggage, and leaves for the airport.

I am working on my homework when I hear The Chinese Knock. *"Stella, come in."*

"Sharon, hello." She walks over to the couch and sits down. "Thank you for the fish and the belt. The fish brought me good luck." She carefully sets the belt and koi brooch on the glass top of the coffee table.

"Stella, please keep the fish. He will bring you more good luck."

Stella jumps up and hugs me. *"Oh, so beautiful. Yes, this fish will bring me more good luck. Sharon, thank you."*

"Stella, you are welcome."

Shortly after Stella leaves, I hear another Chinese Knock. When I open the door, Jin is standing there with a dozen red roses. *"Jin, why are you bringing me flowers?"*

Jin says, *"Oh . . . no, no. Jin is not giving taitai flowers. Martin's secretary gave me some money, and she said, 'Martin wants taitai to have twelve red roses.'"*

"Oh," I say, *"come in, come in."* Jin walks into the living room. I get a tall vase from a kitchen cabinet and run water into the vase. When I set it on the coffee table, Jin puts the flowers in the vase. Each flower is individually wrapped in cellophane. I have never seen flowers wrapped up like this.

Jin, having done his duty, says, "OK, OK. See you tomorrow."

"Jin, thank you for bringing the flowers. See you tomorrow." Jin motions good-bye as he steps through the doorway and pulls the door closed.

I don't want the flowers to be imprisoned in cellophane, and as I begin to free the third rose from its cellophane cage, there is yet another Chinese Knock. I open the door and say, *"Jin, hello."*

Jin says hello and walks over to the roses and puts the cellophane back on the flowers as I watch. How did he know I was taking off the cellophane? I am not going to argue with him or explain why I don't want the cellophane on the flowers, so I let him do what he wants.

"Jin, thank you," I say as he steps into the hallway for the second time and closes the door.

I press my ear to the door and listen to the sound of Jin's footsteps as they fade away. When his footsteps are silent, I listen awhile longer for any returning footsteps, and there are none. After waiting thirty seconds more, I walk over to the roses and strip them of their cellophane. The roses are glad to be free.

September 16, 1997: A Belching Contest

When Jin picks me up for class this morning, I remind him, *"This is the day I go to the Portman Ritz-Carlton. Right?"*

Jin says, *"Right, right. The Portman. Jin remembers. Did Martin give you a call last night?"*

"Yes, yes. Martin called last night. He said to tell you hello." When Martin called me last night, he also said, "So how is my lovely number one wife doing?"

Jin parks the car in front of Fudan, and in accordance with our plan, he corrects my homework and passes it back to me. I look at his corrections, ask him a couple of questions, scuttle into the classroom, and correct my work. With my hands folded on the desk, I wait for class to start. I look as guiltless as a cat that has swallowed a canary.

At the end of our class, Ms. Chang explains the homework assignment in Mandarin and writes the instructions in Chinese characters on the board. I don't understand what I am supposed to do. When Jin picks me up after class, I show him what I have copied down in Chinese from the blackboard.

Jin says, "When taitai is at home, Jin will explain this assignment, but first Jin will take taitai to the Portman." I usually spend two hours at this hotel eating my banana split, getting money from the ATM in the basement, and buying meat at the Australian meat shop. Sometimes I also buy baked goods at the German bakery and other foodstuffs from the little general grocery store at this hotel.

With my shopping done, we return to The Tower. Jin helps me carry my books and groceries upstairs and shows me what I'm supposed to do for my homework. I have prepared an English lesson for him, and we work on that, too. As always, he does well with his lesson. Since Martin is in Japan, Jin doesn't have to go back to the factory, and he walks across the street to go home.

Shortly after Jin leaves, two men from The Tower's maintenance crew come up to hang my paintings. As a result of my shopping efforts, forty two framed paintings lean against the walls of our apartment.

Because I am crawling my way through this culture, I am often unsure of what is appropriate. I ask the two men if they would like a soft drink several times, and finally I just open two cans and say, *"Do you want a glass?"*

They say, *"No glass."* I hand them their drinks in the can, and they thank me.

In Shanghai, people belch and think nothing of it, and these two men decide to have a belching contest. When people belch, I laugh. I have been laughing when people belch since fifth grade. So, when these two guys start their belching contest, I hurry into the bathroom and put a hand towel over my mouth to muffle my laughter.

I don't know who won the contest, but one guy had real talent. He ripped some long ones that made me think of Charlie Colburn in my fifth-grade class. Charlie could let out a burp longer than an opera singer could hold, "O sole mio."

Charlie also had a fondness for worms. He would bring these little creatures to school and delighted in making all the girls scream, including me. I can't even imagine who might have married him. Or maybe he married an exotic dancer, and he owns the Charlie's Creepy Critters worm farm in Cheney, Kansas, and he's a millionaire four times over.

In three hours, these two men drilled forty-two holes in the concrete walls, had a belching contest, and hung all of my paintings. I put one hundred yuan in envelopes for each of them as a bonus for their work.

As they begin packing up their drills, I stand with my back to the door. I am poised to meet the challenge of their refusal of their bonuses. With their tools packed up and their shoes on, they stand in front of me and want to leave. *"Thank you for putting my paintings on the wall,"* I say. *"Your work is terrific,"* and I offer the envelopes to them.

"We can't accept," they say in unison.

I spread my arms across the door and say, *"If you cannot accept, then you cannot leave."*

They say, *"OK, OK. Thank you. Thank you."*

I open the door for them and say, *"Don't be so polite."*

September 17, 1997: No Supper

While driving me to class this morning, Jin says, *"Taitai, did Martin give you a call from Japan last night?"*

I said, *"No, no. Martin did not give me a call."*

After class, Jin helps me with my homework. I help him with an English lesson, and he leaves to have dinner at his apartment across the street.

I am in my kitchen fixing my dinner when I hear The Chinese Knock. *"Stella, come in."*

"Sharon, hello. I have something for you."

I open the narrow box. "Oh, Stella, this is beautiful."

Stella says, *"My mother told me that if I want to give someone a gift, I should give what I like best. I have had this fan for twenty-two years. This fan is the most precious thing I have."* Stella doesn't need to give me anything just because I have given her a brooch, but she is observing the Chinese custom of reciprocity.

I have the fan in my hand as I say, "Stella, thank you. *When I look at this gift from you, I will remember your gift of friendship."* I hug her and say, "Thank you again, Stella. I will see you later."

"*Sharon, you are welcome. Oh, and this is for Martin. Would you please give this to him for me?*"

"*Yes, I will give this to Martin when he comes home.*" Martin's gift is an abacus on a key chain.

Jin picks me up at six thirty this evening. I want to go with him to the airport to pick up Martin. I can always see Jin's eyes in his rearview mirror, and he can always see me as I sit in the backseat behind him. On the way to the airport, Jin says, "*Taitai, will Martin eat dinner when he gets home?*"

"*Martin probably will eat dinner. Martin doesn't like Japanese food or Chinese food.*"

Jin says, "*Right, right. Martin says, 'Jin, McDonald's.'*" I heard a "tsk" from Jin, and he says, "*McDonald's isn't good. Chinese food is very good.*"

"*Jin, do you know Martin only eats sixteen foods?*"

Jin looks surprised. "*What does he eat?*"

"*Martin eats bread, beef, zucchini, cookies, and beans. I brought about twenty kilos of these beans from America. Martin calls them frijoles. Martin will also eat chicken from KFC, and he also eats bacon, pork ribs, eggs, hotdogs, fish, and potatoes. Martin eats four other things, but I don't know these words.*"

Waiting for Martin outside the gate for international flights, Jin and I are standing side by side and looking straight ahead when Jin says, "*So then . . . Martin did not give you a call last night?*" Jin crosses his arms and continues to look toward the gate.

I keep my eyes on the gate, too, as I say, "*Martin . . . did not give me a call last night.*"

Still looking straight ahead and with a stern tone in his voice, Jin says, "*No phone call . . . no supper.*"

September 18, 1997: Happy Feet

This morning, I gave Martin a note for Jin, written in Chinese, which said, "*Jin, I want to leave early for my class because I have something I need to do before I go to Fudan.*"

When Jin picks me up early, he says, "*Taitai's Chinese is very good.*"

I say, *Jin is a terrific teacher.* "Naturally, he shrugs off the compliment.

I have a lot of homework to do for my Chinese class. Jin is an immense help to me, and our plan is working well. Having a perfect score for my homework gives me happy feet that need to dance.

September 19, 1997: Is He Inviting Me to Lunch?

This afternoon, when I step into The Tower's elevator to go downstairs, a Chinese man, wearing a business suit, is already on the elevator. Speaking in English, he says, "Have you eaten today?"

Is he inviting me to lunch? I don't even know this guy. Even though I have not eaten lunch, I say, "Yes, I have."

As I step off the elevator, I remember my Chinese professor, at the University of New Mexico, saying that another way of saying hello is to ask someone if they have eaten. I should have said, "Yes, I have eaten. Have you eaten today?"

Saying hello in this way is not just a greeting but an expression of compassion for another person. This salutation began during the great famine, sometimes called the Three Bitter Years, which lasted from 1958 until 1961. No one knows for sure how many people died, but estimates have been as high as over forty million. People ate bark to fill their stomachs, and there were reports of cannibalism.

Chinese people must think I'm an idiot or rude or maybe both.

September 20, 1997: Cutted Chicken in Shanghai

I have invited Stella to have lunch with me and ask Jin to take us to a notable Chinese restaurant. Because I have invited Stella, I will not only pay for lunch but order for us as well.

Stella and I arrive during the lunch hour, and the restaurant is packed. This dining bistro has blinding-white linen tablecloths and red carpeting. I am the only foreigner in this restaurant. This is nothing new.

After accepting a menu from the waitress as if I can read Chinese, I stare at the characters for a moment to be sure that I am holding my menu right side up. What should I order? The waitress stands by our table.

I am not going to order fish. Not after what happened last week when I went to lunch with some American friends. Since I was the only person at the table who spoke Mandarin, my friends asked me to order two fish dishes and whatever else might be good. Without looking at the menu, since I couldn't read it anyway, I asked the waitress for two different fish dishes. Then I named my four favorite vegetables, and she pointed out my favorite four veggies on the menu. I watched her finger travel over the characters on the menu. I said that the dishes she pointed out to me would be fine. Whatever these veggie dishes were, we would soon find out.

I was trying to concentrate on the conversations spinning around the table, but crinkling and slapping sounds were annoying me, like a persistent fly executing flybys. Someone said, *"Excuse me,"* and I looked up at our waitress who said, *"Are these fish OK?"* Next to my chair were two gasping, flip-flopping fish, slapping around in a large plastic bag. The suffering of these fish horrified me. Of course they weren't OK. Put them back in water.

I watched them as they flipped around and sucked air. She asked me again. *"Are these fish OK?"* These gasping-for-life fish had minutes to live before being slaughtered for the pleasure of our lunch. I looked up at her and said, *"Yes, they're good,"* which made me the slammer-of-the-gavel—the one who condemned two innocent fish to the oven.

The conversations at the table continued to buzz until . . . these eviscerated, descaled, lifeless fish lay hot on a platter, their mouths agape. The eyes of these unlucky fish branded me—GUILTY—which was what I deserved.

I do not want to experience *that* again. What will happen if I order chicken? Will a bird with her legs strapped together be brought to our table? And then? Will she desperately try to make her getaway by ineffectively flapping her wings, which will cause an embarrassing number of feathers to spring from her little body? And will these feathers momentarily hover in the air before they gracefully settle on our table and in my hair and make a feathery nightcap on my head?

I peruse the dining room for evidence of chickens. I don't see any feathers anywhere, and I don't hear any feisty squawking coming from the kitchen. Mentally I place my chip on the chicken. I look at the menu and see gibberish. Where is a chicken dish on this menu? The waitress is still waiting for me to give her our order. Where is *any chicken dish* on this menu? At least the waitress is polite and not tapping her foot on the floor or thwacking her pencil on her little pad of paper. I need to find the Chinese character for chicken, 鸡.

After I locate a dish with the chicken character, I press my finger to the spot and hold my menu toward Stella. "Stella, what chicken dish is this?"

"That is cutted chicken," she says.

Oh . . . so this is cut-up chicken meat. "Stella," I say, "would you like to have this kind of chicken?"

"Yes," she says. "I like this kind of chicken."

The waitress, with her pencil poised and ready, takes my order for cutted chicken and two other dishes—*bocai* and *nangua*. She writes down my order, which means that spinach and pumpkin must be on the menu someplace.

Drink choices are either hot tea or hot tea. OK. We'll have hot tea. I don't drink hot tea, but *mei guanxi*, "It doesn't matter, never mind." The waitress pours tea for us, and Stella taps her index finger lightly on the table. She uses one finger because she is unmarried. Because I am married, I use two fingers to tap on the table. This gesture is like bowing to someone in appreciation for what they have done for me.

There are no knives or forks or sporks in this authentic restaurant. Little bowls of brown vinegar are set in front of us, and then steamed dim sum filled with spinach arrives. Stella picks up one dim sum with her chopsticks, delicately dips the crescent shape into the vinegar bowl, and takes a dainty bite.

My chopsticks and I bravely grapple one dim sum that . . . belly flops into the bowl and splashes vinegar on the blinding-white tablecloth, which is now not so blinding. Stella notices my blooper but says nothing.

The waitress comes over and again fills our tiny teacups. I look at the waitress, point to the splatter pattern of vinegar, and say, *"She did this. She does not know how to use chopsticks."* Stella gives me a warm smile. The waitress, with a slight nod of her head, acknowledges my obvious face-saving lie.

And then the cutted chicken arrives. An eviscerated, de-feathered, lifeless chicken lies hot on a platter, its mouth agape and cutted in half—half a beak, half a head, one eye, one wing, and one foot. The eye of this unlucky chicken brands me—GUILTY—which is what I deserve.

September 21, 1997: An Indian Headdress Flying Out the Window

This morning, on the way to Fudan University, I saw an eight-foot-high pile of garbage on the street, and as Jin drove by this mountain of trash, someone chucked something out a second-story window. With perfect aim, the rubbish landed on the peak of the heap. This reminded me of the time when my mother also threw things out a second-story window, and it was one of the happiest days of my childhood.

In 1952: Tommy, Mom, and Marianne are on the top row. Susann is on the lower left, and Sharon is on the lower right.

When I was five years old, my mother married a widower with three children. When I first met my new brother and sisters, Marianne was twelve years old, Tommy was ten years old, and Susann was six years old. My sisters and I got along well, but Tommy was a nettle in my life. When I would walk by him, he thought it was hilarious to try to trip me. I quickly learned to be ready for him. When he would stick his foot out to try and trip me, I would step over his foot and walk right past him with my head up. I even learned to pretend like he was invisible. Unfortunately, there were no Girl Scout badges for learning how to pretend a brother was invisible or for graceful walking.

Whenever anyone would stand in front of the television and block Tommy's view, he would say, "You make a better door than a window." I was ten years old before I figured out what that meant. Sometimes he would say, "What's the matter with you? You got bats in your belfry?" I was twenty years old before I figured out what that meant. The first German word I learned from Tommy was *Dummkopf*, which means *blockhead*. I thought that was pretty special.

My teachers were flummoxed as to why I couldn't tell time, and one day at school, I was sent to Mr. Kyle's office. He was the school's social worker. He was a kind man and asked me a lot of questions. Then he tried his best to teach me how to tell time. I had no idea what he was talking about. He finally gave up and sent me back to my classroom where I continued to read the encyclopedia.

My time-telling brain cells were hanging out with the same brain cells I used to tell myself anything about directions, like how to get back home or how to get to the grocery store. I often didn't know where I was or how I got there. That was another mystery for me.

One time, I wanted to go outside and play before dinner was ready, and Mom told me to come back in the house at four thirty. I walked out the back door, and I was looking at the two hands on the face of my watch. I wasn't sure if the number twelve on the watch went down by my thumb or if I should turn my watch around and put the twelve up by my little finger, or if it even made any difference.

I was sitting on the porch trying to figure out what four thirty looked like on my watch when Tommy came out the door behind me and said, "What are you doing?"

"Tommy, I have troubles. Mom said I'm supposed to come back in at four thirty, and I don't know what that looks like."

Tommy sat down on the porch next to me and said, "Look, dumdum. It's easy . . ." In sixty seconds, Tommy explained everything I would ever need to know for the rest of my life about how to tell time. He was right. It was easy to tell time. Since then, I have never had a problem with anything having to do with telling time. I can even tell what time it is anywhere in the world. Too bad I didn't ask Tommy how to never get lost.

Tommy was a good teacher, and he knew a lot about a lot of things. He even knew a lot about finance. This was clear to me when Tommy sold Susann and me a stair-walking ticket. The cost of each ticket was twenty-five cents and was good for ten round trips. Tommy would punch this ticket with a hole punch every time Susann or I went up or down the stairs. My mother stopped his financing scheme, but she didn't stop him from giving me a lifelong shower curtain phobia.

The phobia started when Tommy, Susann, and I were playing hide-and-go-seek. I went into the bathroom to hide, but Tommy was already there. He lurched out from behind the shower curtain and walked like Frankenstein. I screamed. The game was over, and the phobia began. From then on, I could never enter an unfamiliar bathroom unless the shower curtain was clear plastic or pushed against the wall.

But I wasn't the only one who found Tommy to be a challenge. My sisters and I were perfect children, but Tommy's slovenliness conflicted with my mother's let-us-be-neat-and-tidy mindset. Sports equipment, clothes, Boy Scout stuff, comic books, and the Indian headdress of a chief were thrown around his room.

To get Tommy to clean up his room, my mother tried nagging and pleading. She tried closing the door and ignoring his room. Then she tried—The Broom. Tommy came tearing down the stairs with my mother chasing after him as she brandished a broom and took feeble strikes at him. He laughed at this great fun as he dashed out of the house with my mother and her broom in pursuit. When he started running down the street, my mother ran out of breath and gave up the chase. Tommy continued to best my mother in her efforts to get him to clean up his room. Nevertheless, I silently continued to cheer for my mother.

And then one day, as I was walking home from school and my house came into view, I saw a flurry of objects flying out the second-story window—the window to Tommy's room. As I walked up the driveway to my house, a chief's Indian headdress flew out the window, followed by Tommy's favorite book, *Flash Gordon and the Perils of Mongo*. Following this book onto the pile were baseball trophies, a Boy Scout pup tent, two rough sticks for starting a fire, and a space-travel Captain Z-RO thingamajig Tommy sent off for from the back of a cereal box. Like most things involved with cereal, it didn't work, and that was the most important thing I learned from Tommy—never trust what is written on the back of a cereal box.

I took my school books to my room, neatly placed them on my desk, and hurried back outside. I sat on the top step of the porch, and from this perch I had a panoramic view of this spectacle. I would also have the perfect view of Tommy as he walked up the driveway.

Perched at my post, I watched baseball bats clink onto the pile, followed by Tommy's Boy Scout uniform with a lot of merit badges, a Captain Midnight flashlight, bed pillows, blankets, Dopey Duck and Wacky Duck comic books, one bag of rock-hard green marshmallows (was that mold?) from a past camping trip, baseball pendants, baseball cards, butch wax for a butch haircut, some yellow stuff in a bottle . . . cologne? Really?

Next onto the pile was a box of magic tricks with no instructions, a magic wand that did not work, a crystal ball that also did not work, one piece of luggage (don't throw that out), pens and pencils no one had chewed on, one Davy Crockett hat in good condition, a Captain Video lunch box with no dents in it until now, and a Flash Gordon ray gun with a man-melter infinity beam projector.

I wanted that ray gun until I found out it came from a cereal box address. After the ray gun came the Magic Eight Ball. When Tommy shook that eight ball, it would give him yes-and-no kinds of answers, but it wasn't good at forewarning—obviously.

Following the Magic Eight Ball onto the pile were wrinkled shirts, an ice hockey stick, ice skates, old movie popcorn bags with some uneaten popcorn in them, three shoes, a Superman super ring, stinky socks, homework reports (my mother was looking for those), clip-on ties, two Lone Ranger six shooters with a real leather holster, a black mask, one turkey feather, a ten-inch plastic white horse with a saddle, the case for his accordion, a Boy Scout survival kit and handbook—*How to Survive in the Woods*.

Finally, his *Polka Music for the Accordion* sheet music landed on the peak of the heap. Only his bed, dresser, and accordion remained in his room. A truckload of presents could not have given me greater joy than the sight of Tommy's stuff airborne.

With a gleeful grin, I anticipated his homecoming. Tommy . . . the boy who gave me a shower curtain phobia . . . the boy who could outrun my mother . . . the boy who had his own room while I shared a room with two sisters.

Tommy took his time walking up the driveway and never even glanced at the pyramid-shaped pile on the lawn. He walked past me and brushed my arm with his leg as if he didn't see me. How could he not see me? I had a gigantic smirk on my face eight inches wide. I was bursting with so much bliss that I was in a state of rhapsody. In fact, I think I was levitating because I couldn't even feel my buttocks touching the porch.

Tommy put his books in his room and came back outside. As he began hauling his things back up to his room, I said, "Tommy, you could just sleep out here on the lawn. Your pup tent is in there someplace. Then you wouldn't have to bring all your thingamabobs back upstairs." Then I could have your room, too.

Tommy might not have heard me, but he finally heard my mother's message, and he never had a messy room again. My mother's victory was my victory and one of the happiest days of my childhood. Even now, the remembrance of Tommy's stuff airborne still has the power to make me smile.

But don't get me wrong. Tommy had a good heart, and he was extremely intelligent. He had a photographic memory, too. For a couple of years, Tommy went to the Quigley Preparatory Seminary in Chicago because he wanted to be a priest—until he met Claudia—and then he became an excellent certified public accountant instead of a priest. He owned his own accounting firm and taught accounting and finance at Northern Illinois University for twenty-nine years. He was a good man who helped many people in his life. Tommy passed away in 2012.

Thank you Tommy for teaching me how to tell the time, for being my brother, and for making me smile when I think of you.

September 22, 1997: Sidewalk Petition

On the way home from class, Jin drives by an old woman sitting on the sidewalk. She is holding a sign with a lot of Chinese writing on it. Traffic is at a standstill. *"Jin, what does that sign say?"*

"This is very bad. Someone has stolen her home. They didn't give her any money. Now she lives on the street."

"Can she get a lawyer?"

"No lawyer. Too much money."

The only thing this woman can do is hold her sign and sit on the sidewalk.

September 23, 1997: Pearl Ladies

A woman in my Chinese class often talks about the Pearl Lady in Shanghai who emigrated from Kyoto, Japan, after the 1995 Kyoto earthquake destroyed her home. This woman's family has been in the pearl business for three generations. The rumor is that the Pearl Lady buys her pearls from someone named Ling Ling in Beijing and from pearl dealers in Suzhou—the City of Pearls.

Last week, Jin took me over to the Pearl Lady's apartment, and there were at least fifteen women there. They were all foreigners in a buying frenzy. I could only see what was available by peering over the shoulders of the two short women who were there. Mostly I watched hands grab and canoodle. At the Pearl Lady's apartment, there were also four Chinese women whirling pearls into necklaces as fast as they could.

*In 2006, most pearl vendors in Suzhou sell pearls
from this modern building.*

Today, I wanted to look at pearls, and I asked Jin to take me to
Suzhou. This is a two-hour drive from Shanghai, and we left for Suzhou
right after my Chinese class.

In Suzhou, we walked into a two-story building on the main street. Pyramids of pearls, at least ten feet high, were on the bottom floor of this building. We went to the second floor where the pearl hawkers were but left when they started pulling me to their tables.

Back outside on the main street once again, I found a little pearl shop I really liked. It is owned by Xue Cai Xia and her husband. Xue Cai Xia, who likes to be called Xia, invited Jin and me to the back of her shop where she brought out a lot of pearls for me to see. I bought ten pairs of pearls to be made into earrings and twenty strands of pearls to be made into necklaces.

September 24, 1997: Female Logic

While Nelli was in the States, she bought egg-crate foam for me, and she called me this afternoon and said that Martin and I could pick up the foam padding at her apartment this evening.

After dinner, Martin and I walk down the hallway to Paul and Nelli's apartment. When Martin and I are sitting in their living room, Paul says, "Nelli plans to do some serious damage on this trip," which means that Nelli is going to raise the economy of Shanghai with the things she plans to buy.

I say, "Nelli, I would love to go shopping with you."

Martin moans. "Not more shopping. Honey, don't you have enough stuff?"

No one bothers to explain to Martin that if I had enough stuff, I wouldn't go shopping. It is obvious to us that Martin does not understand Female Logic, which states that if A, not enough stuff, then B, go shopping.

We also don't explain the "Number One Rule of Shopping" to Martin, which states that a woman can only buy an item if it saves her money, makes her money, or is something that she wants. And finally, we don't explain the real reason for the invention of the restaurant. When a woman (or Paul) gets hungry while shopping, it is time to go to a restaurant. No longer is hunger a reason to stop shopping and go home.

I love to shop with Nelli, and even though Nelli doesn't speak Chinese, she never asks me to be her interpreter when she wants to tell a merchant something. She speaks to them in Portuguese, and this works for her. I have heard Martin speak to vendors in Spanish, but this doesn't work for him. Nelli gets a deal. Martin gets blank looks.

September 25, 1997: How to Make Friends

With the egg-crate foam on our bed, the mattress almost feels like a mattress. Feeling the springs in the mattress never bothered Martin.

In class today, Professor Chang said that we will have a midterm exam in three weeks. I don't like taking tests, especially if they are before ten o'clock in the morning. This all started my first year at Illinois State University, and as a freshman, I declared psychology as my major. Psychology 101 was a first-semester requirement for me.

Being fond of staying up late and sleeping late, I scheduled all of my classes to start no earlier than ten o'clock in the morning. Perfect. Except for finals when my psychology exam was scheduled for *eight o'clock* in the morning. The week before this final, my professor said, "No one shall be late for this exam. If you are late, you better be in the hospital or dead."

Sometimes, when I stayed up too late having a good time, I would fall asleep in the lecture hall, but not because the lectures were boring. At least the lectures I *heard* were not boring. One time, however, I fell asleep, slipped out of my seat, and thumped onto the floor. The cold floor woke me up, and because everyone was laughing, the professor stopped talking. The only good thing about my tumble was that many of the students from Psychology 101 recognized me on campus, and I made a lot of new friends.

The night before my psychology final, I looked out my dorm room window and noticed a beautiful new snowfall. I would be sure to wear my heavy boots for the trek to the lecture hall. First, however, I would have to find my boots, which were in my closet, which was like the Taklamakan Desert in China—what goes in, doesn't come out. Too bad I didn't look for my boots before I went to bed. I set my alarm clock for six thirty, which would give me plenty of time to eat breakfast in the dining hall of the dorm and to dress warmly.

If my alarm clock made any noise, I never heard it because I woke up at a quarter to eight. I jumped out of my warm bed, ripped curlers out of my long hair, and looked at myself in the mirror. My nightshirt barely came to my knees. I found some penny loafers and put them on. I didn't have time to comb my hair and curls sprang around my head. I looked like Little Orphan Annie. I put on my wool coat, which was shorter than my nightshirt. But I was wearing a green coat and a green and red nightshirt, so at least I was color coordinated, which was important to my mother.

I searched for a number two pencil. I found one with a sharp point, but it had no eraser. Oh well. I would have to be careful not to make any mistakes. I looked for my glasses. I had no time to put in my contacts. Where were my glasses? Probably keeping my boots company in the Taklamakan Desert.

The time was seven fifty. Still alive and not in the hospital, would he flunk me for being late? Wind and two feet of snow greeted me as I stepped onto the sidewalk for the twenty-minute walk to the lecture hall. I felt snowflakes falling on my nose and hair. Without my glasses, I had to maneuver through the maze of sidewalks like a blind rat.

Gripping my number two pencil, I finally arrived at the lecture hall, swung open the door, and stepped up to the professor at his podium. He sounded like the Wizard of Oz as he spoke directly into the microphone and said, "Why are you alive?"

Everyone in the class snickered. Did he recognize me as the student who fell asleep in his class? The professor took an exam and held it out to me. I stepped forward and took the sheets of paper as he pointed to a few empty desks way in the back of the lecture hall. The only way to get to the back was by going out the door I came in, walking down the hallway, and entering the rear door to the back of this long classroom.

As I took the exam in my hand, I said thank you and went to the door I assumed I had come in. However, when I opened the door, brooms from the janitor's closet fell on me and clattered to the floor.

The class erupted in laughter. I stepped sideways a few feet, found the correct door, and made the long march to the back of the class.

Even though I was late, my final grade was an A for Psychology 101, but best of all, I made *a lot* more friends.

1997 September 26: Professor or Rat?

My Chinese class didn't start out too well today. Like everyone else, I am supposed to raise my hand, address the professor as *laoshi*, which means *teacher* or *professor*, and ask my question.

Unfortunately, I get my syllables mixed up sometimes. Instead of addressing my professor as *laoshi*, I called her *laoshu*, which means *rat*. Fortunately, I also know how to say, *"Oh, I'm sorry."*

September 29, 1997: You Want What?

After class, I say, *"Jin, today I only want to go to the Portman Hotel."*

Jin doesn't understand me, especially when I say the Chinese word for "only," which is *zhi*. Jin says, *"Taitai wants what?"*

Instead of saying my whole sentence again, I use my index finger to press the five strokes of this character, 只, on his shoulder. I carefully place the strokes in their proper order, and then Jin understands what I'm trying to say.

September 30, 1997: A Fight Broke Out

Driving to the Mandarin Center at Fudan University, Jin and I pass by a long line of well-behaved children dressed in sky-blue uniforms. I can only remember one time when my three children also marched in single file like these Chinese children.

The Texas ranch I lived on was home to my three preschool-aged children, a horse, two black flat-coated retrievers, a cat, a rabbit, a husband, and a dozen chickens.

One day, all three of my children needed new shoes. On this same day, a raccoon ran through the house, in the back door and out the front, chased by two dogs and three children. The cat dove into a pile of ashes in the fireplace. When the chase was over, the cat lazily walked out of the fireplace and tracked ashes over the living room carpet.

T-Bone

Then my oldest son Mikie spilled milk on his last clean shirt and pants. He ran around in his underwear until the washer and dryer finished doing their jobs. Then, in clean dry clothes, Mikie took the watering hose and watered the lawn, his brother T-Bone, and his sister Heather. As I handed Heather dry clothes, Mikie came running into the house. "Mom, T-Bone's eating dog food again."

Outside, the two dogs, Jubal and Shelly, stood by T-Bone and watched him eat their dog food. I scooped T-Bone up into my arms as he clutched his miniature pillow in one hand and a fistful of dog kibble in the other. "T-Bone," I said, "if you're still hungry, tell me you want more food."

Jubal and Shelly followed me back into the house. I felt their warm doggie breath on my legs as I stood at the kitchen sink and pried dog food out of T-Bone's hand. T-Bone pulled his hand away in protest. "But Mom, dog food tastes good." Mikie and Heather giggled. Jubal and Shelly begged for people food.

Adam, the cat, still covered in ashes, hopped onto the kitchen table. "Adam, get off the table," I said. Adam jumped down. At least the cat minded me.

I set T-Bone on a kitchen chair and told him I would get him something to eat. My children had eaten breakfast just an hour before. Each of them had a breakfast of one whole banana, milk, and two eggs. (T-Bone would grow up to be six feet five inches tall. Maybe there was something in the dog kibble.)

I told Mikie and Heather to wash their hands as I cut up a couple of apples, took a pound of grapes off their stems, and cleaned the cat germs off the table. When I placed the fruit in the middle of the table, their hands lunged into the bowl as if they hadn't eaten since yesterday.

"Mom, this grape isn't any good." Mikie held a grape high in the air for my inspection.

"Mikie, if it isn't any good don't eat it." Mikie put his hand under the table and gave the grape to Jubal, who stepped over to the carpeted living room and coughed it up. A grape wasn't Jubal's kind of people food.

I didn't want anyone to step on the grape, so I took a paper towel and picked up the twice-rejected grape with dog slobber on it and tossed it in the trash. I washed my hands at the sink with soap and warm water. Why was I so concerned with clean hands when my youngest son liked to eat dog kibble a couple of times a week, my oldest son just touched Jubal's mouth when he gave him a grape, and who knows what Heather had been into lately. My children had no concern about the raccoon germs, cat-print ashes, and dog slobber on the carpet that I needed to clean up.

When they finished eating, we went outside to my car, and we were off to the town's one shoe store—until a fight broke out. "Heather," Mikie said, "I get to ride shotgun. You rode shotgun last time."

Heather said, "I didn't. Mom . . . Mikie is gonna ride shotgun, and it's my turn."

T-Bone was pouting as he said, "I never get to ride shotgun."

"All right," I said, "settle this by the count of five or no one gets to ride shotgun."

Standing on the living room couch, Jubal and Shelly pressed their noses to the front picture window of the house.

I started counting, "One . . ." The dogs were watching us. "Two . . ." I mentally added, "Dog Nose Prints on Window" to my ever-growing list of things to clean up. "Three . . ." I hope Adam isn't lounging in the fireplace again. Did I remember to feed the rabbit? The chickens? "Four. OK, that's enough. Everyone in the backseat right now." Yes. I fed the horse, too.

Mikie yelled, "I'm not sitting in the middle. T-Bone, you're the shortest. You get in the middle."

Heather said, "Why should T-Bone sit in the middle?"

T-Bone clutched his little pillow. "No, Mikie. I don't want to be a T-Bone sandwich."

"All right," I said, "settle this by the count of three." My patience was now as short as my count. "One . . ." I'm tired already. "Two . . ." How can it only be ten o'clock in the morning? "Mikie, get in the middle."

Mikie said, "Mom, this isn't fair. I don't want to sit in the middle."

My hands went to my hips, and now I felt powerful. "Mikie, my job is not to make life fair. Get in the middle *now.*" The ride from our ranch to Main Street finally began, and my children continued their barrage.

"Stop all this fighting and yelling right now," I said, "or I'm going to pull this car over to the side of the road . . . Don't make me pull this car over." I pulled the car over and turned around in my seat. "I'm telling all of you right now to stop this fighting and yelling. Until we get home, I don't want to hear a single word from any of you. I don't even want to hear a peep, hiccup, belch, sneeze, or cough. In fact, I don't even want to hear loud breathing. You are all skating on thin ice. Do you understand me?"

Mikie said, "Yes, I understand."

Heather said, "Yes, Mom, but—"

I said, "Heather, I don't want to hear it right now. T-Bone, do you understand what I just said?" T-bone looked at his brother and sister and nodded his head as he clutched his little pillow.

They were quiet for the rest of the way to Main Street, and my three angels marched into the shoe store. They silently marched out in single file with new shoes. I held the car door open for them like a chauffeur as they crawled into the backseat and clicked their seat belts into place. I was elated with this peace.

My powerful Pontiac Catalina rumbled back onto Main Street, and Mikie, in a pleasant tone of voice, said, "Mom, may I ask you something?"

"Sure, Mikie, what is it?" I looked at Mikie in my rearview mirror.

Mikie was leaning forward in his seat. This was a serious question. "How come we didn't get ice skates at the shoe store?"

"Mikie, we live in Texas. Why would I buy ice skates?"

"Because you said we were all skating on thin ice."

October 1, 1997: Where Are My Cookies?

After dinner, Martin takes his plate to the kitchen and starts looking in all of the kitchen cabinets. Whatever he is looking for, he isn't finding. I go into the kitchen. "Marty, what are you looking for?"

He is still looking through cabinets as he says, *"Binggan."* Martin acts like he speaks to me in Chinese every day. Leave it up to a man to learn the word for his favorite food.

I say, *"Binggan?* Who taught you the word for cookies?" Martin isn't going to tell me.

"Honey, how come we're out of *binggan?"*

There are no cookies because you ate them, but I don't want to point out the obvious. "Marty, I'll get more *binggan* for you tomorrow. You'll have them by dinner time."

Martin's second favorite food is french fries. Next, he'll be learning how to say *zhà shǔ tiáo.*

October 2, 1997: Who Likes Cookies?

When Jin picks me up from school, I say, *"Martin doesn't have any cookies."*

Jin, forever the problem solver, says, *"Right, right. Martin likes cookies. There are cookies at the Lotus Super Center."* Jin starts the car. *"If Martin has cookies, Martin is happy. Taitai is happy. Then Martin doesn't have any problems. Everyone is happy."*

"Right, right," I say, *"and if cookies could solve all problems, there would be world peace."*

At the Lotus Super Center, Jin and I find six different kinds of Chinese cookies. Perhaps Martin will like some of them. As I am paying for the cookies, the clerk looks at the six packages. Then she looks at Jin and says, *"Someone likes cookies."*

October 6, 1997: That Naughty Smoke Alarm Again

When I came into The Tower this afternoon, someone from the office said that the smoke alarm went off in our apartment. Why don't they fix the alarm instead of just turning it off?

October 7, 1997: I Want My Banana Split

I have a test in two days. Jin helps me every day with Mandarin words and grammar that he knows will be on my test. I have learned a new verb from him this morning on the way to class. This verb is *na,* and it means *to take.* He has also corrected the way I pronounce *Riben,* "Japan," and *zhoumo,* "weekend."

While I am sitting in my class this morning, I decide that I want to have my banana split a day early.

When I see Jin after my class, I say, *"Jin, I want to go to the Portman Hotel."*

He says, *"Jin does not understand what taitai is saying,"* and he starts to drive.

Is this a quiz or does he honestly not understand me? I try to explain. *"Jin, you know. The tall hotel. Fifty floors. The place where I get money and banana splits."*

He says, *"Jin does not understand what taitai wants."*

OK. This is a quiz. I write the characters, 我要去, "I want to go," on his shoulder. I can see Jin's eyes in his rearview mirror, and his eyes are laughing.

"Yes, yes. Now Jin knows," he says. *"Taitai wants to go to the Portman. Taitai's Chinese is very good."*

Jin made me work for my banana split.

October 8, 1997: Buying a Ruler

I like to underline what I want to memorize in my textbooks. I use a six-inch ruler because I want straight lines, but I have forgotten to bring a short ruler with me to Shanghai.

Before I left my Chinese class today, I looked in my little Chinese dictionary for the word "ruler," and I found the word *tōngzhǐzhě*. I practiced saying this word and writing the characters, 统治者, before I left the classroom.

Jin is waiting for me in the parking lot after class, and once I am in the backseat, he says, *"Where do you want to go?"*

I say, *"I want to buy a ruler."*

Jin looks at me in his rearview mirror. *"A ruler? Taitai cannot buy a ruler."*

What is Jin talking about? Bazillions of plastic rulers are made in China. *"Jin, don't you have rulers in China?"*

"Yes, yes. China has rulers, but taitai cannot buy one."

"Can you buy one?"

"No, no. Jin cannot buy a ruler. Taitai cannot buy a ruler. No one can buy a ruler."

"But Jin," I insist, *"you bought a ruler for your daughter to take to school."*

"No, no. Jin did not do this."

"But Jin, in America I have three rulers. At my Shanghai apartment, I have one big ruler."

"You have three rulers? In America? Jin does not understand." Jin looks out his side window and then turns around in his seat and looks at me. *"You have a big ruler in your Shanghai apartment?"*

"Yes, but this ruler in my Shanghai apartment is too big."

"Too big? Jin is confused."

"Jin, is my pronunciation bad? I will write the word for you. I'll give you a look."

"Taitai, put your pencil away. Your pronunciation is good. I am telling you . . . taitai cannot buy a ruler. Jin cannot buy a ruler. No one can buy a ruler. So where do you want to go?"

"I want to go to Babaiban."

"Why do you want to go to Babaiban?"

"Jin, I just told you. I want to buy a small ruler."

"But taitai, I just told you, Jin cannot buy a ruler. Taitai cannot buy a ruler. No one can buy a ruler. Why does taitai want a small ruler?"

"I need a small ruler when I read Chinese. A ruler helps me to remember what I need to know for my Chinese class. My ruler at home is too big."

"When you read Chinese? A ruler helps taitai remember? Taitai wants a small ruler because the one in your apartment is too big?" Jin rolls his eyes, and then I hear a "tsk"—that sound he does so well—and he says, *"Jin does not understand. We will go to Babaiban, but taitai cannot buy a ruler. Jin cannot buy a ruler. No one can buy a ruler."*

We both sigh at the same time. Why is he being so obstinate?

Jin drives in unusual silence, which is good because I am in no mood to hear his monotonous mantra again. Jin keeps looking at me in his rearview mirror. I keep looking at him. Maybe he is thinking he should be in another profession. Maybe *I am thinking* he should be in another profession.

Jin parks the car in the underground parking lot at Babaiban, and we take the escalator upstairs to the first floor. Jin walks over to the elevator, and I follow him because he knows where he is going. As Jin stands in front of the elevator, he stares at his shoes. Whoever is going to speak first, it isn't going to be me. Finally, Jin says, *"What floor do you want?"*

I give Jin a steady look as I speak Chinese like a Shanghai native and say, *"I want the floor . . . that has . . . rulers."*

"But taitai, I told you—"

I put my hand up to stop Jin's relentless mantra. *"I know. I know . . . I cannot buy a ruler. Jin cannot buy a ruler. No one can buy a ruler. OK, OK. What floor has pencils and pens?"*

"The sixth floor, but—"

"Jin, please don't tell me." We ride the elevator to the sixth floor in silence. I am not talking to him.

At the office supply section a young woman who knows I speak Chinese approaches me and says, *"Hello, may I help you?"*

Jin stands behind me and crosses his arms. He doesn't want to talk to me, either. Good. That makes two of us. *"Yes, yes you can help me,"* I say. *"I want to buy a small ruler."*

She looks astonished and says, *"A ruler? We don't have rulers."*

Jin puts his hand over his mouth. I take out a piece of paper and say, *"Perhaps I didn't say this word correctly."* I methodically draw the strokes for the characters for ruler, 统治者, and the young woman watches over my shoulder as each stroke is placed in the correct order. I hand the piece of paper to her and say, *"This is what I want."*

Jin can no longer hold his peace and says, *"Taitai, I will take you home now. You can show me your big ruler from America."*

I am not going anywhere until I find my ruler . . . and doesn't he know that I'm not speaking to him?

The young woman looks at Jin and back to me and says, *"I am sorry. You cannot buy a ruler—"*

I put my hand up to interrupt her. Does *everyone* in this country know this monotonous mantra? *"Thank you,"* I say. *"I will look for a small ruler, and I will buy it."*

I can hear Jin and the saleswoman walking in lockstep behind me as I meander through the aisles of office supplies—until finally—I see a green six-inch ruler for twelve yuan. I hold up the ruler and proudly say, *"This is a small ruler. I will buy this ruler."*

The saleswoman burst out laughing, and Jin is smiling as he says, *"Taitai, you cannot buy Mao. He is dead."*

I pay for my ruler and take a vow of silence. I have spoken enough Chinese for one day. Maybe I have spoken enough Chinese for the whole week.

Once my ruler and I are in the backseat of Jin's car, I look in my small English-to-Chinese dictionary and find only one word for "ruler," which is *obviously* not the word I WANTED.

When Jin is driving down Lao Shan Lu, I break my vow of silence. *"Jin, please roll down my window. Please . . . roll it down now."*

"Taitai, why do you want the window down?"

"Because . . . I want to throw out this bad dictionary."

"Don't throw out the book. Jin will get a ticket. Give that dictionary to Martin."

"That is a good idea. I will give this bad dictionary to Martin. Let him say stupid things."

October 9, 1997: Purses Are a Good Bet

My Chinese test is not easy. Tomorrow we will get our tests back, and our professor will go over the answers.

A woman in my class has given me Mrs. Wang's phone number. She is a seamstress in Shanghai. In the department stores here, there is nothing above an American size six.

Also, there are no dressing rooms to try anything on. I have seen men and women trying on clothes in the middle of a store aisle. As for the return policy? There isn't one. If you buy something, it's yours. Therefore, my solution is to buy purses and have everything else custom made, including shoes and boots.

Mrs. Wang came over this afternoon and measured me for a *qipao*—those figure-fitting dresses with mandarin collars. She will make one red and one black silk *qipao* for me.

October 10, 1997: Ninety-Eight Percent

With one wrong answer on my test, my score is two-percent, which is the same as ninety-eight percent. I must admit, I would have preferred a perfect score, which would have been a score of zero. I try not to beat myself up about it. When I get into Jin's car, the first thing he asks me is, *"Taitai's test? Is it good or not good?"*

"I will give you a look," I say as I pass my exam to him.

I hear a "tsk"—that sound he does so well—and he says, *"The one you missed, you know."* He thinks he has not done his best for me.

"*Yes, the one I missed is one I know.*" Jin hands my test paper back to me. "*Don't worry,*" I say, "*Taitai will do better next time.*" Now he has *me* talking about myself in the third person.

October 15, 1997: My One Affair

This is Wednesday—my Banana Split Day. After class Jin says, "*Portman?*"

"*Yes, yes. The Portman Hotel. Jin remembers.*"

"*Right, right. Jin remembers. Wednesday . . . Taitai . . . Portman.*"

I enjoy my banana split with hot fudge, and then I take some money out from the ATM in the basement of the hotel and buy some groceries. Two hours later, I am ready to go home, and I step outside the hotel into the parking area, which is covered by a gigantic dome.

Jin's car is parked toward the end of a long line of cars, and he is talking with another driver. When he sees me, he pulls his car out of the queue and drives to the front of the line where I am waiting. With my groceries in the trunk, he opens the car door for me. As he turns the car onto the main street, he says, "*James . . . is he doing well?*"

"*Who is James?*" I say.

"*You know, the man you see every Wednesday.*"

"*Oh . . . no, no. I'm not meeting anyone. Every Wednesday, I eat a banana split and shop.*"

I make a mental note to tell Martin that Jin thinks I am having an affair and because there are no secrets in China, people at the company will say, "*You know Martin? The guy with the fake beard . . . he is wearing a green hat.*" In China, when a man is married to a cheating wife, he is said to be wearing a green hat. At least there will be no judgment about my having an affair, so it doesn't matter what anyone but Martin thinks.

Actually, I am having an affair with my banana split. With this kind of affair, I will have Martin wear a brown and white beanie with a whirligig on top made from long toothpicks and Maraschino cherries speared to the ends. Then, as Martin dashes around the factory, the cherries will spin into a blur.

It is getting late and almost time for Jin to pick up Martin, and I say, *"Jin, how about if we go to the factory now? Then you won't have to hurry in this crazy Shanghai traffic. OK?"*

"OK, OK," Jin says. *"This is a good idea because Jin doesn't want Martin to say,' Jin, you are late.' But you know, Martin says, 'Jin, five o'clock, Martin home.' But five o'clock comes. No Martin. Five thirty. No Martin. Six o'clock. No Martin. Jin is not late. Martin is late."*

*"Right, right. Jin should tell Martin that he is the one who is late. In English you would say, '*Martin, you are late.'"Jin nods his head.

When we arrive at the factory, Jin walks with me into the administrative section because the one time I tried to find Martin's desk by myself, I was soon lost. Then Martin, Jin, and another driver looked all over the factory for me. Jin won't let that happen again.

Jin and I are walking toward Martin's desk when a friend of Jin's, who is also a driver, says, *"Taitai, nihao. How is your ruler?"*

I say, *"Not too bad. Thank you for asking."* Does everyone working at this company know about my little ruler?

Martin is at his desk. He says *nihao* to Jin and gives me a hug and kisses my cheek. "Hi, honey. I'm surprised to see you."

"I was late getting my errands finished," I say, "and I wanted Jin to come here first instead of taking me straight home." There isn't any place for me to sit while I wait for Martin other than someone's vacant desk. "Marty, I'm going to go back to the car and I'll wait for you there."

As Jin and I start walking back to the car, we see Yang walking toward us. *"Yang, hello,"* I say. *"Long time no see. Are you doing well?"*

Yang shakes my hand. I'm reminded of his marvelous smile. Yang says, *"Hello. Long time no see. Are you doing well?"*

I am sure Yang has heard the story about my small ruler, but he doesn't mention it. He might even know about my "affair" with banana splits.

The three of us walk to Jin's car, and Yang opens the car door for me. I pat Yang on the shoulder. I look in his eyes and say, *"Yang, good to see you. Until later."* Yang seems happy.

Jin and I play go fish with cards we keep in the glove box. It isn't long before we see Martin walking to the car, and Paul is with him.

Since we live in the same building, sometimes Paul comes back to The Tower with Martin. Paul slides into the front passenger seat, pats Jin on the shoulder to say hello and then looks at me as I sit in the backseat. "Hey, Sharon, how are you? How's the Chinese coming along?"

"Hi, Paul. I'm fine. I'm studying hard. How are you doing?"

"I'm working too hard," he says.

Jin starts the drive toward The Tower, and I'm sitting behind Jin, as usual. Paul reaches down between the front seats of the car and pulls out a Chinese picture dictionary for children. Jin uses this book to help me with my Chinese. Paul casually thumbs through the dictionary. When he comes to the page with pictures of school supplies, his eyes zero in on a picture of a six-inch ruler. Paul turns his head and is looking at me when he says, "So Sharon, I heard you bought a ruler. How did you do that?"

"You know, Paul, I've been wondering. Is there *anyone* who hasn't heard about my ruler?"

Paul pauses to give my question serious consideration, and then, with an angelic expression on his face, he says, "Sharon, everyone who knows anything knows you bought a small ruler. Now, if you had tried to buy a big ruler . . ."

I look at Martin. His face doesn't even show the hint of a smirk as he says, "Honey, I never said anything."

I look at Jin's eyes in his rearview mirror. Jin says, *"Taitai, what did Paul say?"*

"Paul is talking about my ruler."

Traffic comes to a standstill, and Jin turns to Paul. In flawless English, he says, "Taitai did not buy Mao. He is dead."

October 17, 1997: Go Home and Rest

Last night, Martin didn't get home until six thirty. Jin is driving to Fudan, and I say, *"So Jin, Martin was late coming home last night. Did you tell him, 'Martin you are late'?"*

"Oh . . . no, no. If Jin says, 'Martin, you are late,' Martin will say, 'Jin, go home and rest. Don't come back.'"

"I understand. See you after class."

Jin says, "See ya." He sounds just like an American.

While I am in class, I realize I need rubber bands to keep my flash cards grouped together by category. When Jin asks me after class where I want to go, I say, *"I need rubber bands. Could we go to Babaiban?"*

Jin says, *"Taitai, it's Friday. Go home . . . Rest . . . Don't worry. Jin will find rubber bands for taitai."*

Does Jin not want to take me to the office supply department of Babaiban—the home of rulers? I don't argue with a Chinese person, so I drop the subject. I am thankful I can go home and rest.

October 20, 1997: Rubber Bands

It's Monday. As Jin starts driving me to class he says, *"Jin has something for you."* He passes a bag of one hundred rubber bands to me at a stoplight.

"Jin, this is good, very good. Thank you for the rubber bands. How much money were these rubber bands?"

Jin says, *"Mei guanxi, mei guanxi."* "It doesn't matter, never mind."

I want to pay him for the rubber bands and say, *"Where did you get these?"*

"Someplace," he says.

OK. This is yet another time when I am not going to get my way. *"Jin, thank you for these rubber bands. You are good to me."* Jin is thoughtful, and I can depend on him to help me. In keeping with the Chinese custom of reciprocity, I will give Jin something he needs or something he would like to have. I don't know yet what I will give to him, but I will come up with something special.

October 22, 1997: Happy Wednesday

It is my Banana Split Day. After I have my sugar fix, I ask Jin to come with me into the Portman's grocery store to help me carry several bags of groceries to the car. As we are carrying groceries down to the parking garage under the Portman, Jin is humming to himself, and I say, *"Are you happy?"*

Jin stops walking and says, *"Are you happy?"*

"Yes. Yes, Jin. I am. I'm very happy." We both start walking again.

"Then if taitai is happy, Jin is happy. If taitai is not happy, Jin is not happy."

I wink at Jin and say, *"Every Wednesday, taitai is extremely happy."*

Jin stops walking again . . . and then he winks back at me. *"Then every Wednesday, Jin is extremely happy."*

October 23, 1997: What Does a Man Know About Shoes?

Mrs. Wang brought over the two Chinese dresses she made for me, which are a perfect fit. After she leaves my apartment, I wonder what shoes I should wear with this kind of dress.

Wearing my black *qipao,* I put on some heels and look in the bathroom mirror. The mirror is too short for me to see what the heels look like with the dress. Stella will know which shoes I should wear, and I go downstairs to the main office to find her.

At the back of the main office, behind a closed door, there is a room filled with banks of surveillance monitors. Electronic eyes watch everyone entering or leaving the building as well as all offices, hallways, and elevators. Whoever is watching the monitors knows I am on my way downstairs.

The entire front of the main office is all glass. When I step off the elevator, I can see this office and the three plastic chairs that are against the wall. This arrangement of chairs reminds me of the principal's office in my grade school. The entire front of the main office is thick glass. I can see Mr. Guo, the sales manager for the building, as he sits behind his enormous desk. I push on the heavy glass door, and Mr. Guo stands up.

I say, *"Mr. Guo, hello. Is Stella here? I have a question."*

Mr. Guo says, *"Hello, hello. Perhaps I may help you?"*

Kevin and David enter Mr. Guo's office from the door at the back of the office. They must have been in the surveillance room. The three men wait for me to gather my Chinese words so that I can explain what I need. *"I want to ask Stella what kind of shoes I should wear with this dress."* Three more employees of the building appear along with Stella. The room is getting crowded.

Mr. Guo says, *"I can help you, but first I must tell you about proper walking and sitting. It is essential that you not walk like a Western woman."*

"Perhaps you could show me this proper walking and sitting."

Mr. Guo says, *"It would be my pleasure to show you."* Two more employees crowd into the sales manager's office. This is now Chinese theater with standing room only. When Mr. Guo steps from behind his desk, the crowd parts like the Red Sea.

He steps up to the glass door and walks outside the office, where he closes his eyes and mentally transforms himself into an elegant Chinese woman. He takes a deep breath and steps toward the door. With his chest out and his head up, he pushes on the heavy door. Using tiny graceful steps, he glides like a swan, sits on a chair, and crosses his ankles. His back is straight as he sits on the edge of the chair and folds his hands on his knees. Then he leaps up and spreads his arms out like he is about to fly away and says, *"You see? Easy. You try."* Mr. Guo ignores the giggles from the crowd.

Once Mr. Guo was outside his office, that's when he began the proper walking. That is what I am going to do, and I say, *"OK, OK,"* and I clomp in my heels toward the door.

"No . . . no . . . no," Mr. Guo says. *"I will show you again."* Mr. Guo demonstrates more slowly this time. He balances an imaginary book on his head and glides out the door and back. Everyone, including Stella, snickers behind their hands.

"Now you do," Mr. Guo says. *"This time . . . walk with grace."*

I can do this. Chin up, chest out, shoulders back, and tuck that butt. I slowly move toward the door. When my left foot is forward, my right shoulder is forward, and I take a step . . . and reverse . . . and I take another step . . . I walk out of the office, walk back in the office, and sit on a chair. I put my right ankle behind my left ankle, and I am careful not to lean back too far. I tuck my hands together in my lap and say, *"So then, Mr. Guo, is my walk good or not good?"*

Mr. Guo beams with approval, and everyone applauds. I say, *"Thank you, Mr. Guo, for helping me. You are an excellent teacher,"* and then I remember why I came downstairs. *"So then, Mr. Guo, what shoes should I wear?"*

Mr. Guo touches the side of his nose and says, *"I think this does not matter."*

October 25, 1997: I am Martin's Boss

Tonight is our first English Night Party for the administrative and engineering employees. Yesterday, Jin helped me to order enough food for twenty people from my favorite Chinese restaurant, which is Wu Wu Wu, located at 555 Lao Shan Lu. *Wu Wu Wu* means *five five five*.

Earlier today, Jin picked up the cake I ordered from the Chinese bakery and brought it upstairs. Having the food catered is much easier than cooking and worrying about whether or not our Chinese friends will like American food.

Martin and I registered this activity with the management downstairs because Shanghai officials want to know what we are doing. There is no freedom of assembly in China. Also, guests have to sign in downstairs before they can come up to our apartment. Jin doesn't have to sign in.

Martin has already eaten dinner since he won't be eating any of the Chinese food I have ordered. The food arrives at six o'clock, along with our twenty guests. Amy helps me to set out forty pairs of chopsticks along with paper napkins and ceramic plates. When Amy and I have all of the food placed on serving plates on the dining room table, we are ready for dinner.

Martin asks for everyone's attention and says, "Thank you for coming to our apartment tonight. Before we eat, I would like Sharon to say something in Chinese."

What? Martin didn't tell me I was going to have to say anything. *"Hello, everyone,"* I say. *"My name is Sharon, and I am Martin's boss. Thank you for coming to our home."* Our guests laugh as they applaud my effort to speak Mandarin.

After my little speech, one of the engineers, with a forlorn look on his face, pats Martin on the shoulder as he says to him, "So sad."

Dinner is a success. I watch Amy eat cake with chopsticks. Will there ever be a time when I will be as good as she is with chopsticks? I use a fork to eat my cake. After dessert, I put on a Mr. Bean movie starring Rowan Atkinson, who is one of England's greatest comedy actors. The movie has a lot of physical humor.

Martin and I had this English Night Party so that everyone could learn a little more English in a fun and inviting atmosphere. Martin and I loved having everyone to our apartment.

October 28, 1997: She Begged and I Buckled

I hear The Chinese Knock and answer the door. "*Stella, hello. Please come in.*"

"Sharon, hello. I have a favor to ask. Do you know who Mozart is?"

"*Yes, why do you ask?*"

"*I would like for you to be on the Pyramid Quiz Show with us. First they will show us a fifteen-minute documentary film. Then they will ask three teams questions about Mozart. The Tower will be one team.*"

"Stella, I don't know much about Mozart. They will also be speaking Chinese."

"Sharon, your Chinese is good, but you won't have to say anything. We need one more person. The Tower has been chosen to be on this program. Everyone must be from The Tower. You don't need to do anything."

"Stella, are you sure? I can just sit there? I won't have to answer any questions?"

"*Yes, yes. Just sit with us. Say nothing. Do nothing.*" Then she says the magic words, "*Sharon . . . qiu qiu ni.*" "I beg you."

Stella begs and I buckle. "*OK, OK. I'll go, but I will just sit there. I won't have to say anything. Right?*" Stella assures me that I won't have to answer even one question about Mozart or say a single word in Chinese. I tell myself that as long as I will be doing nothing, everything will be all right.

November 3, 1997: The Pyramid Quiz Show

I need to leave class early so Jin can get me to the Shanghai television studio on time. When I stand up from my desk, my professor asks me, in front of everyone, why I am leaving class early. I tell her I am going to be on the *Pyramid Quiz Show*.

She says, "*On what day will the program be on television?*"

"*Next Wednesday.*"

"*Great,*" she says. "*I will watch you on television.*" My professor writes something down in a book, and everyone in class also makes a note to watch the show next Wednesday.

On my way to Jin's car, I imagine my fellow students and professor tuning in next week to the quiz show to watch me do nothing. But if they want to watch me do nothing that is fine with me. Jin is excited that I'm going to be on television, but he also doesn't know I will be doing nothing.

Stella told me that twenty-two million people in China watch this quiz show, which is not a lot of people considering that China's population is over one billion people. The *Pyramid Quiz Show* is ranked as the third most popular television show in the nation.

I keep reassuring myself with my mantra—I don't have to do anything. I am just going to sit there and do nothing.

Jin and I arrive at the station on time and walk to a door where a man is checking off names. Jin turns to me and says, "*Taitai, see you at four-thirty.*"

My name is checked off, and I'm told to sit with my team. Stella waves and calls my name. I climb up some bleachers and sit next to her. "*Stella, hello,*" I say. "*So I don't have to do anything, right?*"

"*Right, right,*" she says. "*Don't worry.*"

Someone passes out size large, long-sleeve T-shirts in red, yellow, and blue to the teams. There is the red team, the yellow team, and The Tower's team, which is the blue team. We put the T-shirts on over our clothes.

In China, a size large is a medium, and my T-shirt is way too small, but I pull it over the thick sweater I am wearing and squeeze into it. I look like a snowman without a carrot for my nose, but it doesn't matter because no one is going to see me. I am going to be doing nothing. So, I don't care.

Finally, Mr. Producer steps in front of the three teams and says, blah, blah, blah in Chinese and then some more of the same, but I don't pay any attention because I am just here to do nothing. Fiddlededee. I start making a mental grocery list. I check my nails. My mind goes to my freezer. I try to picture how many Magnums are in there. I add Magnums to my grocery list. Ho-hum. I check my nails again. They haven't grown since I looked at them the last time.

Each team is seated on four rows of bleachers. There are five people on the top row, followed by four, three, and two people on the bottom row. Stella and I are sitting in the second row from the bottom.

Uh-oh. Mr. Producer is speaking in English. Oh no. I hear him say, "For the first time, we have a foreigner on our program." He extends his hand toward me and says, "Welcome."

I say, "Thank you." Of course no foreigner has ever been on this program before because this show is all in Chinese.

He continues in English as he motions to me. "We will hand the microphone to you and ask you the special question."

Mr. Producer isn't talking to me, is he? I turn to Stella and say, "Stella, who is he talking to? What special question? Stella?"

Stella shrugs her shoulders. She is no help. When I look back at Mr. Producer, he puts a microphone under my chin, but I don't take it because I am here to do nothing. Stella needs to tell Mr. Producer right now that I am not here to answer *any questions*. Stella grabs the microphone and holds it in front of me. Whose side is she on?

Mr. Producer says, "OK, OK, take the microphone."

I take the microphone from Stella and say to Mr. Producer, "You're going to ask me a question during the show?" I speak in English. I don't want him to know I can even say hello in Chinese.

"That is right," Mr. Producer says. "We will ask you the special question. Hold the microphone like you are doing now and give me your answer."

I say, "But I will have to give you my answer in English." If I answer in English, hardly anyone will know what I have said.

"That is not a problem," he says. "We will put your answer in Chinese along the bottom of the television screen."

Oh . . . this is just great! Now twenty-two million Chinese people will see a foreign nincompoop in action. I hand the microphone back to Mr. Producer as if it is a hot potato. Now I am nervous, and I look like a snowman. My idiocy with the ruler is going to be nothing compared to whatever brainless answer I am going to give to this special question.

The three teams watch a fifteen-minute documentary in Mandarin on the era during which Mozart lives. I can understand most of it. We see the house where Mozart lived, the clothing worn during this time, and we learn a little about Mozart's musical history.

Mr. Producer says that we are going to start in fifteen minutes, and then he asks Stella, *"What is wrong with her T-shirt?"*

Stella says, *"It's too small."*

Mr. Producer points toward a dingy hallway. *"OK, OK. I want everyone to go to wash hands room. Take off what you have on under your T-shirt."*

Taking the sweater off helps the T-shirt to fit a little better. When we return to the bleachers, the program begins. Each team is asked questions in Chinese about Mozart and his era. I don't know the answer to any of the Mozart questions. I am pretty sure that the documentary had none of these answers.

Then Mr. Producer hands me a microphone and asks the dreaded special question, which is, "During the time Mozart lived, women wore a ceramic item under their billowing hooped skirts. This item had holes in it. What was the purpose of this item?"

I have no idea what the answer is, but I say, "You put perfume on a cotton ball and then put the cotton in this ceramic item." Bong! Wrong answer. The red team and the yellow team are given a chance to answer the same question. They don't even have a guess. The answer? The ceramic item is a flea trap.

Fortunately, our team wins even with my wrong answer, and I assume that I am done. Nope. Someone draws a name out of a fish bowl. The studio lights twirl around dizzily until they settle on a spinning wheel, and then a voice from the void says, *"Let's see what Mr. and Mrs. Wei have won."*

Mr. Producer helps me down from the bleachers and walks with me to the center of the stage, where I face a large spinning wheel. He hands me a dart. I am grateful he didn't hand me any glue. Mr. Spinner is standing next to the wheel and continuously pulling down on the wheel to make it spin. Mr. Producer says to me, "It is time to throw the dart."

I ask Mr. Spinner in Mandarin to step aside, and he says, *"It doesn't matter, never mind. Throw the dart."* OK. I throw the dart, but not too hard, because if I hit Mr. Spinner, I don't want to kill him, especially on television. A newspaper headline flashes in my mind, "Foreign Nincompoop Kills Man on Quiz Show." The dart touches the spinning wheel and slides to the floor. I throw the dart again, this time harder, and Mr. and Mrs. Wei have won a vacation.

The program ends, and everyone on our winning team is given a watch with the logo of the show on its face. We are also told that we can keep our T-shirts. As we go out the door, cookies are passed out. Martin would have liked this part. Stella and I walk to Jin's car where he is waiting for me. I hug her and tell her I will see her later.

When Jin is getting ready to drive off, he says, *"How was it?"*

Still wearing my blue T-shirt, I say, *"The blue shirts won. They gave us watches."* I hand the watch I have been given as a prize to Jin. *"Please give this to your daughter."*

Jin says, *"She will like this. She will show this to her friends at school. Thank you."*

I say, *"Don't be so polite."* I have now given something to Jin in return for the rubber bands. As each day passes, I am becoming more Chinese.

November 7, 1997: Hairy Crab Party

The company is sponsoring a hairy crab party in a private dining room of a restaurant tonight. Martin comes home late, so there is no time for him to eat anything before we leave for dinner. There is also no way Martin will be eating any of the Chinese food at the restaurant, so he will have to wait until we are on our way home from the dinner party to get something to eat.

With Martin's help, I put on the black *qipao* Mrs. Wang made for me. The dress fits every curve I have and is comfortable. The two slits up the side of this long dress make it possible for me to walk, and I know how to do the proper walking and sitting in this dress, too. I am wearing Stella-approved heels.

The mandarin collar of this dress is a good style for me. Blue bamboo fronds and miniature phoenixes in gold, blue, and bits of red are interwoven into the black background of this silk fabric. The phoenix is one of the four mystical animals of China. The other three are the unicorn, dragon, and tortoise. Buttons are also made from this fabric. They are handmade frog buttons, and they are placed diagonally across the top of my dress starting from the middle of my throat and ending under my left arm. This diagonal cut is on the opposite side of the traditional *qipao* because, as Mrs. Wang said, *"This cut is the opposite for you because you are a Western woman."*

This is one of several wet markets in Shanghai where live fish, turtles, hairy crabs, and other sea creatures can be purchased for dinner.

Jin drives us to the restaurant and shows us to the door of the private dining room. Martin and I are the last guests to arrive, and when we walk in everyone applauds. Are they applauding because we have finally arrived? After I sit down, I remember that applauding is a kind of greeting. Paul, Martin, and I are the only Westerners attending this dinner for thirty people.

Paul is seated at the back of the room facing the door, and the only two empty seats in the room are next to Paul. As soon as Martin and I sit down, Paul stands up to say a few words. He talks about how much he is enjoying Shanghai, and then he asks if everyone is enjoying working for the company. Naturally, everyone says that they love working for the company. Then Paul looks at me and says, "Sharon is studying Chinese. This is wonderful." Paul is on Martin's right. I am on Martin's left.

Paul

Everyone applauds in appreciation for what Paul has said, and then Martin stands up. He introduces himself, says blah blah blah, and holds his hand toward me and says, "This is my wife. She is now going to say something to you in Chinese."

Martin has blindsided me. He will pay for this. I have nothing prepared to say in any language.

Rascal is his name. He lives in me, and he has now awakened. I take a deep breath. My brain spins around in my head as it gathers up my entire Mandarin lexicon and puts it in a pile before me. I stand up. My brain has done all it can and shouts, "You can do this." Rascal is sitting comfortably on my shoulder. He has never let me down, and no one can see him.

"Good evening. My English name is Sharon. My Chinese name is Wen Li Xia." I hold my hand toward Martin and say, *"Everyone knows Martin does not speak Chinese."* I touch my forehead as if I am having a profound thought and say, *"Oh . . . I made a mistake. Martin knows enough Chinese to say hello, ask for a hamburger and cookies and then . . . tell a woman she is beautiful.*

"I am sure he gazes into her eyes like a puppy as he says this." I demonstrate what this might look like, and then I say, *"I should know, but if that doesn't work, he knows how to say, 'I beg you.'*

"Then he will say . . . thank you, bye-bye, airport . . . and leave the country."

The women in the room cover their mouths as they try not to laugh. The guys break out in toothy grins that reflect the shenanigans they know are coming up next. Almost everyone in the room got to know me a little when they attended our first English Night Party. Amy is smiling and loving every moment of this.

I say, *"Everyone knows Paul does not speak Chinese, so then Martin and Paul don't know what I'm saying . . . Too bad."* Rumbles of snickers are gaining momentum as they swirl around the room. Paul hardly knows me, so he is clueless as to what I might be saying, but Martin . . . well . . . he is now looking at me with apprehension and a dash of regret that has come too late.

I say, *"Everyone knows Paul thinks he is Martin's boss. No, no. Paul is not Martin's boss."* I put my hand over my heart, and with encouragement from my Rascal, I say, *"I . . . am Martin's boss."* Rocking laughter shakes the thin walls of the room. We are disturbing the other diners. Some of the guys slam their hands down on their table and stomp their feet on the floor as they laugh. Because of the ruckus in this room, few hear my final remarks when I say, *"Tonight it is my pleasure to be here with everyone. Thank you."* I sit down. My little Rascal is tittering as he goes off to take a nap until I need him again. I love him.

Everyone applauds with enthusiasm, including Paul and Martin who look around the room for someone to tell them what is so funny. It takes a while for the laughter to die down, and no one is willing to tell on me. The young Chinese man, Allen, who is sitting next to me, leans toward me and whispers, *"You were hilarious."*

A vegetable dish is served, and then two waiters come into the dining room. They are carrying large platters piled high with pyramids of hairy crabs, which are also referred to as teddy bear crabs because of their furriness. Everyone except for Martin tries the vegetable dish and takes a hairy crab.

The camouflage of these animals is hair that looks like floating seaweed when these crabs are in the water. But when these crabs are on a platter, this hairy camouflage looks like mud on their joints.

There are no tools on the table to help me open this animal. Allen shows me how to break open a crab and says, *"The males are harder to open."* He shows me which crabs are females. *"Sharon, here . . . take this female. Don't eat the lungs. Very bad for you."* Allen rips off one of the claws from his crab and shows me how to use the claw to pry the shell open. *"Now you try,"* he says.

I have some success opening the crab with the claw, and Allen points to something inside the crab. *"Those are the lungs,"* he says. *"Don't eat them."*

Martin looks at my crab and shivers. I look over at Paul who is opening his crab as if it's a new toy. Martin leans toward me and whispers, "There is no way I could eat one of those." Everyone in the room knows Martin does not, will not, and cannot eat Chinese food, and his queasiness around teddy bear crabs makes it all the more delightful to tease him. We all know Martin's first stop after dinner will be either McDonald's or KFC.

Amy shouts in English from across the room. "Sharon, have Martin open the crab for you."

Allen hands a second female hairy crab to me, and everyone is watching as I turn to Martin on my right. I hold up the crab and shake her flopping legs in front of Martin. His expression of revulsion makes all of us laugh, and I say, "Honey, would you open my teddy bear crab for me?"

Paul yells out, "Sharon . . . love . . . will only go so far."

Martin turns to Paul and says, "Actually, Paul . . . Sharon is talking to you." Our laughter disturbs the other diners again.

I try to open the claw of the teddy bear crab using my front teeth. I don't want to touch the claw with my tongue because the joint of the claw has a lot of hair on it. Allen sees me struggling with this teddy bear claw and says, *"Sharon, use your back teeth to open the claw."* I do as he suggests and holy cow. When I put the claw on my molars, I can feel the hair of this crab on my tongue. I do not like this feeling.

A large platter of turtles, piled high in a pyramid, is brought into the dining room. I pass on eating them. I don't even want to know how to eat them. A few more dishes arrive, most of which I don't recognize, and soon everyone is ready to go home. Martin's dislike of Chinese food has been solidified with this teddy bear crab party.

On the ride home, Jin asks me how dinner was, and I tell him, *"Martin said, 'Sharon, stand up. Say something in Chinese.' So I told everyone that Paul is not Martin's boss. I am Martin's boss. Everyone laughed."*

I can see Jin's eyes in his rearview mirror, and he looks concerned. *"Does Paul know what you said?"*

"No, no. He doesn't understand Mandarin. Paul and Martin wanted to know what was so funny. No one would tell them."

Martin is looking out the window and ignoring our conversation. Jin says, *"Does Martin want to go to McDonald's or KFC?"*

"Whichever is closer to home would be good."

Jin, still pondering my little speech at the dinner, says, *"So taitai is Martin's boss. Right, right . . . Jin likes this."* Jin speaks with conviction when he says, *"In my home . . . Jin is the boss."*

"So, Jin, does your wife know you are the boss at home?" Jin smiles but says nothing.

Jin pulls into McDonald's, and I say, *"Martin wants the third hamburger on the list with a soda, fries, and catsup."*

November 8, 1997: A Banquet

Lu is from Wuxi, China. He was working on a PhD in Chemistry at the University of New Mexico when I was taking classes in Chinese at this same university. He volunteered to help me learn to speak Mandarin. In exchange for his help, I showed him around Albuquerque and took him to lunch or dinner now and then.

Last week I received a letter from Lu's mother in Wuxi, and I asked Jin to read it to me. The letter was an invitation from Lu's parents for an early afternoon dinner. Jin called Mrs. Lu and accepted on my behalf. He also told her that he would be bringing me as well as my friend Stella. Jin helped me to pick out appropriate gifts to give to Lu's parents, which were four boxes of candy.

Today, Jin drove Stella and me to the home of Lu's parents. We all dressed up for the occasion. Stella wore the koi fish brooch on her vest.

On the way to Wuxi, I asked Jin and Stella to correct me at this dinner if I was doing something I was not supposed to do or if I was failing to do something I should be doing. I touched Jin on his shoulder and said, *"You know, Jin, I don't understand your culture."*

Jin looked at me in his rearview mirror and said, *"Taitai, don't worry. I don't understand it, either."* His comment was not reassuring, but Jin and Stella promised me that they would keep me from doing something inane as long as I didn't try to buy another ruler.

On the long drive to Wuxi, the three of us talked about Martin's and my dog, Jakie. Then Stella told Jin how I dropped dim sum in my vinegar bowl, splashed vinegar on the tablecloth, and told the waitress that Stella was the one who splattered vinegar on the tablecloth.

"You know, Jin," Stella said, *"Sharon has told me that nothing is ever her fault."*

"That's right," Jin said. *"It is never taitai's fault. It is Martin's fault, Jin's fault, Stella's fault, or Jakie's fault."* Jin and Stella weren't saying that I could never be at fault. They were saying that they were willing to take the blame for me, so I could save face. They knew this dinner was going to test my Chinese social and dining etiquette—what little I had.

I said, *"Jin and Stella, thank you for coming with me."* Jin had no choice, but I didn't mention that.

When we arrive in Wuxi, Lu's father is waiting outside his home for us. He welcomes me with a firm handshake and a heartfelt smile. He motions for us to walk through the front door, and we step into a room that is about twelve feet square with a round table and six chairs. Stairs lead to a second floor. Behind the front room, there is a kitchen and a door that opens to a bathroom. The two-story brick house is about six hundred square feet and connects to a long row of two-story houses.

Lu's mother smiles with tenderness as she greets me. When she takes my hand in both of her hands, I feel like one of her long-lost relatives. Jin hands me the gifts I brought for Lu's parents, and I give the boxes of candy to Mrs. Lu, using both hands as I give her a slight bow. She also bows slightly as she receives the gifts with both hands.

Then she gestures toward the chair where she wants me to sit. This is the chair facing the door—the place where the most important guest sits. Lu's mother, as the hostess, sits on my left, and Lu's father sits on her left. Stella is on my right, and Jin sits next to Stella. As soon as everyone is seated, dinner begins.

Lu's mother serves everyone green tea, which I don't drink, but I thank her and drink some anyway. Then Jin says something to her I can't understand, and a soft drink appears in front of me. I thank her again.

Next, Lu's mother brings out a vegetable dish, and I say, *"This looks good."* I am waiting for someone to tell me to start eating or for someone to take food from the plate with the chopsticks that have been set in the dish with the vegetables. Everyone sits and stares at me. The steaming vegetables are in front of me, and everyone's plate is empty. I don't know what to do.

In the States, the hostess will say, "Dig in," or some other similar command. Jin and Stella have a quiet conversation, and then Stella says in English, "Sharon, do you want to wash your hands?"

I do want to wash my hands, but this isn't why I'm not eating. I still don't know what to do about the plate of veggies in front of me, and now I don't know what to say about washing my hands. I know I will use my chopsticks in such a way that I won't touch my food with my hands, so I'm not that concerned with washing my hands. But before I can figure out what to say about washing my hands, Mrs. Lu brings out a large wooden bowl of warm water and holds the bowl to my side. A white washcloth is in the water. Stella says, "Take the towel. Wash your face and then your hands."

I do as Stella suggests, and then Lu's mother invites me to start eating. Oh . . . I am supposed to start eating first.

Jakie

Once everyone has vegetables on their plate, Lu's mother asks me how many children I have, and I say, *"Three children."*

Jin says, *"No, no. She has four."* Everyone stops eating, stares at Jin, and waits for him to explain. *"Taitai has Jakie,"* he says. *"He is a dog but like one of her children."*

I say, *"Right, right. I have a dog. We call him Jakie. Your son met my dog Jakie. He also met my other dog, Wolfgang, and my husband and friends, too. Lu was at my birthday party."*

She says, *"What did you do for your birthday?"*

"We ate food and cake. I played a song on my piano. My piano teacher was there, too. She played three songs on my piano. Everyone likes your son. He is an outstanding young man. Two of my friends gave your son a talk. They told him to stay away from women, especially American women."

Lu's mother leans toward me, and Lu's father leans toward his wife as Lu's mother whispers to me, *"Does Lu have a girlfriend?"*

I lean toward Lu's mother and whisper, *"He has never mentioned a girlfriend."* I am grateful I know nothing about Lu having or not having a girlfriend.

Stella tells Lu's parents about the cutted chicken lunch she and I had and how I dropped dim sum in my vinegar bowl and told the waitress Stella was the one who made the mess. Lu's parents laugh when they hear this story, but they are not quite sure if this story is true. However, they don't know about the Rascal who lives with me and is napping right now.

Lu's mother next serves a shrimp dish, and I say, *"I love shrimp."* Lu's mother has now served two dishes, and they are excellent.

Jin looks at me with an unblinking stare—he does this so well—and says, *"Taitai, these dishes are very good . . . aren't they?"* Jin is keeping his promise to help me mind my Chinese manners. In the States, when a guest finishes a meal, she compliments the cook on the superb dinner, but in China, I am supposed to compliment the cook on every dish, not just at the end of a meal.

I say to Jin, *"Yes, yes. Everything is very good."* I turn to Lu's mother and say, *"The vegetables and shrimp are delicious. These are the best dishes."*

Jin sits back in his chair and compliments Lu's mother, and Stella joins in Jin's praises.

Lu's mother whisks the plates away and serves another vegetable dish, which is fabulous, and I tell her so. Then she serves teddy bear crabs. I reach for a female crab and fumble around with it until Lu's mother takes it away from me and skillfully cracks it open in seconds. She points to the lungs and says, *"Don't eat those."*

I use my chopsticks to pull the meat out of the crab. *"Oh, this is extremely good,"* I say. *"The other dishes were fabulous, but these crabs are even better. You are the best cook."* Everything I say is true, and then I realize this isn't just a dinner. This is a banquet, and I am the guest of honor. I am touched by the generosity of Lu's parents and their kindness.

I ask Lu's mother how long they have been married. Lu's father looks over at his wife and continues to look at her as he tells me the story of how they worked as laborers during the Cultural Revolution and didn't live together for many years. He never takes his eyes away from his wife as he talks about their trials and tribulations, and he speaks without bitterness. Lu's mother listens as she looks at her hands folded in her lap. They seem to love each other. When Mrs. Lu is speaking, Lu's father looks at her with admiration and smiles. When Mr. Lu is speaking, Lu's mother respectfully listens to him.

Another vegetable dish is served, and then a barbeque meat is placed on the table. I tell Lu's father, *"This food is so good, you should be too fat to walk through the door. You are a lucky man to have such a wonderful wife."* He nods his head and agrees with me. Mrs. Lu shakes off the compliment and goes to the kitchen for more food.

Another vegetable dish comes out of the kitchen as well as a whole chicken, but without a head or a foot—thank you very much—and I am not sure how to get the meat off the chicken with my chopsticks. Jin sees my hesitation, takes some clean chopsticks, pulls off a wing, and puts it in my bowl of vinegar. I fumble with my chopsticks as I pick up the wing, and Jin says, *"Hold your chopsticks like this. Take a bite of chicken."*

Mrs. Lu takes my right hand and helps me to position my chopsticks better. My chopstick lesson is helpful, and just as I am getting the hang of it, Jin drops the piece of chicken he is eating, and I say, *"That is Stella's fault."*

"Not my fault," Stella says. *"Martin's fault."*

Jin says, *"No, no. Not Martin's fault. Jakie's fault."*

I finish the wing, and I still don't know how to get meat off the chicken with chopsticks. Jin picks up the communal chopsticks again and pulls off some of the breast meat and puts it on my plate. *"Jin, thank you. That is my favorite part."*

Jin looks at Stella and says, *"Jin knows the part of chicken taitai likes best."*

Stella looks at Jin with a charming expression and says, *"Stella doesn't know what Sharon likes best."* Now Jin has Stella talking about herself in the third person.

Mrs. Lu asks me about Martin's work, and I don't know how to explain his job. I look at Jin for help, and he says, *"Martin's job is to work. Taitai's job is to shop. Taitai says, 'Jin, we are going shopping.'"* Jin punches the air to emphasize the word "shopping," and his English is perfect. He has my Midwestern accent down.

Stella interprets for Lu's parents what Jin has said, and Lu's parents are impressed that Jin can speak some English.

The conversation then turns to The Martin Food List and Martin's nine-word Mandarin lexicon as Jin says, *"Martin only eats sixteen things, and he only knows nine Mandarin words."*

Stella nods and says, *"This is true."*

Lu's father wants to know what is on The Martin Food List.

Starting with his index finger on his left hand, while his right hand still holds his chopsticks, Jin says, *"Martin eats pizza, McDonald's, KFC, french fries, cookies, spaghetti, bacon, eggs, catsup, beans, lettuce, bread . . . no Chinese food."*

Lu's parents look at each other with an expression of wonderment. Lu's father says, *"What words does Martin know?"*

Jin says, *"Martin can say hello, cookies, KFC, McDonald's, beautiful, I beg you, thank you, bye-bye, and airport."*

Stella says, *"Martin knows how to say 'lazy sleeper' too, because yesterday Martin said, 'Stella, you are shui lan jia.'"*

I say, *"Stella, I told him to say you're a lazy sleeper."*

Stella says, *"Who taught you how to say lazy sleeper?"* I look at Jin, who gives everyone a sheepish grin as he begins to eat with gusto.

The final banquet dish is rice and soup. Lu's father scoops from the bottom of the soup bowl and pours the broth with meat and vegetables over my rice, which is the perfect end to a meal. I tell Lu's mother, *"This soup is delightful."* I am now out of adjectives to express how delicious her food is and out of room for any more food in my stomach.

Mrs. Lu gives us apples, and I ask her if I can take the apple home with me because I'm too full to eat anything else. The fruit and vegetables in China are the best I have ever eaten. Peasants pick fruit and harvest vegetables in the morning. Before lunchtime, peaches, plums, pumpkins, cherries, watermelons, and deep green vegetables are sold in open-air markets.

Stella, Jin, and I express our appreciation to Lu's mother for taking so much time to make such a spectacular dinner, and we thank Lu's father for inviting us to their home.

Lu's mother suggests a stroll around Taiho Lake in Wuxi. A walk is a good idea, and Jin drives us to the park. Stella takes my right hand, and Lu's mother takes my left as we walk around the park. Jin and Lu's father stroll behind us and talk.

When Jin drives us back to their house, Lu's father and mother present me with a teapot and cups made in Wuxi along with tea. Lu's parents also give some tea to Jin and Stella. I shake hands with Lu's father and embrace Lu's mother.

November 12, 1997: My Fifteen Minutes of Fame

Most Chinese people at the company, everyone in my Chinese class, and Jin's family, as well as his daughter's class at school, watched the *Pyramid Quiz Show* on television last night—aside from the usual twenty-two million viewers. Jin said that when he saw me on television, he yelled, *"That's taitai."*

November 20, 1997: I Am a Bad Person

When I attended the Shanghai Expatriate Association meeting this afternoon, one of my friends, Cheryl, was there. She doesn't speak any Chinese, and she said that a few days ago, when her driver opened the car door for her, the door hit her in the head. Ever since then, her driver has been saying, *"Wo bu hao ren . . . Wo bu hao ren."*

Cheryl asked me, "What does *wo bu hao ren* mean, and why does he keep saying this?"

I told her, "He is saying that he is not a good person. This is his way of asking you to forgive him." Cheryl looked puzzled, and I said, "The next time he says he is not a good person you might tell him that he is a good person. Maybe he will feel forgiven."

I wrote in pinyin on a piece of paper for her, *"Bú duì. Nǐ shì hǎo rén."* "Not correct. You are a good person," and I explained the tones to her.

Cheryl called and said that when she told him that he was a good person, he smiled for the first time in days. Since then she hasn't heard him say anything more about being a bad person.

November 22, 1997: Squids Lice and Fish Gills

I wanted to meet Ling Ling who lives in Beijing and sells pearls to people from all over the world. Because I easily get lost, Martin and I bought a plane ticket for Jin so he could go with me.

For lunch, on our flight to Beijing, everyone is given a cardboard box with packages of dehydrated food. The label on one package reads, "Squids Lice." Even though this is a typographical error, this doesn't make squid slice any more appealing to me.

Jin and I check into the Great Wall Sheraton Hotel and put our luggage in our rooms. We take a cab to Hong Qiao, also referred to as the Pearl Market and walk into a four-story building where Ling Ling's office is located on the third floor. On the first floor of this building, venders sell tourist kitsch. On the second floor, there are over one hundred kiosks manned by pearl dealers. At the back of the second floor, there are some antique dealers. One vendor is selling counterfeit Beanie Babies. Another shop is selling leather goods.

Hong Qiao International Pearl City in Beijing

Jin and I walk up a gloomy unlit stairwell to the third floor where we find Ling Ling's pearl shop and office. Because I don't know what Ling Ling looks like, I walk up to someone in Ling Ling's shop and say, *"Hello, I would like to speak with Ling Ling. Is she here?"*

The young woman looks toward the back of the shop and shouts, *"Ling Ling, someone is here to see you."*

Ling Ling soon comes up to me, shakes hands with me, and says, "Hello. I'm Ling Ling. May I help you?" Her English is good.

I say, "Ling Ling, it is a pleasure to meet you. *This is my friend, Mr. Jin.*"

Ling Ling greets Jin, who says, *"Ling Ling, I am also happy to meet you,"* and then he says to me, *"So then, you will stay here, right?"*

I assure Jin that I will stay put. He seems to be happy to be leaving girlie-territory and doesn't want to stick around and model pearl necklaces and earrings for us. Sometimes, he is just no fun.

At the back of the shop, which is Ling Ling's office, three women are stringing pearls. There is also a door in the interior of the office, similar to the door on a bank vault. Around the walls of the shop, necklaces are hung on pegs. Bins are stacked against the wall, and each bin is piled high with strands of unstrung pearls.

Unstrung strands of pearls fill bins in Ling Ling's shop.

I select two strands of high-quality, eight millimeter pearls to be made into an opera-length necklace. I also purchase one hundred strands of white pearls and a few strands of unusual colors of pearls, along with some strands of oddly shaped pearls, which I am told are called baroque pearls. I have never seen pearls in so many colors, shapes, and sizes. I purchase a few readymade pearl necklaces and bracelets. Unlike other pearl dealers in China, the prices for pearls at Ling Ling's shop are marked on a tag tied to the pearls.

Ling Ling opens the door to the interior vault. *"Sharon, please look in here. Perhaps you can find something you like."* The vault has gray metal drawers that go from the floor to the ceiling like the drawers in a safe deposit vault. I open drawers at random and see pearls with even more unusual colors and shapes. I find a few strands I have to buy. Several of these strands of pearls are cobalt blue with sparkling luster.

Some pearls are shaped like the front teeth of a horse. These are Biwa-type pearls. Before shopping in Ling Ling's shop, I have never heard of or ever seen Biwa pearls. Biwa is the name of a lake in Japan where these pearls were first cultured.

I hand Ling Ling the pearls I want to buy and say, *"I must stop shopping or I won't be able to buy lunch."*

"OK, Sharon," Ling Ling says. *"Let's have lunch."* Because Ling Ling has invited me to lunch, she will be ordering for me as well as paying. Ling Ling and I walk up to a restaurant on the fourth floor where she orders two vegetable dishes and fish. The dishes are quite tasty. (By 2006, Ling Ling owns a pearl shop in Shanghai as well as in Beijing.)

When Ling Ling and I return to her office, she points to a chair where I can sit and watch her while she strings my pearls into an opera-length necklace. To combine two strands of pearls into one necklace, she uses a beading needle to take a pearl or two from one strand of pearls, and then, using this beading needle, she slides these pearls onto a string. Then she takes a pearl or two from the other strand of pearls and slides those pearls onto the string. She repeats this process until the two strands of pearls are blended together onto one string. This method puts the the largest pearls in the center of the necklace. Then, using just her hands, Ling Ling puts a knot between each pearl, and every knot is exactly the same size. She does all of this while carrying on a conversation with me in English and Chinese.

Ling Ling learned to speak English from a book and then practiced her English with English-speaking customers. Ling Ling has a Chinese-English dictionary on her table that has been worn into a delicate frazzle.

After I purchase over fifteen pounds of pearls, I ask Ling Ling if someone can teach me to string pearls because I want to start a pearl business when I return to the States. One of Ling Ling's stringers shows me how to turn a strand of pearls into a necklace, and then it is my turn. The necklace I put together looks horrible, but practice will give me the skill I need.

Ling Ling gives me everything I need to string pearls—beading needles, string in black and white, and some french wire. After I pack up my pearls and supplies, I am hungry again, and Jin appears like magic. He looks at my packages and then looks up at the ceiling. Ling Ling and I look up at the ceiling, too. What is he looking at? And then he says, "Oh . . . I can hear Martin. He is saying, 'Jin, don't take Martin to Beijing again.'" This is a mystical side of Jin that I have never seen before.

As I tell Ling Ling that I will be back soon, Jin lifts the bags of pearls with a grunt. "So heavy," he says. The pearls aren't *that* heavy.

Jin and I take the elevator downstairs instead of walking down the dark stairwell, and I say, "Jin, I'm hungry. Could we talk about food?" Jin wants to discuss a taxi.

We take a cab back to the hotel, and after Jin sets my pearls down in my room, I say, "Jin, can we talk about food now? Let's eat someplace where they only have a Chinese menu." I want to eat at a good Chinese restaurant where the locals eat because the people who live in Beijing demand fresh and reasonably priced food. Restaurants for locals don't have menus in English. If a restaurant has a menu in English, this is a restaurant for tourists who most likely don't even know what real Chinese food looks like.

Jin searches his memory and says, "Jin knows a good place. Do you like fish?"

I give Jin a thumbs-up and say, "I like fish." I am once again eating animals. Some Buddhists do not want to contribute to the suffering and death of animals, and they observe a no-meat rule. And then there are Buddhists who are fickle-minded about the no-meat thing. I am in this group. We are on-again off-again like a blinking traffic light. My only excuse is that I feel better when I eat some meat. I do, however, observe the no-eat-piggy rule. That should count for something.

Jin and I walk a few blocks to a restaurant with an all-glass façade. We are seated at the front of the restaurant by the floor-to-ceiling windows. A waiter gives us menus and stands by our table. I open my menu as if I can read Chinese as Jin orders two vegetable dishes and a fish dish.

When ordering dishes, it is customary to count the number of people at the table and add one, so for three people, order four dishes, and one or two of these dishes will be an animal source of protein unless there are Buddhists in the group who are observing the no-meat rule.

Traditional Chinese food is not like American Chinese food. In China, vegetables, fruits, animal flesh foods, tofu, rice, and soup are separate dishes and served one at a time. Chinese people don't plop rice on a plate along with a main dish, and rice and soup are served at the end of a meal rather than at the beginning. Then, after you pay your bill, fruit in season is served.

Also, traditional Chinese cooking offers a variety of sauces rather than just brown sauce, white sauce, soy sauce, and sweet and sour sauce. The biggest difference is that a meal in China is a time of celebration, not something to get through in a hurry so everyone can go back to work.

Outside this restaurant, there are a lot of people walking by the floor-to-ceiling window. Some people slow down as they walk past the window, and sometimes they even stop and peer through the glass to see what they can see.

The waiter brings a large fish to our table, flopping in a bag, gasping for life. Jin nods to the waiter. *"Good, good,"* he says, and the fish is taken off to the kitchen.

A vegetable dish soon arrives, and Jin asks for an extra pair of chopsticks, which will be our community chopsticks. The chopsticks used for taking food from the community dish are not the same ones we use to put food into our mouths. Using the community chopsticks, I lift vegetables from the main dish onto my plate, and Jin follows suit. A second vegetable dish arrives, which is even better than the first.

Then the fish arrives in one whole piece and his mouth is open. Is he dead or just in shock? I stare at the fish to see if he will move, and Jin says, *"Is there a problem? You said you like fish."*

My eyes are glued to the fish as I say, *"Is he dead? I think he wants to say something."*

Jin takes the community chopsticks and pokes him. *"He is dead. He has nothing to say. Let's eat. First, you eat the gill."*

"The gill? Jin, why eat the gill?"

"Fish gill is the best part. Taitai should eat the gill."

If I eat the gill, I might throw up, and I say, *"No, no. Taitai should not eat the gill. Jin should eat the best part."* In my desperation, not only am I referring to myself in the third person, but I am arguing with a Chinese person, which is against my rule.

Perhaps reasoning with Jin will work, and I say, *"First, I will eat some fish. Then my tummy will be full. There will be no room for the gill in my stomach. Taitai wants Jin to have the best part."* It isn't that I am being generous. No, no. I am desperate.

Jin finally agrees with me, and when he eats the gill, the eye of the fish turns blue.

November 24, 1997: Stringing Is a Skill

I tried to string pearls into a necklace this evening, but I can't remember how to make the knots. This means I will have to go back to Beijing for another lesson. Learning this skill will take a lot of practice.

November 28, 1997: A Gaggle of Guys in The Sacred Circle

It is Friday. The company is treating everyone to an evening of bowling, and Jin drives us over to the bowling alley. He walks with us into the bowling alley and then goes back outside to talk with his driver buddies who are in a huddle just outside the bowling alley. I stay inside the bowling alley for ten minutes to at least make an appearance.

Martin's administrator, Mary, comes up to me, and we talk briefly. She is a sweet person and treats me with kindness. I say hello to a few other people and then find Martin who is having a good time bowling and say, "Marty, I'm going to get something to eat."

"OK, honey, but have Jin take you or you'll get lost. T.G.I. Fridays is two or three streets down." Martin hugs me and kisses my cheek. In China, this is scandalous behavior.

Wearing a sweater and blue jeans, I step into the Shanghai night. The air is cool, and vehicles slowly drive down the wide street as they bump through a bottleneck of cars, trucks, and motorcycles. Thousands of lights, from shops open for business, blink and beckon buyers. Impatient drivers honk their horns.

I find Jin in a huddle talking with five other drivers. His back is to me as I approach him. I stand to his side and wait for him to notice me. When the men stop talking, Jin turns toward me. *"Taitai, why aren't you bowling?"*

"I don't like bowling, but I'm hungry."

The gaggle of guys looks amused. I don't know why. Without a word, Jin guides me by my elbow away from the huddle. Is this a Sacred Circle? Once we are out of hearing distance, he says, *"Where do you want to go?"*

"Do you want to go to T.G.I. Fridays? Martin says it isn't too far, two or three streets."

At T.G.I. Fridays, when we are seated, we are given menus in English, and Jin's eyes roll around the menu as if he can read it.

"Jin, do you like strawberries?" I say.

"Yes, strawberries are good," he says as he continues to peruse his menu with interest. I don't point out what is on the menu since I know he trusts me to order something he will like. I order a virgin strawberry daiquiri and a Jack Daniel steak with mashed potatoes and a side of veggies for both of us. Everyone on the wait staff speaks excellent English.

Our meals arrive quickly. *"Jin,"* I say, *"this steak tastes just like an American steak."* There is an English lesson on the table, and I say, "This is an American steak with mashed potatoes and veggies, and this is a strawberry daiquiri." I go back to speaking Mandarin as I point to our drinks. *"Usually these drinks have liquor, but I ordered them without liquor. You're driving, and I don't like liquor."*

Speaking in English, Jin says, "I like this strawberry daiquiri and American steak with mashed potatoes and veggies." His pronunciation is perfect, and I quietly tell him so. Just as we finish our meal, Jin's phone rings, and Martin is ready to go home.

After I pay the bill, Jin and I walk the few blocks back to the bowling alley. The gaggle of guys is still in The Sacred Circle, and they go silent as we walk toward them. Loud enough for them to hear, Jin speaks English and says, "The strawberry daiquiri and American steak with mashed potatoes and veggies are very good!"

November 29, 1997: Suzhou, the Vienna of China

I wanted to see Suzhou today, especially the art galleries. Suzhou is famous for its canals, and Martin agrees to come with me, which is rare since he isn't into sightseeing. For Martin, sightseeing is sigh-seeing. He sighs when he sees. He doesn't even want to see the Great Wall.

The drive to Suzhou takes about two hours, and Jin, Martin, and I walk around Suzhou's tourist area. We see large meditation stones and a scholar's house with round doorways and roof corners that swoop up toward the sky. The round doorways keep evil from entering. If evil tries to enter through a round doorway, it gets caught and spins around and around until it dizzily spins away.

Even now, roof corners on some Chinese homes slope up, which causes evil to flip toward heaven and away from the house. Headboards on beds are curved so that evil slides off.

Sometimes when I walk through the doorway of a shop, I have to step over a board that could easily trip me. The Chinese believe that if you step on the threshold of a doorway, you will have bad luck. In temples, the boards over thresholds are sometimes eighteen inches high. The height of this board forces everyone to step over a threshold. I think the purpose of a board like this is to keep evil from flowing into a room or a shop.

Western mannequins modeling Western clothing

The tourist area of Suzhou has more than fifty open-front shops with no doors or front walls. Each shop has a retractable door, similar to a garage door, which is pulled down at closing time. Most of the mannequins for the clothing stores have blue eyes and light-colored hair.

When we pass by a shop with American chocolate candy bars, I buy a couple of them for my survival kit. I can spot these candy bars from twelve feet away.

I want to shop for art, and as we walk down Artists' Alley, I find an amazing artist. His name is Xu Ai Liang. When I step into Ai's gallery, someone from Hong Kong has just purchased several of Ai's paintings. I introduce myself to the artist, and he asks me to call him Ai, 爱, which means love.

Suzhou artist Xu Ai Liang

I purchase three watercolor paintings of women as well as the only tiger watercolor painting Ai has ever done. He said that he struggled with the tiger painting for six weeks.

Ai has won many awards. He is also a talented calligrapher, and his calligraphy can be seen on most of his paintings. Ai enjoys painting Buddhist subjects. He said he would paint a levitating Buddha for me as well as a horse galloping on stormy clouds. The paintings will be ready in one month.

I am about to leave Ai's gallery when he reaches under his work desk at the back of his shop and pulls out his monograph. He lays open the front flap of the book, picks up a calligraphy brush, dips it in black ink, and calligraphies, *"Wen Li Xia, this book is for you. Xu Ai Liang."* Only a few of the paintings shown in his monograph are hanging in his gallery. The rest of them have already been sold.

At lunchtime, Jin wants to check on his car while Martin and I eat some lunch. We stop at a little café by the canal, and as we look out the window of the café, we have a view of the canal where houses are built right off the water just like in Vienna.

A canal in Suzhou

A house on the canal in Suzhou

While Martin and I wait for our lunch to be served, the locals stand by the edge of the canal and wait for the lunch special, which is eel. This doesn't appeal to either Martin or me even though Jin says eels taste good. Eels can be found in most wet markets on the streets of Shanghai, and they are purchased alive, just like fish, turtles, chickens, and insect pupae.

Martin and I watch the fishermen as they lean over the railing of their boats and scoop eels out of the water with nets. On the decks of these boats, fires burn under steaming pots. Lunch customers look on as eels are cooked on these floating kitchens.

Our lunch arrives, and Martin eats one thing on his plate. This will have to hold off his hunger until Jin can stop at a McDonald's or KFC on the way home.

After lunch, we walk to the art gallery next door. I purchase a traditional mountain scene painted on a scroll, which has been painted by a seventy-five-year-old artist. Chinese people are starting to gather in this gallery.

I also purchase an oil painting of a rose painted by an artist who happens to be working in the gallery today. The elderly artist holds his painting as Martin videotapes this artist and me as we talk.

More people gather as Martin is videotaping us. Chinese people enjoy hearing me speak Mandarin, and sometimes I hear echoes of everything I say pass through the crowd.

The Mandarin that the rose artist is speaking is heavily accented with the soft Suzhou dialect. I think I heard him say that his painting is beautiful, but this doesn't make sense because Chinese people are modest about their own accomplishments. Although it is true that his painting is beautiful, just to make sure that I understand what he has said, and I ask, *"Did you say the rose is very beautiful?"*

"No," he says. He holds his hand toward me as he says, *"You are very beautiful."*

I say, *"Nali, nali,"* which means *where... where is this beautiful woman about whom you speak?* The audience is surprised by what I have said, and they laugh as they applaud my practice of the Chinese custom of modesty.

My favorite photo of Jin

Martin and Sharon in Suzhou

As Martin and I wave good-bye to everyone and walk out of the gallery, Jin appears. I say, *"Jin, have you eaten lunch?"* He nods his head and the three of us walk single file down a narrow sidewalk by the canal.

There is no railing to keep us from falling into the canal, and I am in no mood to fall into murky water with eels and other wiggly creatures. The narrow sidewalk curves away from the canal and off to a dirt road where Jin takes a picture of Martin and me. I take a picture of Jin standing by a tree.

We continue going down this narrow path until we come to some antique furniture shops that go down both sides of the walkway. Lots of them. Jin is walking next to me as Martin is leading the way, and just as I step into one of the shops, Martin says, "Honey, you've already seen the shops this way."

Silent universal man-speak passes between Martin and Jin, and Jin says, *"Right, right. You don't want to see these shops again, do you?"*

While I don't know how to get back to Shanghai from Suzhou or where Jin has parked his car, I know I haven't seen those shops. Obviously, the guys don't want me to shop anymore.

If the men of the world were the only people who shopped, stores would only need to be open for one hour a day—except for Paul.

December 4, 1997: The Smoke Alarm

The smoke alarm has gone off again. How many times do the men from maintenance need to come up here and turn off the alarm before they're motivated to fix it? Or replace it?

December 5, 1997: My Greatest Find

Estelle is an American who works for the company, and she loves pearls, so of course, she wants to meet Ling Ling. She also wants to see the Great Wall and shop in Beijing.

Last night, which was Friday, we flew into Beijing, and when we arrived at our hotel, the Great Wall Sheraton, we hired a private car to take us to the Great Wall, Ling Ling's, and Beijing's famous flea market, Pan Jia Yuan.

Today is Saturday. This morning we met our driver, Mr. Gao, who told us he is married, has one child, and lives in a central Beijing apartment along with his little dog, Peter. He showed us a picture of his son, who is cute and has long hair.

On the drive to the Great Wall, Estelle and I see a market in a wide open area, out in nowhere. People are selling clothing, housewares, and other goods, which are spread out on blankets. Estelle says, "Let's stop and see this place."

Gao stops and gets out of the car with us. He tries to keep track of us, but Estelle and I go in different directions while Gao stands in the middle of the flea market doing his best to watch in two different directions at the same time. Once in a while, we wave to him. This market has over a hundred sellers spread out over an acre of farmland. Estelle finds a lot of things to buy.

*At the Great Wall, this is the view from a
lookout window at a sentinel station.*

The photographer is standing on the steps of the Great Wall
photographing Sharon as she looks out a window at a sentinel station.

When we arrive at the Great Wall, we invite Gao to go with us to see this wonder of the world. A Chinese person is customarily obligated to refuse the first two invitations but may accept the third invitation. If a Chinese person is only invited one or two times to do something, this is not an invitation. The person who is extending the invitation is only being polite. We ask him three times to go with us, and he refuses each time. Gao says he would rather wait by his car for us.

We tell him we will return to the parking lot by twelve thirty, and Estelle and I take the tram to the Great Wall, which is over five thousand miles long.

Gao

There are a lot of hawkers on the Great Wall. I buy a T-shirt and a few Great Wall pins. One of the pins is misspelled, typed in all capital letters, and has no spaces between the words. I purchase every misspelled pin I can find. "MEMEMTOOFTHEGREATWALL" is printed on the pins.

The hawkers know a few words of English, but to allow them to rest from trying to speak English, I speak to them in Mandarin. When Chinese people hear me speak Mandarin, their usual first reaction is to laugh because they're surprised. This reaction is similar to hearing a joke. When the listener has not predicted the punch line, he laughs because he has been surprised.

Estelle and I take a lot of pictures at the Great Wall. When Estelle sticks her head through one of the windows cut out of the Great Wall, an American says, "Look out. That's Chinese cement."

At twelve thirty, Estelle and I notice the time and hurry over to the tram, which is pretty far away. We have to wait for over twenty minutes to catch the next tram going back down, and we are late getting back to Gao. When we arrive at Gao's car, I say, *"We are sorry we're late."*

Gao says, *"I was worried. I wondered what happened. In thirty minutes more, I was going to go up to the Great Wall to look for you."* Gao smiles at us, and all is forgiven.

We are hungry, and Gao stops at a KFC where we all eat spicy chicken. Estelle and I walk over to the restroom at KFC where a long line of women wait. In Chinese, "restroom" is euphemistically called the, *"xĭ shou jiān."* "Wash hands room." Outside the restroom, there is one roll of toilet paper. From this roll, the women in front of us are taking two squares. Estelle and I don't take any sheets of toilet paper because we carry little restroom purses with us, which can be purchased anywhere in China. These purses have two compartments. One is for a package of tissues, and the other compartment is for money and credit cards, which are necessary things from which a woman should never be parted.

After lunch, Gao drives to the building where Ling Ling's shop is located. When Estelle and I walk into this building, we are on the ground floor. We see a large shopping area that is closed and wonder why someone would close their shop. We take the elevator to Ling

Ling's shops and do some serious pearl shopping. One of Ling Ling's stringers gives me another stringing lesson. When I have practiced stringing pearls for six months, I think my knots between pearls might be the same size.

Around dinner time, when we are leaving the building, we notice that the shop on the first floor, which was previously closed, is now open. We step in and discover that this is a grocery store that specializes in selling live animals. What catches my attention the most are the turtles, cicadas, crickets, insect pupae, and most awful, the centipedes. We don't stay long.

On our last day in Beijing, Gao takes us to Pan Jia Yuan, which is a flea market spread out over at least a square mile. When Estelle sees a painting of a man in a barren field on his knees, she asks the salesman if he has more paintings like the one she likes. If this is the only one, this suggests that this painting is an original. He assures Estelle by saying, "Not have more. This only one." Vendors often shout out in English, "Good quality. Only one."

Estelle buys this painting that is thirty-six by forty inches, and the painting is taken off its stretcher bars and rolled up, so she can take it on the airplane. An hour later, when we pass by this same vendor, there is another framed painting like the one Estelle just purchased from him.

Estelle purchases a three-foot-square bag and fills it up. I buy some old advertising postcards and a few ceramic items I like as well as a set of plates that, most likely, were made in the 1800s during the Qing Dynasty. I know something about the age of a ceramic piece by looking at the foot.

In Beijing, the best place to buy art is Artists' Alley, which is located in Pan Jia Yuan. This alleyway is a long stretch of little slapped-together art galleries. Today, when I walk down Artists' Alley, there is an antique book dealer, seemingly out of place in this row of galleries. I don't know how to evaluate old books, but I enter this quaint shop anyway because something is summoning me. The three men in the shop stop talking when I enter.

I say, "Hello everyone." My eyes survey a row of books at shoulder level. I don't know what I'm looking for. As I put my hand on the spines of some books, I can feel the eyes of these men follow my hand as it travels down the row.

By touching these books, I will find what wants to come home with me. My fingers bump into a piece of poster board placed between two old books. I gently pull out a sketch of a simple house using penciled squares measured in meters. When I turn the poster board over, there it is—powerful and igniting—a graphite drawing that represents the Massacre of the Manchus in 1911, the massacre that ends the Qing Dynasty.

In China, during the 1600s, the Manchus, from Manchuria in northeastern China, are the ethnic minority while the Han Chinese people are the ethnic majority. Nevertheless, the Manchus rule over China from 1644 until 1911. Shortly after taking power, the Manchus declare that all Han Chinese men will adopt the Manchu hairstyle of a shaved forehead and a braided pigtail.

A rebellion led by Sun Yat-sen and others instigates the Massacre of the Manchus. This is the end of the Qing Dynasty. Most likely, this drawing is a portrayal of a Qing Dynasty loyalist—one of many who were slaughtered in 1911.

The eight-by-ten-inch work shows a man tied with ropes to a tall post. His forehead is shaved and a long queue loops down his back and over his shoulder. With his head turned to his left, he stares directly at me with defiant eyes. His hands are covered by the sleeves of his long white robe. Below his eye is a shadow in the shape of a star on his cheek. This original graphite drawing, executed with realism, precision, and detail, stirs my heart like no other drawing I have ever seen. I hold the drawing out to the men and say, *"May I buy this?"*

The men talk among themselves and say things like, *"We shouldn't let her buy the drawing. What will she do with it?"* One man says to me, *"Not for sale."*

I say, *"This work is good. I will give you eighty yuan."* I have no idea what the drawing might be worth. It seems to have been tossed between the books as an afterthought.

The man who refuses to sell the drawing turns to the other two men and says, *"She speaks with a Shanghai accent. What do you think?"* I am not able to hear any other parts of their conversation, and then they stop talking and study me. I calmly stand there and hold the drawing as the three men stare at me and say nothing . . . and then the one who does the talking for them says, *"Little Sister, where are you from?"*

"I live in Shanghai. Did one of you draw this? This is superb. I will give you one hundred yuan. Is this price good or not good?"

The speaker of the group looks at the other two men and back to me. *"OK. One hundred yuan."*

I don't press my luck and ask why they were reluctant to sell the drawing to me. I give the speaker one hundred yuan, and the three men wave their hands in a gesture of good-bye.

The drawing is unsigned.

December 14–28, 1997: A Miracle Happened

When Martin and I return to New Mexico, fresh snow is on the ground when our plane lands in Albuquerque. It had been snowing for several days. Our dog, Jakie, went berserk when he saw us. He howled and yapped as he twirled around and around. (Our dog Wolfgang died shortly before we left for Shanghai.)

Martin was invited to have lunch with several of his friends from work, and they told him that they would meet him at the restaurant. No one wanted to ride in his truck with him because Martin hasn't driven a vehicle for a while. Martin went out to his truck in our garage to drive to the restaurant, but I didn't hear him leave.

He soon came back into the kitchen and said, "You know what? I thought a miracle happened."

"Really?" I said.

"When I went out to my truck, I noticed that I was taller, and I thought, it's a miracle. But then I look at the front of my truck, and my tire is flat."

One evening, Martin and I had ten of our friends over for dessert. I never noticed before how fast people talk.

In China, it is customary to take gifts back from one's travels for family and friends, so Martin and I bought gifts to give to Stella and

Jin. We bought Stella a couple of sweaters, and we knew Jin wanted American cigarettes.

Martin and I also stocked up on some groceries and packed everything into three large boxes. We bought cans of tuna, chili with no beans, Demi Moore Stew, whey protein powder, and jars of peanut butter. Most importantly, we bought cookies to take back to Shanghai.

Once we return to Shanghai, we will be eating fresh salads because I will have access to organic vegetables. An American farmer contacted the Shanghai Expatriate Association. He owns a vegetable farm just outside of Shanghai, and he is willing to bring fresh vegetables to Shanghai once a week. So, Martin and I bought a lot of ranch salad dressing.

We also bought toilet paper, hair spray, and shampoo to bring back to Shanghai because these items in Shanghai are quite expensive. We packed several packages of tortillas and twenty pounds of pinto beans and stocked up on books and VHS movies. Our time in the States went by quickly, and we were sad to leave Jakie again.

Back in Shanghai, Jin picks us up at the airport, and he is as happy to see us as we are to see him. Once we are in the car, I say, *"Jin, what did you do while we were gone? Did you miss shopping?"*

Jin's eyes check his rearview mirror. *"Jin missed shopping with taitai. Shanghai is boring. Jin stayed in the driver's room. Box lunches at the factory aren't good."*

Martin has never eaten the lunches provided by the factory for the employees. Either Jin or another driver gets something for Martin to eat from KFC or McDonald's. Sometimes I make a sack lunch for Martin. I can get him to eat a sandwich for lunch if there are cookies included with his sandwich.

Jin parks his car in the parking lot for The Tower. I come upstairs to our apartment and unlock the solid wood door. The heels of my shoes click on the wood floor as I step into the entryway. I stand for a moment in our living room and notice how warm and inviting our apartment is with its blond wood floor, red wool carpets, Chinese antique furniture, and colorful paintings on the walls. I look in my kitchen, which is waiting for me with its tiny oven and four gas burners.

Jin and Martin bring the boxes and luggage upstairs. They unpack the three large boxes and set what they can on the counter in the kitchen and then put everything else on the dining room table.

I unzip my luggage and pull out cartons of American cigarettes for Jin, who smiles a big smile as I hand them to him. I know he is quite happy to receive them, and that he will joyfully share this gift with his driver friends. For Jin's wife, I have some earrings made in Hawaii. I also give Jin a gift for his daughter.

While we were in the States, we also bought Jin a camera, which we will give to him later as part of his Chinese New Year's gift. I will give Stella her sweaters tomorrow. Jin looks happy as he leaves to walk to his home across the street.

I step into my kitchen and look out the window at the night lights of Shanghai. I can't see the Huangpu River, but I can hear the foghorn of a passing ship.

When I was back in the States, I missed Shanghai. I missed the foghorns on the Huangpu River, our high-rise apartment, the bustle of the city, speaking Chinese, and my Chinese friends. I missed my Chinese friends the most.

As I start to walk out of my kitchen, the smoke alarm goes off, and it is saying, *"Thank you for coming home."*

I say, *"Don't be so polite."*

January 2, 1998: Yearning for a Love Match

The movie *Titanic* came out in December when Martin and I were in the States, but I didn't see it because I don't like disaster movies. This movie is also being shown here in Shanghai and having an impact on young Chinese people. The theme song for this movie is, "My Heart Will Go On." I have heard this song on Jin's car radio. People are singing this song in karaoke bars. While it is a beautiful song and well sung by Celine Dion, I am already tired of hearing it.

The appeal of this lost-love song might have something to do with the desire young Chinese people have to marry for love. The story of *Titanic* revolves around two people who fall in love. One of them dies while the other one lives. Love is cut short for these two lovers when the ship goes down. For the Chinese, marrying for love is a new idea in a land where arranged marriages have been the norm for centuries.

The book Chinese people are talking about is *Bridges of Madison County*, written by Robert J. Waller. This book, like the movie, *Titanic*, speaks to a passionate love cut short. Before I left Shanghai for the States, I had lunch with my Fudan University professor who said, *"The Chinese translation of Bridges of Madison County has all of the good parts expurgated."* When I was in the States, I easily found a copy of this book at a Barnes & Noble bookstore.

Today, I asked Jin to take this book to my Chinese professor's home. When he gave her the book, she gave him a book to give to me—*Modern Chinese Characters*, by Binyong and Rohsenow. She told Jin that she would not be teaching at Fudan University this coming semester. I will miss her.

January 3, 1998: One Egg Is Broken

Jin drives Martin and me over to Babaiban. There is a grocery store on one of the eleven floors. Because I only need eggs, this will be a quick trip. I ask Martin to stay outside the store because I don't want to spend more time looking for him than shopping for one item.

I am in a hurry as I walk to the egg section. If I take too long in the store, who knows where Martin might wander. Uh-oh. There are no eggs. I see a woman who works there and say, *"Hello. May I trouble you to ask if you have eggs?"*

She looks annoyed and says, *"Do you see eggs?"*

I silently give this young woman the sobriquet of Miss Persnickety. *"No, I don't see eggs. Perhaps there are some in the backroom?"*

She looks at me with a stoic expression. No doubt, this cantankerous attitude of hers is the consequence of her daily ritual of kerplunking her feet into a bucket of ice water as soon as her eyes pop open in the morning. Determined to get what I want, I ask again. *"Do you have eggs in the backroom?"*

She shrugs her shoulders and says, *"Wo bu zhidao."*

While she literally says that *she does not know* if she has eggs or not, what she actually means is that *she doesn't want to be bothered with me.* She also could have said *mei you,* which literally means *we don't have* any eggs, but this doesn't mean that she doesn't have any eggs. This means that *if she has any eggs, she doesn't have any eggs for me.*

The Chinese have other sayings such as *bu xing,* which means *no way.* Similar to the Spanish saying of *mañana* is *mingtian ba,* which means *perhaps tomorrow,* and tomorrow never comes. Another Chinese saying is *kao lu,* which means *I will think about it.* My favorite saying is *mei ban fa,* which means *this cannot be done,* and even if it can be done, this will not be done for you.

The problem is that I have no *guanxi* with Miss Persnickety. *Guanxi* is a relationship or connection with someone who can get things done. When I do someone a favor or give something to someone, I receive *guanxi,* which is like a poker chip I can turn in when I need something—like eggs.

I pull every ounce of my waning patience into my voice as I say, *"Could you please look in the backroom for eggs?"*

Miss Persnickety says, *"I could look,"* but she doesn't budge.

Maybe if I have a conniption fit, right here, right now, this would speed her up a bit. I say, *"Would you please look now?"*

"OK, OK," Miss Persnickety says.

I watch Miss Persnickety do a lackadaisical ankle-rolling stroll. I have never seen a human being amble along like that before. Twenty . . . minutes . . . later . . . she returns and says, *"We have eggs."*

I am so exasperated that I want to slap my forehead, but I stay calm as I say, *"Could you get some for me?"*

Miss Persnickety rolls her eyes and says, *"How many do you want?"*

I tell her, I want thirteen. She turns on one toe like a ballerina, and her feet scuff off to the backroom.

Now . . . as I watch her . . . I want to smack her in the noggin. Then a little snotty voice in my head says, "Well, Miss Cheeky, you aren't as far up on the evolutionary tree as you thought."

Thirty minutes later, she returns with a pyramid of thirteen eggs piled in a square cardboard box. A broken egg is vaingloriously displayed at the top of the pile, and chicken poop secures adorable white feathers to the eggs. I am certain that these eggs have been chosen just for me, and I say, *"Thank you for these eggs,"* Miss Persnickety.

I pay for my eggs, and I am pleased that there is no extra charge for the feathers and chicken poop.

When I walk out the door, I see Martin where I left him—thank you very much—and he is pacing like an expectant father. "You were in there for two hours," he says, "and you only bought eggs?" Martin looks at the eggs and says, "Is the egg on top broken?" I give Martin a don't-mess-with-me look. "OK, OK," he says. "I guess we're ready to leave."

"Marty," I say, "I suggest that you don't even say the words 'broken egg.'" Martin puts his fingers to his lips and makes a zipping motion.

When we get to the car, Jin glances at the eggs as he holds the car door open for me. Martin opens his own door and sits on my right in the backseat of the car as usual. Jin turns the key in the ignition and looks at me in his rearview mirror and says, *"Taitai, one egg is broken."*

The hard-won eggs sit in my lap. I look at Martin and say, "Jin just said one egg is broken."

Martin burst out laughing. The car is idling, and Martin reaches over and touches Jin's shoulder to get his attention. Jin turns toward Martin who says, "Jin, for your sake, I hope you can understand me. It would be a good idea if you didn't say anything more to taitai about a broken egg."

Jin turns to me. *"What did Martin say?"*

"He said, 'Taitai had trouble getting eggs. Next time, Jin can help taitai. Martin is no help with Chinese people.'"

Jin says, *"Yes, yes. Jin can help taitai. No problem."*

The broken egg stares at me. This egg is a mirror of my own imperfection. Martin takes my hand and doesn't let go until we arrive home.

January 4, 1998: Electric Eyes

Jin and I are on The Tower's elevator, which has a microphone and camera, and we are coming up to my apartment. When I say something to Jin about the Dali Lama, Jin elbows me and says, "Shh."

I know the bookstore manager at the Barnes & Noble bookstore in Albuquerque. She has sent many boxes of books to our Shanghai address, and some of the books are about Buddhism. These boxes are first opened up at a Chinese postal bureau and inspected before they can be delivered to me, and so far, I have received all of the books that I have ordered.

Before I left New Mexico, I explained to the manager at Barnes & Noble that I couldn't import any books with a picture of the Dali Lama. If any of the books I ordered had such pictures on the covers or inside, I asked her to cut out those pictures and save them for me. I told her that I would tape the pictures back in my books when I returned to New Mexico. Practicing Buddhism in China is not illegal, although I have heard that Tibetans can be imprisoned for possessing a photo of the Dali Lama.

Although the Chinese Censorship Bureau is invisible to me, I am aware of this officialdom. Before we moved to Shanghai, Martin was frequently on business trips to Shanghai. One time, he sent a postcard to me from Shanghai and wrote his message in Spanish. Martin was home for six weeks before I received his postcard. Perhaps the Censorship Bureau doesn't have many Spanish linguists.

On this same business trip, Martin called me several times from Shanghai, and I heard strange music in the background and clicking noises during our conversations.

Now that I am living in Shanghai, sometimes when I want to make a phone call from our apartment, I lift the telephone receiver, and there is no dial tone, but I hear strange music. I yell into the phone, *"Wei? Wei!"* "Hello? Hey!" After that, I hear a dial tone.

January 5, 1998: Politics

I don't ask anyone in China about his or her politics, and I don't say anything about mine. I was, however, asked by one of my Chinese friends about some of President Clinton's policies concerning Iraq.

I gave her the same response I always give when Chinese people ask me about my government or its officials. I say, *"The president never calls me to ask my opinion."*

Her response was, *"But you can vote."*

Apparently, some Chinese people think because Americans can vote government officials into office that we have a say on every aspect of our governance. The political system of the United States isn't easy to explain to someone who has never elected a national official.

I never talk about the power of the vote, freedom of speech and assembly, or the due process clauses of the US Constitution found in the Fifth and Fourteenth Amendments—safeguards from arbitrary denial of life, liberty, and property by the government.

January 9, 1998: Miss Persnickety's Cousin

I am back in Beijing again to see Ling Ling. My Chinese class won't start until February—after the Chinese New Year—so this is a good time to shop for pearls.

On my flight to Beijing, I take a book to read about Buddhism. This book, *Dzogchen: The Self-Perfected State*, is written by Chögyal Namkhai Norbu, has no pictures of the Dali Lama, and has been written in English. So I have little concern about an airport official taking my book away from me or having any kind of problem because of it.

On the airplane, as I am reading my book, the Chinese man sitting to my left is also reading a book. The title of his book is in Chinese, and I glance at the characters on the cover. Two of the characters, 菩萨, on the cover say, *"Pusa,"* which means *Buddha*, and he sees me looking at the cover of his book. I mark my place in my book and hand it to him as I say, *"Can you read English?"*

He smiles as he looks at the title of my book. "Yes, I can read English, but not as well as you can, I'm sure."

"Your English is excellent," I say. "I couldn't help but notice what you are reading. As you can see, we have something in common."

"Yes," he said. "It would seem that we are both Buddhist. I have never before met an American Buddhist."

In my purse, I have name cards that are similar to business cards. These cards have Martin's and my Shanghai and Stateside address and phone number. I give him my card using both hands, which is the Chinese custom with such things.

He presents his card to me in the same way. His card has his name and the company for which he works in Beijing. His family name is Wang, and because I am not certain how to pronounce his first name, I address him as Wang. He takes his business card back for a moment and writes his home telephone number on the back of the card. "Here," he says, "call me the next time you are visiting Beijing. You can meet my family."

We talk for a while about his work and his home in Beijing as well as my life in Shanghai and the Chinese language. Then I say, "There is something I would like to ask you." He nods to let me know I can ask my question, and I say, "My Chinese friends privately tell me of their political discontent with China, and my experience is that I can pretty much do what I want and the city of Shanghai is much safer than big cities in the States. Why is there this discontent?"

He hesitates for a moment while he carefully chooses his words and says, "The answer is that Chinese people cannot vote."

I thank Wang for answering my question, and I don't enter into a discussion about the power of the vote or freedom of speech and assembly.

And then we talk about Buddhism. Wang tells me that his father-in-law, who lives with him and his wife, is the real practitioner of Buddhism in his family. For many hours a day, his father-in-law meditates in their dining room. On two occasions, Wang has seen him levitate two inches off the floor.

I say, "When I meditate, I have monkey mind."

"Me too," he says.

Meeting Wang was a delightful coincidence

Against my better judgment, I book a room at a three-star hotel because a friend in Shanghai has told me that this is a good hotel and much less expensive than the Sheraton. However, as is the case with three-star hotels, this one is not without a problem or two, and I have renamed this hotel The Green Eggs Hotel.

Gao picks me up at the Beijing airport, and on the drive to the hotel, Gao and I talk about our favorite things to eat. Gao loves peaches. I love strawberries and dip them in sugar.

Gao helps me carry my bags to my room, and we agree to meet in the hotel lobby tomorrow morning at nine o'clock. Our plan is to go to Ling Ling's shop, have lunch, and then I want to see Mao's mausoleum. Even though the day will be busy, I don't want to get up too early. If I eat breakfast around eight o'clock, I can meet Gao by nine o'clock.

When I check in at the hotel, I hear a lot of French being spoken in the lobby, and a large tour bus is parked out front. I have dinner at a restaurant in the hotel and go to the hotel gift shop where a man and a woman are having a discussion in French.

As I pay for a couple of candy bars, I briefly speak to the clerk in Chinese, and when I turn to leave the shop, the woman speaks to me in French. *"Excuse me. We want to buy bottled water, but these are out of date."* She puts a bottle of water in my hand and points to the date printed on the bottle. *"Please ask for us if they have water with good dates."*

I take a deep breath and approach the clerk who is most likely a relative of Miss Persnickety's in Shanghai. *"Hello,"* I say. *"May I please ask if you have any other bottles of water? This bottle of water has an old date."*

Miss Persnickety's cousin says, *"Mei you."* "Don't have," which means that *even if she has any other bottles of water, she is not about to go and get anything for me or anyone else.*

I hand the bottle of water to the clerk to show her the old date on the bottle of water, and she says, *"This bottle? I will look."* Miss Persnickety's cousin looks annoyed with me as she pretends to check the date and says, *"This is good water,"* and she hands the bottle back to me. In China, anything within six months past the expiration date is good. What is six months compared to China's five-thousand-year-old history?

I pass the bottle back to the couple as I say in French, *"I am sorry. She said they don't have any other bottles of water. Outside the hotel, the little shops have bottled water."* I hold up my American candy bars and say, *"These candy bars are good."*

January 10, 1998: The Green Eggs Hotel

At the Western breakfast bar in this hotel, there are scrambled eggs, pancakes, and French pastries as well as fruit, yogurt, juice, knives, and forks. Not bad. I take a plate, napkin, and flatware and step up to the scrambled eggs queue where a woman from England heaps a large spoonful of eggs onto her plate. We gawk at her scoop of eggs that are half yellow and half green. In her British accent, she says, "I don't believe I fancy these eggs."

I say, "I don't think I care for these eggs, either."

She sets her plate of mint-green and yellow eggs down and takes a clean plate. As we step into another line, I name this hotel The Green Eggs Hotel. I assumed that Dr. Seuss was being imaginative when he wrote about green eggs in his book, *Green Eggs and Ham*. Nope. Green eggs are not a fiction.

As we stand in another line, there is no pushing and shoving, unlike lines where Chinese people are involved. Chinese people don't wait in lines. They push and shove to be first.

I choose a glass of orange juice, some fruit, and yogurt, although I would have preferred eggs. I sit at a two-top table in this crowded breakfast room. As I take a sip of juice, a Chinese man approaches my table and says, "*Bonne matin. Puis-je vous rejoindre?*" "Good morning. May I join you?"

I am so surprised to hear a Chinese man speaking Parisian French that my orange juice almost goes down the wrong pipe. I motion to the vacant chair at my table as my mind scurries away from the Chinese Language Bureau in my brain and scurries over to the French Bureau. "*Bien sûr,*" I say. "*Asseyez-vous.*" "Certainly. Please sit down." Now I know what it's like when I surprise Chinese people by speaking Mandarin.

Breakfast passes with the usual pleasantries about our families, where we live, and why we are in Beijing. He is visiting from Paris, of course, because he lives there.

Around eight thirty, I go to the front of the hotel, and Gao is already in the lobby waiting for me. In the car on the way to Ling Ling's, Gao says he is going to stay with me while I look at pearls. I tell him that there is no need for him to stay with me, and that I will be all right, but I drop the subject since I don't want to get into an argument with him.

We are soon at Ling Ling's shop. Gao and I go to the back of the shop where Ling Ling and I begin to look at pearls.

On a previous trip to Beijing, I met a jade dealer whose name is Ke. She speaks no English. When she hears that I am at Ling Ling's shop, she stops by to see me. I don't have time to talk with Ke while I am at

Ling Ling's, and I ask Ke to have dinner with me. I tell her that we can go to her favorite hot pot restaurant in Beijing. I introduce Ke to Gao, who tells Ke that he will pick her up around dinner time outside the building and take Ke and me to the restaurant.

After Ke leaves, Ling Ling and I look over at Gao who is leaning forward in his chair. He has his elbows on his knees as he looks at his folded hands, and his feet take turns tapping on the floor like a ticking clock. *"Gao, it isn't necessary for you to stay here,"* I say. *"You can come back later. We can eat lunch. OK? I would like to eat lunch outside this building."*

Gao looks uncertain and glances at Ling Ling who says, *"Sure. You can leave. Sharon will stay right here. Later you can come back. Take Sharon to eat."*

I say, *"Gao, this is a good idea. Two o'clock you can come back? Take me to eat lunch? OK?"* Gao is my friend, and I don't want to boss him around.

Gao stands up from his chair. *"Wen Li Xia, you will stay here, right? You won't go downstairs?"* I pinkie promise him I will stay at Ling Ling's shop.

Many pounds of pearls later, Gao returns and looks relieved when he sees that I'm still at Ling Ling's. As Gao and I leave the shop, we say good-bye to everyone by saying *zaijian*, "See you again."

We step outside the building, and the Beijing sky is gray, which is typical. Gao puts my pearls in the trunk of his car, and when we start walking, he says, *"I will take you to my favorite place. It isn't expensive."*

The last time I was in Beijing, Gao learned that I am terrified of crossing streets. So when we're across the street from his favorite place, which is a "hole-in-the-wall joint" as people would call it in Chicago, he says, *"OK, close your eyes."*

I put my left hand over my eyes, and Gao takes my right hand and pulls me across the street. Nothing bad happens. The entrance to this eatery is a narrow door with undersized red Chinese characters scribbled with a paintbrush above the entrance. This is a place frequented by locals because only the locals would know this is a restaurant.

Gao and I walk through the doorway single file. A lone naked light bulb dangles from the ceiling. A small dusty window by the door allows some light into the room. High on a wall behind a long counter, scrawly Chinese characters in chalk are spread across a blackboard menu. I give

Gao one hundred yuan for lunch, which I assume will be enough since this is a neighborhood restaurant for the natives and food is inexpensive.

Gao brings over two soft drinks, which are safer to drink here than water or tea. When Gao's name is called, I hear the slam of plastic. Our meals are served on one-piece molded trays like the cafeteria lunch trays used in my elementary school. Gao places the tray in front of me. Everything looks and smells good, but the only food I recognize is the rice. When Gao sees my hesitation, he says, *"This is a good meal. They give this kind of food to Buddhists."*

Oh, good. This means that there are no dead animals on my tray. I pick up my chopsticks and dig in. As I point to something on my tray, I say, *"Gao, what's this dish?"*

Gao points to each dish. *"Tofu with sauce . . . steamed rice . . . vegetables in sauce . . . fruit with sauce . . . wheat pancake. Wen Li Xia, do you like this food?"*

"Yes, yes. This tastes exceptionally good. No dead animals, either. I like that." The total cost for the two of us is forty yuan, or about five US dollars, and Gao places my change beside my tray.

After lunch, I tell Gao that I would like for him to go with me to see Mao Zedong's mausoleum. Gao doesn't want to go inside the mausoleum with me, but he walks with me to the ticket booth to help me buy a ticket. The woman at the counter says I have to check my purse with her before I can enter the mausoleum.

I am wearing a fanny pack, and I pull out four thousand yuan, which I hold out to Gao because I want him to keep it for me. I am not going to check my fanny pack with anything valuable in it. When the young woman sees the money, she says, *"I won't check your purse. You can tuck your purse under your shirt."*

Gao pulls the tail of my shirt over the back strap of my fanny pack, and I pull the front of my shirt over the fanny pack. Will anyone notice I have something hidden under my shirt? Gao takes me to the end of the long line for the mausoleum, where only Chinese people are waiting. There is no pushing and shoving in this line.

Twenty minutes later, I enter a large cold room. Thick protective glass encircles the center of the room where Mao, wearing his military uniform, is laid out in a peaceful pose. He is about fifteen feet away from me, and I wonder if he is made of wax. The walkway for the viewers is three feet wide, and like pallbearers in lockstep, we slowly and quietly shuffle past Mao. We exit at the back of the mausoleum where objects of veneration—Mao memorabilia—are sold from many kiosks.

I look at a cigarette lighter with Mao's photo. When the flame flares up, the lighter plays the Chinese national anthem. Merchants have Mao flags, Mao photos, and the *Little Red Book* of Mao's sayings for sale in English and Chinese. When I am looking at some Mao buttons, Gao appears next to me.

Gao and I next go to Pan Jia Yuan where I want to buy artwork. But before we enter this favorite alleyway of mine, I give him four thousand yuan, so that he can buy the artwork I like. Gao will pay less than I will pay, and we have a plan—or plot. As I walk in front of Gao down Artists' Alley, we will pretend like we don't know each other. If I like a piece of artwork, I will tap on the work two times and step away. Gao will come behind me, bargain for the artwork, and purchase it at a good price.

After buying art for about an hour, I see a painting I especially like of several gold koi fish. Four feet above my head and clipped to a line across the aisle, this painting is too high for me to tap. I turn around and find Gao only a few steps behind me. I tell him I want the painting of the fish high above us and say, *"Gao, please ask if this koi fish painting is the only one. If this is the only one, let's buy it."* Gao is told that this is the only painting with koi fish.

After Gao pays for the koi fish painting, we make a trip back to the car to unload the paintings we have before we buy more. When we return to Artists' Alley, there is another koi fish painting like the one Gao just bought. When we see the duplicate painting, I say, *"Mei guanxi."* "It doesn't matter, never mind." After that, we don't bother to ask if a painting is the only one. When we take the second round of paintings to Gao's car, it is time to pick up Ke for dinner.

Gao drives to the pearl market where Ke is waiting outside the building. With Ke seated next to me in the backseat, I ask Gao several times to join us for dinner, but he declines. Not insisting Gao join us for dinner is my first mistake. Even though I am paying for dinner, I ask Ke to order for us, which is my second mistake.

I am once again trying to avoid eating animals. Speaking in Chinese, I tell Ke I am a vegetarian. Perhaps I didn't say this word correctly or Ke doesn't know what vegetarians eat because she orders meat.

One dish, however, is not just meat. The gray mound shivers on its platter, and Ke cuts off a few chunks and throws them into the hot pot to cook. Not only is Gao not there to explain to her what being a vegetarian means, but there is no dog at my feet to gobble up what I don't want to eat. Will a sauce soon arrive at our table? I can pour that over the convolutions and disguise the taste and feel of this pig brain in my mouth. Nope. No sauce.

When Ke has determined that this piggy part is cooked, it is with delight that she places a hunk of it on my plate with a thud. I have trouble picking up this awkward lump with my chopsticks. Not even my chopsticks want to touch this piggy part, but with tremendous effort, I finally manage to put this lump to my lips, and I take a bite. This pig brain has no flavor and does not feel good on my tongue. I swallow without chewing and hope I don't choke or throw up.

Ke says, *"How do you like this dish?"*

I say, *"I'm full. You can have it all,"* and she devours this piggy brain with glee. Good.

Gao picks us up around seven o'clock and takes Ke home first. After dropping her off at her home, Gao says, *"How was dinner?"*

"Gao," I say, *"Ke ordered pig brain."*

"Wen Li Xia, I'm sorry," he says.

Gao parks outside the hotel and helps me carry my artwork upstairs. After he sets everything down in my room, he holds out a plastic bag. *"Wen Li Xia, I have something for you. My wife washed them."*

When I open the bag, I am sure I hear angels sing. Cuddled inside is a little bit of heaven in the form of large, ripe, flawless fresh strawberries with perky green leaves on their tops. *"Gao, these are magnificent. Strawberries are my favorite thing to eat. Thank you. Tonight I can eat these."*

"Yes, I know you like to eat strawberries," he says, *"but not without this,"* and he passes a bag of sugar to me.

"Gao, thank you, thank you. Now when I sleep, I won't be hungry. Please also tell your wife thank you."

Gao is hardly out the door when I plow into my favorite food, almost too beautiful to eat. I have a sugar buzz when I go to sleep.

January 20, 1998: Sacred String

There is a flea market in Shanghai, a four-story building called the Sunday Market, which is only open on the weekends. New and old things can be found there, as well as a nearly blind old woman who sits by her goods in a dusty corner of the second-floor stairwell landing. She used to sell sheets of sandpaper, which I would buy, and now she sells string in red, black, and turquoise.

I have found various uses for this string. No use, however, is more special than as a reminder of her sweet face and its map of wrinkles. I wonder what her life was like when Mao was alive, and does she have a family? I would love to see a picture of her as a young woman.

Every time I go to this flea market, I look for her, and when I find her, we act out this same play. Act I begins when I address her with the respectful hello, which is *ninhao*, instead of the *nihao* I use with everyone else. I begin with my first line and say, *"Ninhao."* I point to a piece of string, forgetting that she can barely see through graying cataracts. *"How much is this?"* I say.

People begin to gather around us. She nods her head to my question and holds up one finger, which means *one yuan*.

"Good," I say. I pick up a wad of the strings and ask, *"How many are here?"* I know her answer by heart, but I must say my part.

She smiles a near-toothless smile. She knows who is talking to her, and she knows her part, too. She makes a cross with her index fingers because this is the Chinese character, 十, for the number ten.

Act II begins and more people gather as our performance continues. They have seen this acted out many times before, and they never tire of watching.

The permanent Chinese vendors on the first two floors of the market know I live in Shanghai, know I study Chinese at Fudan University, and know I drive a hard bargain. What happens next, therefore, is perplexing to them.

I reach for the string for which I have no need and say, *"I will buy these, OK?"* I am politely asking her permission to buy at the first asking price.

She peers through foggy eyes, and with the deliberate nod of an empress, she grants my request. Perhaps she can see some colors and knows that I have blond hair.

Act III begins when I place a bill worth one hundred yuan into her outstretched hand. She puts the money one inch from her left eye. Everyone looks from me to her, from me to her. This is the audience's favorite part, and they must wonder if I will ever change the script, which I won't. Our math tells us that the total cost is ten yuan for ten pieces of string.

As she slowly moves her right hand to give me change for one hundred yuan, which I know she does not have, I say, *"Zaijian."* "See you again." I hastily leave and go about my business. I know she will soon get up and return home. I am happy to give her this pleasure of leaving work early.

The look on everyone's face says—how does this old woman do this? Do I feel sorry for her? No. I admire her greatly, and when I hold her string in my hand, I see her face and whisper to myself—a great woman held this string before me.

When life is difficult, I imagine being in this woman's arms. As she holds me, she says, *"Mei guanxi. Dou hao."* "It doesn't matter, never mind. Everything is all right," and I think . . . she should know.

January 24, 1998: George the Oyster

Last week a toy tiger has appeared in Jin's car, and I tell him that his tiger needs a name. Jin has named his tiger Da Lao Fu. Because *da* can mean *great*, *lao* means *old*, and *fu* means *man* or *elder*, the translation of the name of his tiger is Great Old Man. In Chinese, the word "old" has the flavor of stateliness with a dash of wisdom and bravery. This tiger wears a red bow tie, and he swings from Jin's rearview mirror.

Jin and I go to Suzhou to see my favorite artist. We step into Ai's gallery where Ai shows me the five paintings he has done for me, and they are exceptional. One of the paintings is a remarkable watercolor and ink painting of a levitating Buddha. Jin takes some pictures of Ai and me, and then Jin and I continue down the alleyway where I buy eighteen more paintings. Art is an investment for me. I can enjoy these works of art now and perhaps sell them later on.

Jin and I see a gallery that sells artists' supplies, and we go in. I see some exquisite calligraphy brushes. Some of the brushes have white hair and some have brown hair. An elderly woman comes over and asks Jin if he wants to see any of the brushes. The woman assumes I don't speak Chinese. That's OK. I assume she doesn't speak English. Jin says, *"Taitai, what brushes do you want to see?"*

I point to some brushes with long wooden handles and say, *"I want to see the brushes with brown hair."* The woman takes the brushes out of the glass case, and I ask her, *"What kind of hair is this?"*

She says, *"Songshu."*

I look at Jin and say, *"I don't know that word. What kind of animal?"*

An elderly man, most likely this woman's husband, walks over to her. Trying to help her explain this animal to me, he says, *"This animal has a long tail,"* and he gracefully gestures with his hand to show me the long tail of this animal.

I say to Jin, *"Oh, this animal is the one that makes ponds and chews wood?"*

Jin shakes his head no and says, *"This is like a rat."* Jin points up and says *"I like trees."*

"Oh, I know," I say. *"I like to eat nuts, too."*

Jin says, *"Right, right. This animal."*

I pay for the brushes and then spy a painting of a fierce-looking tiger hung on the gallery wall. As the woman gives me my change, I say, *"Jin, look at the painting of that tiger."*

Jin says, *"That isn't a tiger. That is Da Lao Fu."* The husband and wife look confused when Jin corrects me.

I look at Jin and point to the tiger on the wall. Speaking with firmness in my voice, I explain to him, *"Jin . . . that is a tiger. You . . . are Da Lao Fu."*

The couple howls with delight, and the wife says to Jin, *"So then, you are a great old man?"* Jin blushes as he laughs.

On our previous trip to Suzhou, the manager of a pearl farm has invited us to stop by and see him the next time we are in Suzhou. Jin drives to a farm located off a dirt road, and after parking his car, we walk down a narrow path toward a tiny one-room mud-brick house. We see the manager who waves hello to us. Twelve-inch-wide rows of vegetables are planted on both sides of the footpath, and there are large ponds to the right and the left of this path.

A restaurant owner is fishing in one of the ponds, and as we watch him, he catches fish after fish and puts them into buckets of water. These fish will soon find their way to aquariums in his restaurant.

Most of the ponds have different kinds of fish in various stages of growth. One of the ponds is for hairy crabs, and a high fence surrounds their pond to keep them from wandering off. A few crabs scuttle along the edge of the fence desperately looking for a way out.

The farthest and largest pond to our left is the oyster pond, which is spread out over an acre of land. Bamboo poles in neat rows mark the spot where a net of oysters can be found. Oysters live their whole lives in these nets, which only a strong man can lift. Nets must be frequently lifted to check for dead or diseased oysters.

To the right of the oyster pond is a one-room hut where a woman sits by the front door and shucks oysters. She throws oyster meat in one bucket and pearls in another. When the oyster meat bucket is full, she pours the contents into the oyster pond, and a troupe of minuscule shrimps engulfs the oyster meat.

About twenty feet from the hut is a small, sturdy brick house. I peek through the open window of this house and meet eye-to-eye with the biggest pig I have ever seen. Her snout is the size of a dinner plate. She is curious about me and sniffs the air. Jin yells, *"Taitai, get away from there. She will have you for lunch."*

The manager of the pearl farm takes me out onto the pond in a flat-bottom boat. He rows up to a bamboo pole, pulls up a net of oysters, and takes out two. When we are back on dry land, the manager opens one oyster with a shucking knife and says, *"This oyster is five years old. See the rings on his shell?"* He hands me the five pearls from the oyster and gives me the other oyster and says, *"Here, take this one home."*

The oyster's shell is covered with a moss-like scum. I have never had a pet oyster before, and I say, *"Thank you for the oyster. Will he die if he is not in water?"*

"No, no. Put him in water when you get home."

"OK. Thank you," I say. *"I am going to name him George."* His shell needs a good cleaning with a toothbrush.

The manager wants to show us the pearl factory, and Jin drives the three of us to a large two-story building. We go up to the second floor where there are ten long tables in a row. Pearl stringers sit at these tables where they sort, size, and slip the appropriate size pearls onto a temporary string. The largest pearls must be in the middle, and each completed strand of pearls is sixteen inches long. I look toward the stringers as I say, *"Dajia hao."* "Hello everyone."

Stringers are sorting, sizing, and stringing pearls at the pearl factory

The manager takes us to the drilling room where I try my hand at operating a pearl drilling machine. This requires the simultaneous operation of a foot pedal and a hand lever. The driller must know how to place a pearl between clamps, so that the hole is drilled in the best spot. If a hole is drilled through a flaw, the value of the pearl goes up because the flaw is removed. The most demanding pearls to drill are tiny pearls. A sixteen-inch strand of four-millimeter pearls requires over one hundred pearls. Odd-shaped pearls, such as rice-shaped pearls and baroque pearls, are also difficult to drill because angles must be balanced between two concave-shaped clamps.

A pearl drilling machine has two drill bits that must be coordinated in order to keep the bits from meeting in the middle of a pearl at the same time. This is a mechanical dance that also requires the drill bits to be a certain length. If the bits are too long, metal will grind on metal, and if the drill bits are too short, the hole won't go all the way through the pearl. Additionally, the metal drill bits are soft and must be frequently sharpened on a stone wheel that throws sparks as it whirls.

Behind me is a broom made of sticks for sweeping. A fine mix of metal and pearl dust powders the table after I have done my best to drill a few pearls. This experience has given me an appreciation for the labor-intensive process of producing pearls. The manager tells me that there are over sixty steps to produce one pearl necklace.

We walk to another section of the factory where the manager uses a seven-inch key to unlock an eight-inch-thick metal door that screeches as it opens. We step into a room that looks like it belongs on a science fiction movie set. Three-gallon glass jars are filled with large white pearls. These jars are set on metal shelves that go around the perimeter of this small room. Fluorescent lights hang overhead as motors buzz and bubbles fizzle up from surgical tubing that goes to the bottom of these jars.

This is the bleaching room where bleaching agents are used to create uniformly white pearls. The liquid in these jars is a top-secret bleaching agent, which was invented by a Japanese pearl producer and subsequently stolen by a Chinese man who is now in hiding. Unlike the harsh chemicals used in the past, this is a gentle bleaching agent.

Jin and I thank the manager for taking time from his busy day to show us around the pearl farm and factory and especially for giving George to me.

We arrive back in Shanghai late at night. Jin carries my paintings up to the apartment, and I carry five-year-old George upstairs and into the kitchen. I take out a shallow ceramic bowl and place it on the counter. Jin comes into the kitchen to help me with George and pours fresh drinking water into the bowl.

I hear Martin's footsteps coming down the stairs. When he comes into the kitchen, he says, "What's that?"

I carefully hold out my pet oyster and say, "Marty . . . this is George. He's an oyster." I look at George as I cradle him in both of my hands and say to him, "George . . . this is Marty. Don't be afraid."

Jin looks sad as he turns to Martin and says, "I am sorry."

I am elated with my new pet and say, "Marty, I need to borrow your toothbrush. George's shell needs a good brushing to make him pretty."

January 28, 1998: The Year of the Tiger

Chinese New Year has arrived, and it is the year of the tiger. A few days ago, I bought a red, green, and gold cardboard koi fish cutout for our front door. Red is for good luck, green is for fruitfulness, and gold is for money. The single fish in this cutout is surrounded by the characters of *fu*, 福, for good fortune, and *xi*, 囍, for double happiness. A tassel with a lucky eight-knot hangs from the fish.

Tonight the company is sponsoring a Chinese New Year's party. When we are ready to go downstairs, we hear The Chinese Knock, and it is Jin. He presents us with a ship in a bottle, and the ship is in the shape of a dragon. We appreciate Jin's thoughtful and beautiful gift. He also gives us a gift basket from the company. This basket is filled with jams, jellies, cheeses, and other good-to-eat things. We give Jin the camera we purchased while we were back in the States as well as some money in a red envelope.

After the gift exchange, Jin takes us to a restaurant for the party. The managers, engineers, and administrators of the company are already there when we arrive. The food is good. Some of the guys dance around the restaurant in a twelve-foot-long dragon suit. Being with our Chinese friends is even better than the food.

When we come back to our apartment, I look out my kitchen window. Being on the twenty-seventh floor of our building, I have a good view of booming fireworks shooting into the sky and turning the Shanghai skyline into flares of dawn. Martin takes the video camera up to the roof of the building and stands on the ledge to record the spectacle.

I keep asking him to get down, and he keeps saying that he is fine. I hope he has captured some good footage because I wasn't watching the fireworks.

January 31, 1998: Tootsie

Tonight was our second English Night Party, and my favorite restaurant catered dinner. We also enjoyed cake from a nearby bakery. Martin and I showed the movie *Tootsie*, which our guests loved. We hope to have at least one more party before we leave Shanghai.

1998 February 16: How Do Mommy and Daddy Go?

My Chinese homework was to prepare a joke to tell in Mandarin to the class. Jin didn't know a joke, and I didn't remember any jokes, not even a blonde joke. Last night, I asked Martin if he could remember a joke, and he gave me a blank look.

A new professor is teaching our Chinese class, and I am coming to class unprepared because as Jin is driving me to class, I still don't have a joke. But as I am sitting in the backseat of Jin's car, a picture of a dog, a cat, and a mother and father form in my mind, and I say, *"Jin, how does the dog go?"*

At the stoplight, Jin turns around and says, *"What do you mean, how does the dog go?"*

"Jin knows. What sound does a dog make? How does the dog go?"

Jin says, *"Ruff, ruff."*

"How does the cat go?"

Jin now eyes me with suspicion as he says, *"Meow, meow."*

"How do Mommy and Daddy go?"

"Oh . . . Jin does not know!"

"Mommy and Daddy go . . ." and I imitate the sound of kisses.

Jin laughs loud enough for the car next to us to hear him, and he says, *"Taitai can tell that one to the class."*

February 18, 1998: An Alien Spaceship

At dinner, Martin and I keep hearing a buzzing sound, like the noise an alien spaceship might make. Martin helps clear the dishes off the table before he goes upstairs to his office, and after I clean up the kitchen, I can still hear this buzzing sound. I decide I should crack open the front door and peek into the hallway using only one eye. If aliens are out there, I can slam the door shut and yell for Martin. It is his duty as a man to protect me from fierce animals, bugs, and aliens.

I bravely step up to the door and say to myself, I can do this. I am woman. Hear me roar. I turn the knob . . . and slowly . . . ever so slowly . . . I open the door . . . and the sound of the fire alarm is deafening. I stick my head into the hallway to see if there is fire or smoke. Nope. No smoke. No fire. I go upstairs to Martin's office. "Marty, I'm going downstairs to tell management the fire alarm is going off."

"Is there a fire?"

"I don't think so, but I should let the night manager know about the fire alarm. Are you coming with me?"

"No. I've got work to do. You aren't going to take the elevator, are you?"

"Marty, do you know how long it would take me to walk down twenty-six flights of stairs? And if there is a fire, you want me to leave the building while you stay here and work?"

I put my hand on my hip, just one hand, not two hands like I do with my kids. "Martin, you are exhibit A of male logic." I am calling him Martin now instead of Marty. He has to know he has gotten my dander up. Martin once told me I had gotten his dandruff up, but as he says, English isn't his first language.

With my hand still on my hip, just one hand—but I'm getting ready to use two—I say, "People with degrees in computer science are supposed to have good logic. If A, there could be a fire, then B, get out. I'll be back unless there's a fire."

Martin looks back at the work on his desk and says, "OK, honey. Be careful."

Honestly, how can a man as intelligent as he is stay here instead of going downstairs with me? But I am pretty sure there is neither smoke nor fire, and I go downstairs using the elevator.

As I step off the elevator onto the first floor, I realize that I have forgotten to take a Chinese dictionary with me, and I don't know the word for fire alarm.

I push on the heavy glass door to the main office, and the night manager, who has his head down, leaps up from behind his desk and says, *"Nihao."* He wasn't sleeping, was he?

"Nihao," I say. *"My husband and I live on the twenty-seventh and twenty-eighth floors. There is this thing in the hallway, outside our front door. Right now, this thing is making a noise."* I do my best to imitate the fire alarm.

"Taitai, I'm sorry. I don't understand." Of course he doesn't understand. I sounded like a cow in labor. He takes out a little pad of paper from his desk drawer, and a newly sharpened pencil no one has chewed on, and says, *"Please write for me."*

I want to slap my forehead. In front of me is exhibit B of male logic. How can I write something for him I don't even know how to say? But as I take the pencil and paper from him, I have an epiphany. I know the character for fire, 火.

Each stroke of a character should be drawn in a prescribed order. Not bottom before top, and not right before left. I take my time as I meticulously place the strokes on the paper in the correct order.

The night manager stands behind his desk and watches me intensely as this character, loaded with meaning, takes on a life of its own. I pass the pencil back to this young manager and then returned his pad of paper. He glances at the character I have written and yells, *"Whaaaaaa!"* as he runs out of the office.

I speak to his back as I say, *"Wait a second. Where are you going?"* Is he leaving the building?

By the time I return to our apartment, the fire alarm is silent. This is good because I have a lot of homework to do. Then, just as I sit down to work on my assignment, the smoke alarm goes off in my kitchen.

February 26, 1998: Chinese Medicine

Martin is in the Philippines, so he isn't here when I wake up in the middle of the night with food poisoning. Around six thirty this morning, I call Jin from the phone by my bed. He is still at home and answers his phone. *"Jin,"* I say, *"this morning I'm not going to my Chinese class."*

Jin says, *"Why? What problem does taitai have?"*

I don't know how to say I have been tossing my cookies all night and want to be put out of my misery. I say, *"Jin, I have a bad flu. Very bad."* The blackout drapes in the bedroom are drawn and the sliver of light coming from the top of these drapes changes from dim to bright and back again. The room is spinning.

Jin says, *"Do you want to go to the hospital?"*

The thought of bouncing in a car as it bumps through Shanghai traffic makes my stomach feel queasy. *"I don't want to go to the hospital. I want to sleep,"* like forever. I can feel my heart pounding. I am thirsty, but water won't stay down.

"OK, OK," Jin says. *"One o'clock, I will be at taitai's door. Jin will make you better."* Jin hangs up before I can tell him I am beyond fixing and don't want him to come over. I go back to sleep.

In my dream state, I hear pounding and shouting. I wake up. It's one o'clock. I am still alive. Jin is pounding on the front door and yelling, *"Taitai . . . Taitai . . . Taitai."*

I put on a robe and my bunny slippers. I feel dizzy, and I carefully go down the stairs. If I don't answer the door, Jin will find Stella and have her unlock the door.

I say, *"Jin, nihao,"* as I open the door. At least now the pounding and shouting has stopped.

Jin holds up a plastic bag, steps past me, and walks into the kitchen and says, *"Now, Jin will make taitai better. I brought you hun den."*

Whatever is in the bag isn't moving, but that doesn't mean it isn't alive. I close the front door and say, *"Jin, is this something to eat? I can't eat anything."*

He ignores my objection and pretends to be deaf. I watch as he searches my cabinets, takes out a large pot, adds drinking water, and turns the gas burner on under the pan. A yellow and blue flame whoosh into life, and Jin says, *"Where's the salt?"* Since he is supposedly deaf, I point to a container with no label.

Jin says, *"Taitai, go go . . . sit sit. I will bring hun den out to you."*

What can *hun den* possibly be? My bunny slippers scuffle to the dining room table only a few feet away from the kitchen. I sit on the long side of the rectangular table in the dining room and rest my head on the heels of my hands. I put my elbows on the table.

My mother says I should never, ever put my elbows on the table because Emily Post says so. I can see my mother now with one hand on her hip, while the other hand points to a page in her old Emily Post book on etiquette, and I think, "Well, Mother . . . I don't care what Emily Post says. She is dead, and you are thousands of miles away. If I live through this food poisoning, I will put my elbows on the table whenever I want, and I don't care if I get a carbuncle on both elbows."

In the kitchen, I hear the rustling of a plastic bag and plopping sounds of something dropping into water. Chinese people think some animals have medicinal properties. At least whatever has plunked into the water doesn't sound like a tiger's paw, or pig's feet. If there is one thing I do not want to eat, it is any kind of pork because pigs don't have lymphatic systems, and Jin knows I don't want to eat pork—no ham, no Spam, no bacon, no chops, no ribs, nothing like that—not ever—in any form.

Oh . . . and please let *hun den* not have any rat, cat, snake or dog meat or have any chicken heads, fish heads, fish gills, turtle legs, turtle heads, wings, tails of any kind, fish scales, feathers, brains, entrails, mountain oysters, slippery-slimy snails, insect pupae, insect larva, crickets, chicken feet, tiger meat, bear meat, cock's comb, chicken wattles, chicken beaks, eyeballs of any kind, meat or feet of an alligator, paws or claws of any kind from anything, centipedes, millipedes, or blue pigeon meat floating in some soup. Have I forgotten anything that could be in this soup Chinese people might consider medicinal?

Jin putters in my kitchen while he hums a tune I often hear on his car radio. Is humming part of some mystical healing ceremony? I hear Jin using a chopstick to stir whatever is in the pan. Maybe he can wave a magic chopstick over my head and yell, *"Be healed!"* I feel so bad I never want to eat again. If I try to explain to him why I can't eat anything, he will just pretend to be deaf again. He has a talent for that kind of thing.

Jin opens a drawer, closes a drawer, and comes into the dining room. *"Taitai, here is a soup spoon and chopsticks."* Jin disappeared back into the kitchen. More puttering ... more humming ... more stirring ... cabinet doors opening and closing. A ceramic bowl clinks onto the counter. More pouring and plunking sounds. Whatever has gone into the bowl sounds small and slippery. Uh-oh.

I grab a handful of paper napkins from the far end of the table and set them close by me just in case I take one look at whatever is floating in that soup and hurl. I rest my head on my hands again and defiantly put my elbows back on the table.

I hear Jin's footsteps coming closer and closer. He sets the soup in front of me. Still resting my head in my hands, the aroma of the soup hits my nose, and it is delightful. When I dare myself to look down at the bowl, no eyeballs stare back at me. No crickets or chicken wattles are floating on top, either. Suspended in the soup are fat, fluffy pillows stuffed with something. *Hun den* has passed the look and the smell test.

Jin picks up my soup spoon and hands it to me. He says, *"First, drink some broth. Taitai will feel better."* He sits down on the short side of the table, not even an arm's reach away. He puts his elbows on the table, makes his hands into fists on which he rests his face. His knuckles push up against his cheeks and give his face a puffy look. How blessed he is to have never heard of Emily Post.

With my spoon lingering over the bowl, Jin watches me with the demeanor of someone who could watch over a ward for the anorexic. If I don't scoop up some broth with my spoon, he will do that for me. I sit up and dip the spoon into the steaming soup. I take a little sip and then ... tip the whole spoonful in my mouth. *"Jin, this is good,"* I say.

"Have some more," he says, and I dip my spoon into the broth three more times. As the soup slides to the bottom of my empty stomach, it feels warm and soothing. *"OK, OK,"* Jin says. *"No more broth."* He takes my spoon away from me and hands me chopsticks and says, *"When Chinese people are sick they eat hun den. Now you will get better."*

Jin wants me to eat the soft pillows that look like Italian ravioli. Using my chopsticks, I pull out one of these Chinese raviolis and bite it in half. The whole ravioli is too big to eat in one bite. I say, *"Jin, this is good. My stomach likes this."* I look at the uneaten half of the ravioli held in my chopsticks. There is green stuff and some meat tucked in there. *"Jin, what's this green stuff?"*

Jin, with his knuckles still pushed against his cheeks, says, *"Spinach. Jin knows taitai likes spinach."*

"Jin, this is very good," I say. *"What kind of meat is this?"* I put the other half of the ravioli into my mouth. While I chew and wait for his answer, my chopsticks are poised over the bowl, ready to lock and load the next ravioli. Jin says nothing as I pull out the second ravioli and bite it in half. As I chew, I look at Jin and wait for his answer.

Jin sits up in his chair and says, *"That is . . . a little something to eat. It doesn't matter, never mind."* This is Jin's way of saying that he isn't going to tell me what kind of meat I have eaten.

Aside from the spinach and the meat, there are a lot of indistinguishable and flavorful green herbs in the broth. Apparently, some of the herbs are perfect for a poisoned digestive system because I am feeling better.

The second ravioli is as delectable as the first, but I stop chewing when the image of a smutty snarky pig pops into my mind. Am I eating pig meat? I finish chewing and swallow.

After eating my third ravioli, Jin pats my forearm. *"OK, OK. Stop eating. At five o'clock, taitai can have a little more hun den. It isn't good to eat too much at one time."* Jin takes my chopsticks and bowl away from me and puts the leftover *hun den* in the refrigerator. *"OK, OK. Tomorrow, taitai will be all better. Jin will see you tomorrow."*

When I stand up from the table, I am no longer dizzy. My stomach feels good. The pounding in my chest has stopped, and my heart is now beating in a gentle rhythm. Shuffling in my bunny slippers, I walk with Jin to the door and open it for him. I have strength back in my arms. *"Jin, thank you for the hun den. I feel much better. This hun den is good stuff."* I place my hands together and bow to him. *"Jin, thank you."*

Jin returns my bow and steps out the door. He waves good-bye and starts walking toward the elevator.

Once his back is to me, I say, *"Jin."*

He turns around. *"What?"*

"Why didn't you tell me pig tastes so good?"

Jin has been found out, and he laughs. He turns away from me once again and throws his index finger high into the air as he says, *"Taitai, see you tomorrow."* I hear my American accent.

"Yes," I shout, *"and tomorrow we will have pig for lunch."* Tomorrow, I will treat Jin to lunch—anywhere he wants to go.

February 27, 1998: What Makes a Sourpuss Smile?

On the way to Fudan University this morning, I tell Jin I am treating him to lunch and say, *"We will go anyplace you want."*

When Jin picks me up after school, he says that he would like to go to the Hard Rock Café by the Portman, where I order for myself what Jin wants to eat. We each have a T-bone steak, corn on the cob, a baked Idaho potato, and a virgin strawberry daiquiri. This meal is more than scrumptious. It has the power to soothe a weary soul and to make a sourpuss smile—not that either one of us is a sourpuss.

In China, to show that we have had plenty to eat, it is customary to leave food on our plates. We are, however, eating at an American restaurant, so not a morsel of food was left. When we walk out of the Hard Rock Café, we are smiling like Cheshire cats.

March 1, 1998: A Dirty Chinese Dragon

Because I am missing that shopping-gathering gene many women have, I have never cared for shopping in the States, but as I cross the ocean to Shanghai, something has caused me to love shopping in China. So, it isn't my fault that there has been a slight rise in the economy of Shanghai because of my new spending habits.

I usually bargain for what I want, and one of my favorite places to shop is the Sunday Market. The permanent vendors on the first and second floors have seen me many times and use Mandarin when they speak to me, but the temporary vendors on the third and fourth floors think of me as a dumb blond foreigner.

Now that my Chinese is passable, I enjoy listening to Chinese people talk about me, and I can keep a straight face, too, as I listen to what they have to say. My blond hair and green eyes are a curiosity, and according to Chinese mythology, a woman with green eyes is the daughter of a goddess. Chinese people have put their face right in front of mine to look at my eyes, and sometimes they have even touched my hair. While it is annoying, I am getting used to this behavior.

The Chinese assume all foreigners love old stuff, and one of the things they do to give something an antique look is to bury it in dirt for a month or two. When a seller says to me in English, "This old, very old," sometimes, just for fun, I say, *"Lao de bu hao,"* which means *old is not good.* One Chinese guy once replied to my *lao de bu hao* with, *"It isn't too old. Do you like it?"*

Another one of their favorite sayings in English is, "This only one. No more." When I turn my back, another object just like the one I bought pops into place. Sometimes they also bark out, "This cheap," or, my favorite, "Good quality."

Bargaining is entertainment for the Chinese, and I have learned to keep my sense of humor and to never be so attached to something that I must have it at any price. Also, if I even ask the price of something, and nothing is marked with a price in a flea market, the bargaining must begin and go to the end when I either purchase or forgo.

Before I start to bargain, I decide how much I am willing to pay for something, and I don't go above that price, no matter what. The Chinese think every foreigner is rich and will throw away money on just about anything. Chinese retailers are amazed at what a foreigner will buy. Even I, at times, am amazed at what some foreigners will buy and how much they are willing to pay.

Because Jin can't find a parking spot, he drops me off in front of the Sunday Market. The first and second floors of this market are open all week long, but the third and fourth floors are only open on the weekend. Today is Sunday afternoon, and the merchants on these two temporary floors will soon return to the countryside with their wares, and whatever they have for sale today, I might never see again.

I walk up to the fourth floor and see a twenty-four-inch-high dragon covered in a dirty beige film. He beckons me. I want him. With a good shower back at the apartment, he will be as good as new, and I'm willing to pay three hundred yuan for this dragon and not one yuan more. I look at the vendor and say in English, "How much?"

A dirty Chinese dragon

In his best English, he says, "This three thousand yuan. Very good price."

Three thousand? As I tap my finger on the head of this dragon and try to figure out what kind of material is beneath the dirt, Dragon Vendor says, "This very old."

I look at him, and he stares at my eyes. Most likely, he has noticed that my eyes are dark green. I say in English, "This is very dirty." He doesn't understand me, and then I continue to speak in English as I say, "Three hundred yuan."

Dragon Vendor turns away from me and calls out to the other vendors. Speaking in Chinese he says, *"Ha! This door scratcher is so cheap that she would take the shirt off my back and pay me nothing."* His fellow merchants guffaw and point at me as if I can't see them. I keep a straight face and don't let on that I have understood every word he has said . . . and . . . that he has called me a door scratcher, which is quite an insult. A door scratcher is so cheap she won't buy a door handle for her own door. She scratches on her door until someone lets her in.

His fellow vendors move in closer to see this door-scratching woman. This is Chinese theater. The devoted Rascal in me awakens and gets comfortable on my shoulder. He never lets me down. No one can see him.

I take out my calculator, punch in three hundred, and pass my calculator to him. He punches in twenty-five hundred. I type in three hundred. He types in two thousand. I type in three hundred. He punches in eighteen hundred. I type in three hundred. He punches in fifteen hundred. I type in three hundred. His fellow merchants laugh nervously as they watch the calculator flying back and forth and back and forth like a tennis ball.

When he types in one thousand, I type in three hundred, and he turns away from me again, and as he tugs at his shirt collar he yells out, *"You see, I told you. This door scratcher wants the shirt off my back for nothing. What am I to do with her?"* They nod in sympathy and give out a chortling kind of laughter as they chatter among themselves and point to me as if I can't see them.

Dragon Vendor turns back toward me and throws up his hands in defeat. "OK, OK. Three hundred . . . three hundred." My Rascal is already tittering because he and I know that Dragon Vendor will remember this day forever.

Everyone's eyes watch my hands as I slowly count out three hundred yuan into Dragon Vendor's hand. Then, it is my turn to look into his eyes. I give him a gleeful smile, and with a voice loud enough to be heard in this Chinese theater, I say, *"Hao a! Xianzai ni keyi ba ni de chenshan gei wo le ba."* "Good! Now you can give me your shirt, too."

His eyes pop. His mouth drops. The eruption of laughter is heard on every floor of the market as he stands there and sucks air. I wish I had a picture of his face when he realized I wasn't a typical foreigner . . . but he should have known that when he saw my dark green eyes.

March 2, 1998: The Lingerie Department

Yesterday I was going to wear a skirt to class, but when I put on my half-slip, it fell down around my ankles . . . while I was still at home.

After class today, I ask Jin to take me to Babaiban. I want to go to the lingerie department to buy a new half-slip, but I don't want Jin to escort me. When Jin parks in the underground parking lot of this large department store, I say, *"Jin, please wait here."*

I have been getting lost since I was five years old, and Jin knows by now that I seldom know where I am going, how I arrived someplace, or where I have been, and he says, *"But taitai will get lost."*

If I were a rat in a maze, I couldn't find the cheese, but I could make a dime disappear and pull it out of my ear. This talent, however, is no help in this situation, and I am not even sure where the lingerie department is located among eleven floors. It could take me the rest of the day to find this department, not to mention that I am not sure if Jin's car is on the first or second parking level, but I can figure that out. I see an escalator and point to it as I say, *"I will take the escalator up. In thirty minutes, I will be back."* This is an obvious lie, and I am not even wearing a watch.

The problem for Jin is that if I am lost for too many hours, he will have to report me as a missing person to the Shanghai police. And what's even worse is that he will have to find out how to tell Martin in English, "I lost your wife." "To lose" is an irregular verb, and I haven't taught that verb to Jin yet.

But at least I have a plan on how to get back to Jin's car, which is parked close to the escalator going up. Once I purchase my half-slip, I will take the escalator going down, and then find the escalator going up, next to the last escalator I took going down, and locate the car from there. How hard can that be? How many pairs of escalators can there be?

Jin walks with me to the escalator going up, which is as far as I want him to go with me. Standing at the bottom of the escalator, Jin pulls on his left ear a few times. He does that when he is anxious. I am determined to go it alone.

When I reach the first floor of Babaiban, there is a store map, which indicates that women's clothing, 女装, and lingerie, 内衣, are on the eighth floor. There is also an elevator on the first floor, just to my right, but I don't take it. I might take too many turns and lose my way, and besides that, the escalator is my anchor.

I make my way to the eighth floor where I stand at the top of the escalator, and I see racks of women's dresses with a sign that says "90 percent," which means that the discount is 10 percent. I also see two mannequins with just legs and two large fingers in the symbolic sign of peace. These are peace mannequins.

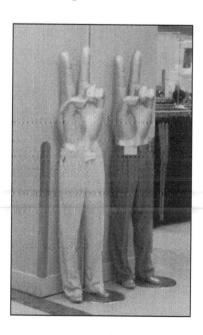

Peace mannequins

I turn to my left, only because there is a twenty-five-percent chance that the lingerie department is this way. I wander down a wide aisle that happens to end in the lingerie department. How lucky is that? This is a straight shot for me from the escalator going up, and I make a mental map of how I have arrived at the women's intimate apparel department, which is actually an alcove.

As I stand in one place, I can see everything in this tiny lingerie shop. I see those nylon socks that Chinese women wear that only come up to their ankle. And there are girdles and bras. Girdles? These zero-to-size six Chinese women wear girdles? As for getting me into a girdle, I wouldn't put on one of those life-sucking things unless I was dead.

I don't see slips of any kind—not full-slips or half-slips—which are called underskirts in Mandarin.

A saleswoman comes up to me and says, *"May I help you?"*

"Yes, I want to buy an underskirt."

"An underskirt?" she says.

"That's right," I say. I pull up my skirt to show her what I mean and say, *"An underskirt that I wear under my skirt."* She continues to give me a blank stare. I reach into my purse and pull out my dictionary. I find the English word for slip and then point to the Chinese characters, 衬裙, as well as the pinyin, *chèn qún,* for underskirt.

She places her finger under the Chinese characters for underskirt in my dictionary and says, *"We don't have underskirts."*

I look down at the clerk's skirt, which is sixteen inches long. This is when I realize that the miniskirt will always be the fashion in Shanghai. If tiny Chinese women wear long skirts, they will look like they are playing dress up. I thank the young woman and make a mental note to call my mother and ask her to send a half-slip to me from the States.

I start walking down the broad aisle looking for the peace mannequins. Where are those dresses with the 10 percent discount? I reach the end of the aisle. The dresses on sale and the peace mannequins are gone.

Then I hear someone shout, *"Taitai."*

That's Jin's voice. I turn around, and he is about thirty feet behind me. He is swinging a plastic bag with a rectangular object in it. When I stop to wait for him to catch up with me, he raises the bag high above his head and shouts, *"Jin needed a box of tissues."*

March 6, 1998: Martin Buying an Underskirt

Stella has come to our apartment for a quiet dinner. There is soft music playing in the background, and I have made lasagna and a salad. The three of us are drinking red wine, enjoying our dinner, and everything is calm ... until without warning ... Martin stands up from the table to show us how to buy an underskirt in Shanghai.

He does an exaggerated feminine swagger with the hip-bump walk of a runway model—only better. I did not know he could walk like that. Then, he abruptly stops and "sees" a large crowd of Chinese people watching him. He looks pleased. He waves like the Queen of England and smiles at them. He checks his hairdo in a "mirror." And his teeth, too.

He looks down at his long imaginary skirt and smooths out the fabric over his slim hips. And then, as he keeps eye contact with the "crowd," he lifts up this "skirt" in a languorous and sexy way—I didn't know he could do that, either—and he points to his "skirt" and hairy leg as he mimes something to this crowd of people. We know that everyone in the "crowd" is looking at his bushy leg with interest. Stella and I are laughing.

Out of an imaginary purse as large as a suitcase, Martin heaves a huge invisible Chinese dictionary. He opens this tome and as he licks his thumb and index finger, he desperately flips back and forth through the pages while he occasionally glances over at the crowd. He continuously babbles in audible gibberish-Chinese using staccato syllables.

During this demonstration, Martin doesn't even crack a smile or acknowledge that Stella and I are in the same room with him. We are laughing so hard we can hardly breathe.

Now, my sides hurt from laughing. Stella has the same complaint. This is all Martin's fault.

March 8, 1998: Love Affair

Jin takes me to the Hua Bao Lou Building, which has a flea market in the basement. I often find fascinating artifacts in this dark and musty market. A merchant, who frequently has interesting things to show me, invites me into his tiny shop. We greet each other by saying *nihao*, and with his finger to the side of his nose, he says, *"I have something special. I will give you a look."*

There is just enough room in the middle of his shop for two chairs. He sits on one chair and invites me to sit down on the other one, which is directly across from him. My back is to the front of the shop. There is a tall Parsons table to his left. It is covered with a floral bed sheet draped to the floor. His top-secret items are behind this sheet. He peers around me to make sure that no one is peeking into his shop, and then he lifts the sheet and carefully takes out a little cloth-covered book.

Until Mao came to power, books were read from the back cover to the front, from the right to the left of each page, and from the top of a column of characters to the bottom. The title of this book, 风花雪月, *Wind Flower Snow Moon*, is written vertically on the back cover. The translation of *Wind Flower Snow Moon* is *Love Affair*.

When something is special, the giver holds out the object with both hands. The receiver who recognizes the specialness of the object also holds out both of her hands. The shopkeeper places the book in my palms. With a nod of his head, he gives me permission to open the book.

As I hold the book, I can see that the uncut pages are folded onto one another. When I open this book, the eight pages are evenly spaced by parallel folds, which are like the bellows of an accordion. Each page is a singular watercolor painting of a man and a woman in the throes of passion. None of these paintings has any writing on them. Why write anything when a picture is worth a thousand words.

During the Cultural Revolution, the Red Guard was determined to destroy everything that was old. *Love Affair* escaped this destiny. This kind of book would not have been owned by the average person or even owned by a woman. Most likely, this book belonged to a high-ranking official who was a man of considerable wealth and possibly a member of the imperial ruling class.

After Sun Yat-sen's revolution in 1911, a provisional government was put into place, and this was the end of the Manchus who had ruled China for 267 years. This was also the end of the imperial rule that had lasted for two thousand years. This book was created sometime before Sun Yat-sen's revolution in 1911.

I say, *"How much is this?"* I lean back in my chair and try to look as nonchalant as possible.

He says, *"You say how much you will pay,"* and he starts to pour some tea for me. Is bargaining going to take so long that we have time for tea? I decline his offer of tea by saying, *"No thanks. Just ate. Feel stuffed."*

He does not know the value of the book, and I don't know how much it is worth, either. To force him to give me a price, I move the book toward him as if to give it back, which shows a disinterest on my part.

He says, *"OK, OK. One hundred and fifty yuan."* I raise my eyebrows in shock at the low price. *"OK, OK,"* he says, *"one hundred and twenty yuan."* The cost is not quite fifteen US dollars. Some people only make eighty yuan a day, so perhaps this is a good sum of money for him. I pay the second asking price.

He shakes hands with me and says, *"Come back, OK?"* Vendors who shake hands with me know something about doing business with foreigners.

"Yes, I will come back," I say. I don't say his name as I leave his shop because I don't know his name. Older Chinese people don't have the custom of sharing their names when they meet someone.

March 11, 1998: One Husband to Pay and One to Play

Everyone at Fudan University addresses me as Wen Li Xia, and we respectfully address our professor as *laoshi*. I don't like talking in class and do what I can to avoid responding to *laoshi's* questions.

Last week our professor went around to each of us and asked us about our families. Wanting to cut this conversation short, I said, *"Laoshi, I have three children and two husbands. One to pay and one to play."*

My classmates were laughing as *laoshi* said, *"Wen Li Xia, you are very bad."* Our decorous professor did not want to hear more details about my interesting family, and he went on to talk to the woman sitting next to me who was still laughing.

Unfortunately, our professor wanted to hear us speak more Chinese that day, and he launched into another linguistic exercise. *Laoshi* pretended to make a telephone call to each of us. When *laoshi* came to me, he said, *"Ring, ring."*

I said, *"Wei?"* "Hello?"

"Wen Li Xia zai nali ma?" "Is Wen Li Xia there?"

I said, *"Wen Li Xia bu zai nali. Mingtian ba."* "Wen Li Xia is not here. Maybe tomorrow," and I hung up.

Today, *laoshi* wants each of us to present a short Chinese lesson to our class. The first presenter gives us a food list written in Chinese and English. The next presenters give us lists of Chinese verbs with pictures, pictures of objects from magazines along with their measure words, and so on. I am the last presenter.

Is our professor saving the best for last or hoping class will be over before I can present my lesson? I don't have any magazines, and I have no way to print out a list, so I draw a scene of a Chinese veterinarian's office on a sheet of paper. Nothing I say about this picture is true, but truthfulness is not one of the requirements.

On the first day of class, *laoshi* told us that we could make up anything. I have taken him at his word—to his detriment.

When I am in front of the class with my picture, I say, *"In Shanghai there is a veterinarian. His name is Dr. King. His specialty is guinea pigs. I take my guinea pig to see Dr. King. The name of my pig is Laolao-Daodao."*

Laoshi interrupts me and says, *"Wen Li Xia, please tell the class what laolao-daodao means in English."*

This is a rare dispensation for me to speak English, and I say, "This is my favorite Chinese word, and it means *blah . . . blah . . . blah.*" Everyone grabs a pencil to write down this word, which I write on the blackboard in Chinese characters and pinyin, 唠唠叨叨, láoláo-daodao.

I continue my spiel. *"On the door of the doctor's office is a sign that says—'Everyone: Sit. Stay.' The doctor asks Laolao-Daodao, 'How are you?' The doctor is wearing bunny slippers. Dr. Wang has his name written on his scrubs. He is giving my guinea pig some medicine. The medicine that he is giving to him is an apple and some lettuce.*

"The doctor has a tattoo on his arm. This tattoo is in English. It says, 'I love Mom.' Dr. Wang got this tattoo when he went out with his American navy friends. They went to a karaoke bar. They drank too much beer. Then the doctor and his friends did some things I don't know how to say, but the next time I talk about Dr. Wang, I will know more Chinese. I will tell you all about this adventure."

When I mention the American navy, *Laoshi's* forehead starts to sweat, and at this point I decide to give this nice guy a break. There is, after all, a microphone and camera in the classroom.

I continue with my flapdoodle. *"Dr. Wang is a good doctor. He is not a very good karaoke singer, but if you ever want to hear Dr. Wang sing, first you must have a few beers. Then you will think he is also a good singer.*

"I should tell you that Dr. Wang is looking for a wife. His phone number is 8899-9988. As for Laolao-Daodao, he is looking for a girlfriend. If you have a lady guinea pig, Laolao-Daodao's phone number is 9988-8888. Laolao-Daodao's housekeeper answers his phone. Thank you."

I am happy to be finished, and *Laoshi* is even happier. He looks exhausted. I hope this is the last lesson I will ever have to present.

March 14, 1998: Whaaaaaa! So Many Wives

Jason, who is an American, is visiting Ellen and her husband in Shanghai. Ellen and I decide to take Jason for a shopping experience and then to dinner.

Jin drives the three of us to a large tourist section of Shanghai called Old City on Fang Bang Lu. This is the location of the Hua Bao Lou building, which has the flea market in the basement.

Ellen goes to the basement flea market while Jason and I are just outside the Hua Bao Lou building at a little shop that sells delicate tissue cutouts. Jason buys a few packages of cutouts. The saleswoman gives Jason his change, and as he studies the coins in his hand, the saleswoman becomes concerned. She looks at me and says, *"Does he have a problem? I gave him the correct change."*

"He is only looking at the coins," I say. *"There is no problem. This is the first time he has ever seen Chinese coins."* She smiles with relief.

Jason says, "What did you tell her? 'He is a moron'?"

"Oh no, Jason. She said you're handsome, and I agreed with her."

"Did she really say I'm good looking?" Jason looks over at the saleswoman who gives him a big smile.

I say, "Jason, ask her what she said if you don't believe me." His deadpan expression tells me that it is time for dinner.

We are meeting two other Shanghai Expatriate friends at a restaurant in Old City, and we all arrive at the restaurant at about the same time. The five of us are seated at a large round table in the middle of the restaurant, and a waitress comes over to our table. She passes out menus written in Chinese and stands by me. Ellen asks me to order since I am the only person at the table who speaks Mandarin.

Jason is conspicuously the only man in our group, which does not go unnoticed by the woman who is waiting on us. Just for fun, I say to the waitress, *"We're all his wives."*

She says, *"Whaaaaaa! So many wives."* Her eyes roam around our table. Her pencil is poised over her pad of paper and waits to take our order.

I am careful not to order dog, 狗, or brains, 脑子, or pig, 猪, or live octopus, 活章鱼, or anything unusual. The waitress looks at my menu as I point to one beef, 牛肉, dish, two chicken, 鸡, dishes, and several vegetable dishes as I say, *"We'll have these meat and vegetable dishes. We would also like something special just for the husband."* I close my menu. *"He needs to keep up his strength. Whatever you suggest, this will be good."*

My Rascal has been sitting comfortably on my shoulder since Jason purchased his tissue paper cutouts. Rascal likes Jason, and while my friends don't know about my Rascal, they know I like to have fun, and they never discourage me.

The waitress takes our order to the chef, and then several men come out of the kitchen and look at everyone at our table. Jason notices and says, "OK, Sharon. I'll bite. What did you say to her?"

"I told her . . . we are all your wives."

My women friends laugh, but Jason is not sure if this is funny or not, and he says, "Sharon, I can't believe a word you say."

I shrug my shoulders and say, "That's OK." My women friends know I have told him the truth. They can hardly wait to see what will happen next.

Minutes later, a chef brings out a plate of something and sets it before Jason. As the chef looks at Jason with admiration, he makes a fist and says, *"Good luck with your wives. Eat this. Will keep you strong."*

Jason watches the chef walk back to the kitchen with a spring in his step. Then Jason looks at his plate and says, "Sharon, what is this?"

I put my elbows on the table and say, "Something just for you, Jason. I have no idea what it is. Maybe Rocky Mountain oysters?" I don't even want to look at what is on his plate. Whatever this dish is, it is believed to be good for a man's virility, and I am not eating any of it.

"OK, Sharon, tell me the truth. What did that guy say when he shook his fist at me?"

I still have my elbows on the table. Ellen and another friend also put their elbows on the table, and we all stare at Jason like loving wives as I say, "Jason, he said, 'Good luck with your wives. Eat this. Will keep you strong.'" Rascal laughs the loudest, but no one can hear him.

March 16, 1998: A Pot of Glue

When I check our mailbox at The Tower, I find a white slip of paper with Chinese characters scribbled on it. I can't even begin to read this writing. I hand this piece of paper to Jin when he picks me up for class. *"Jin, what does this say?"*

"Taitai has a package at the post office. After class, Jin will pick up for you."

I have some postcards to mail, too. *"Jin, these postcards, can I also mail these?"* I show Jin the cards, and he nods his head as he takes the postcards and places them in the front passenger seat along with the piece of paper.

After class, Jin drives to the post office. Inside the postal bureau, the only source of light is from a few windows at the front of the building.

As Jin and I step up to one of the postal clerk stations, every step we take on the old wood floor sounds like the croak of a swamp frog. This is the first time I have ever been in a Chinese post office.

Each postal station has iron bars separating the clerks from their patrons. This postal building reminds me of the bank buildings in old B Western movies. Roy Rogers and Gene Autry would have felt right at home. I give Jin one hundred yuan to purchase international stamps for me.

After Jin receives the stamps, he presents the piece of paper to the clerk, and the fireworks start. Jin and the postal clerk shout at one another in Shanghainese, and Chinese people start to congregate around us. This is Chinese theater.

I am beginning to understand Shanghainese as Jin asks the clerk, *"Why must you open?"*

Jin turns to me and calmly speaks in Mandarin when he says, *"This package from the States, what is in the package?"*

The package is most likely the half-slip my mother has mailed to me, and I say, *"The box contains an underskirt."*

Jin turns back to the clerk, and again, arms fly and voices yell. I must say, Jin is better at the shouting and flailing than the clerk, which is probably why Jin prevails and obtains my package for me without anyone opening it.

Since Jin and I have arrived at the post office, everyone who is *already in* the post office or has *come* into the post office is *still* in the post office. It is getting crowded.

The clerk hands Jin my package with a huff. As Jin hands the package to me, I say, *"Jin, thank you for getting this package for me."*

"No problem," Jin says. *"Now we can mail the postcards."* Jin points to a little pot with glue and a whiskery brush with splayed bristles resting in the pot. When I look at the little pot of glue, I see my nemesis. Glue and I don't get along well. Jin doesn't know that.

As Chinese eyes watch us, Jin shows me how to put glue on a stamp and affix it to a postcard. One stamp is done. I set down my package and take the glue brush with confidence. I can do this. I put enough glue on the stamp to keep it from peeling off as it crosses the humid Pacific Ocean. When I press the stamp onto the postcard, glue squishes out from the edges. I can fix this. Four edges. Four fingers. I'm right-handed, so I use the fingers on my left hand to wipe off the glue from around the edges of the stamp.

When Jin takes the frazzled brush away from me, I hear a "tsk"—that sound he does so well—and he says, *"Taitai, use a tissue. Clean your hand."* The watchers smirk as they snigger.

The glue has defeated me as it often does. I take out a tissue from my purse with my right hand and swipe my left hand. Now I have glue on my right hand too, and bits of tissue on both hands. I hear a few chuckles.

Jin finishes the gluing process and gives the postcards to the clerk, who turns them over and sees that they are written in English. As I stand next to Jin, the sneering clerk contemplates us with a squinty eyed look.

Jin stands tall and ready for a face-off as he holds the clerk's eyes in a steady stare—which he also does well—and then the clerk turns his beady eyes on me. Being careful not to get glue on my clothes, I put one hand on my hip. I consider using two hands, but I don't want to be obvious. The clerk realizes that the next round will be two against one, and with a snort he tosses my postcards into a basket behind the old battered counter.

Jin doesn't want me to glue my hands to my purse, so he takes the strap to my handbag off my shoulder. As he takes my purse, he picks up my package and says, *"OK, OK. Let's go."*

I hold my hands away from my clothes as Jin opens the door for me, and once I'm outside, a gentle breeze ruffles the tissue stuck to my fingers.

Back at The Tower, two guards open the doors for us. With my purse slung over his shoulder, Jin carries my postal package and Chinese books upstairs for me. The guards smile as we enter the building. I am holding my hands away from my clothes. The tissue paper on my hands is obvious, and I say, *"Hello, everybody."* Let them have their fun.

At my kitchen sink, the glue easily washes off with soap and warm water. Jin helps me with my homework, and then we work on his English lesson.

Once Jin leaves, I open the package from the States and find a lacy half-slip. Before I moved to Shanghai, I left one hundred dollars with my mother in case I needed her to send something to me from the States.

March 17, 1998: The Whisker of a Tigress

Jin drives to Old City. I want to shop at the flea market in the basement of the Hua Bao Lou Building. Because Jin can't find a place to park, he drops me off as close to the building as he can.

When I step down the stairs leading to the basement market, it smells musty as usual. I walk down the first aisle on my right, only because I haven't been down this aisle for some time. When I am almost to the end of the aisle, there is a little shop with two sales counters pushed together. These counters are set three feet away from the wall. On one of the counters, there is a six-inch-high statue of a young man standing with his hand on the neck of a tiger. On the forehead of the tiger is the Chinese character of *Wang*, 王, which is a family name and means *royal*. I assume that the statue refers to a Chinese myth.

The merchant sees me admiring the statue, and in heavily accented English, he says, "You like?"

I look at his kind eyes and rest my forearms on his counter. I decide to skip the game of pretending that I don't speak Chinese and say, *"What is the story of this statue?"*

He says, *"If I tell you the story, will you buy it?"* Standing behind his high counter, he smiles at me.

"If I like the story, I will like the statue," I say.

He leans on his counter with both of his forearms, too, as if to settle in for a long conversation with a friend. A few Chinese people gather around us. They are amused that I speak Chinese and have blond hair. The merchant looks at my eyes. *"You have dark green eyes. Very beautiful. Very rare. Your mother is a goddess, right?"*

I am pretty sure that he isn't asking me a serious question, but I answer him anyway. *"Thank you for the compliment. No, no. My mother is not a goddess."* Some of the people in the gathering crowd want to see my eyes, but he waves them off so they won't bother me.

"*Please tell me the story of this statue,*" I say.

He closes his eyes to search his memory and says, "*The man in the statue loves the most beautiful girl in the village. Actually, this girl, Song, is the most beautiful girl to have ever been born. Of course, all the young men in the village want to marry her, but none of them dare to ask for her to be his wife, except for one young man. His name is Qian.*

"*When Qian is of marrying age, he asks his father to arrange a marriage for him with Song. His father tells him, 'Qian, you don't have what it takes to be married to Song. Let her be.'*

"*Qian tells his father, 'If Song cannot be my wife, I will marry no one and die of a broken heart.' What else can a father do but see if a marriage can be arranged?*

"*Qian's father knocks on the door where Song lives and asks to speak to Song's father. Song's father invites him into his home and pours some tea for him. After some polite conversation, Qian's father says, 'My son would like to marry your beautiful daughter. He tells me that he will have no one else for a wife. If he does not marry your daughter, then I am afraid he will die of a broken heart.'*

"*Song's father says, 'I am sorry to hear of your son's determination because there is no young man who has what it takes to be with her. Song would only give your son heartache.' But after much discussion, Song's father relents and allows the marriage to take place.*

"*Song is indeed most beautiful with long black hair, green eyes, a beautiful shape, and a graceful walk. The villagers say that she can heal someone with her smile—if she chooses to smile.*

"*The day of the wedding arrives, and Song becomes Qian's wife. Qian takes his bride to a little house on the edge of the village, and as the sky darkens, he lies down on their bed and says, 'Song, come to bed now.' Song sits in a chair, unmoved and unsmiling. Qian hopes he will have better luck tomorrow night.*

"*On the following evening, when Qian lies down on their bed, he says, 'Song, come to bed.' Song rises from her chair. She warms water on the kitchen fire and fills a large wooden bath bowl. Her dress drops from her shoulders.*

179

She steps into the large bowl, and as she stands there, she pours water over her hair as Qian watches from their wedding bed. Qian hopes he will have better luck tomorrow night.

"The following evening, Qian lies down on their bed and says, 'Please, Song, come to bed with your husband.' Song gets up from her chair and opens the front door. She goes over to the bed, plucks Qian up by the collar of his nightshirt with one hand, and grabs his shoes with the other. She throws the shoes and Qian out the door. She shuts the door with a slam.

"Qian walks to his parents' house and knocks on the door. Qian's father greets his son at the door. Over tea, Qian tells his father what has happened and says, 'Father, I don't know what to do.'

"Qian's father pours more tea into his son's cup, and with a weary sigh, he says, 'My son, you don't have what it takes to be with her, but perhaps there is one thing you can do. When it is daylight, go to the Buddhist monk who lives at the foot of Tiger Mountain. Perhaps he can advise you.'

"After Qian has walked for several hours, a wooden shack comes into view. Qian knocks on the door several times. When no one answers, he peers inside. With a prayer mala in his hand, the monk is sitting in front of his fire pit, meditating and levitating a few inches off the floor. Qian sits across from the monk and waits for him to open his eyes.

"The monk's body levels to the floor. 'Qian, what do you want?'

"'I have come for your advice. I have taken a wife, and she hates me.'

"'Ah, yes. The beautiful Song with the dark green eyes. She does not hate you.' The monk puts his finger to the side of his nose. 'The problem is . . . you do not have what it takes to be with her.'

"Qian's body slumps. 'I know this now, but what can I do?'

"The monk again puts his finger to the side of his nose. 'You must go up Tiger Mountain and find the she-tiger who rules the mountain. Bring back one of her whiskers without harming her.'

"Qian's eyes show fear, and he says, 'But the she-tiger has eaten many villagers.' The monk shrugs his shoulders, picks up his prayer mala, and begins to chant.

"Qian searches and searches for the she-tiger—until one day he sees her. He watches her as she pounces on her prey and tears it to bits. From this day on, he follows her wherever she goes, and then one afternoon, during the heat *of the day, he stands only a foot away from her. His heart is beating so hard that he can hear pounding in his ears.*

"The she-tiger sniffs him. While fearing for his life, he puts out his hand and touches her head. As he feels the softness of her fur, she begins to chuff. Then she pushes her head hard against him, lies down at his feet, and takes a nap.

Qian pets her tummy while she sleeps and whispers sweet words in her ear. The she-tiger's paws are as large as platters, and her claws, which she flexes in her sleep, are as long as chopsticks.

"From this day on, Qian stays by the she-tiger's side while she takes her nap. He strokes her fur and whispers in her ear. He tells her how much he admires her, how beautiful she is . . . and how much he loves her.

"Then one day, Qian reminds himself that he must have one of her whiskers, and on this day, as she sleeps, he whispers in her ear, 'My dearest beauty, may I cut off one of your whiskers?' She opens one eye. She closes one eye. Qian takes out his knife and cuts off one of her whiskers. The she-tiger opens one eye. She closes one eye. Qian secures her precious whisker in his pocket.

"He remains by her side, strokes her face and her ears, touches her foreleg, and lifts her heavy paw. As he is petting her tummy for the last time, he whispers in her ear, 'My magnificent she-tiger, you are beautiful. I love you, and now I must leave you.'

"As Qian stands up, she awakens and begins chuffing. The she-tiger gets up. Qian strokes her face and her ears. He puts his hands on the sides of her head and smooths his palms over her eyes. She closes her eyes, twitches her whiskers, and chuffs. She does this when she especially likes something Qian does.

"He puts his arm around her neck, kisses her forehead, and turns away from her. She is still chuffing as he begins to walk. Tears that are like rocks on his heart flow out his eyes—eyes that have seen her for the last time. He wonders if she is watching him as he walks away. He sees her face and her eyes in his mind.

"After walking for several hours, he reaches the monk's door and knocks and knocks and knocks. Finally, Qian pokes his head through the doorway. The monk is in front of his fire, meditating and levitating. Qian sits across from the monk and waits.

"When the monk opens his eyes, he says, 'Do you have something for me?'
Qian gives the whisker to the monk who examines the whisker and throws it
in the fire. The monk says, 'Return to your wife. Now you have what it takes
to be with her.'"

I wait a few moments to see if the merchant will finish the story.
The crowd listening to the story also waits, and I say, *"So what happens*
when Qian goes home to Song?"

He says, *"This is all I know of the story. So do you want to buy or not buy*
the statue?" The audience and I applaud. He waves off the appreciation
from his audience.

"OK. I will buy it. How much?" I gladly pay for the statue. The story
alone is worth the price of one hundred yuan.

April 8, 1998: The Vulcan Salute

Stella is sitting with me at my work table this afternoon. I am using
super glue to attach fourteen-karat gold posts onto pearls to make stud
earrings. With a slip of the tube, I glue my thumb and index finger
together on my right hand, which is not a problem as long as I have
acetone. I do not have any acetone.

Stella says, *"Whaaaaaa! How you do?!"* Then she starts laughing so
hard she can hardly talk. Stella gently tugs at my fingers. She thinks I
am playing a joke on her, but she can't pull my fingers apart and says,
"Whaaaaaa! What you do?!"

I say, *"Stella, please look up a word."* I spelled the word "acetone" for her,
but none of my six Chinese dictionaries has this word. I tell her I need
to buy some stuff, and that I only know how to say this word in English.

Stella dials Jin's cell phone number and says, *"Jin, Sharon needs you.*
Can you come over right now? . . . She has a problem . . . She glued two
fingers together."

I can hear Jin laughing on the other end of the phone and Stella
says, *"No, no. I'm telling you the truth . . . Her fingers won't come apart . .*
. It happened just now . . . She was gluing something. Now her fingers are
stuck . . . Yes, two fingers . . . with glue . . ." and then Stella looks over at
my hand and starts to laugh again. *"No, no. I didn't do it,"* she says. *"This*
is not a joke . . . I don't know. She says she needs some stuff . . . I don't know

what she is talking about . . . No. She doesn't know how to say it, either . . . OK, OK. Bye-bye."

Stella assures me Jin is coming over, and she goes downstairs. In five minutes, everyone working at The Tower will know that I have glued two fingers together.

Fifteen minutes later, my apartment intercom phone rings. One of the guards says, *"Taitai, can you come down? Jin is here."* There is a smile in his voice.

I go downstairs. As the guard opens the door for me, he presses his thumb and index finger together in a new type of Spockian greeting and says, *"Nihao."*

I smile and return his Vulcan salute with my glued fingers. *"Nihao,"* I say. *"Live long and prosper."* Let him have his fun.

Jin drives me all over Shanghai looking for acetone. At every shop where we stop, I say, *"I need some stuff, but I don't know how to say."*

And they say, *"Why do you need this stuff?"* This is when I show them my hand.

Every salesclerk has the same response. *"Whaaaaaa! How you do?!"*

Jin and I find acetone at the fourth shop.

But I learned two new Chinese words today. The first word was acetone and the second word was . . . idiot!

April 9, 1998: A Piano for Ruth

A few days ago, Jin and I went to a music store where I paid to rent a piano. This morning the piano arrived, and I took my sheet music out from the cubbyhole under the stairs. As I played my rented piano, I thought of my grandmother and the piano she gave to me when she died. Some of my sheet music used to belong to her.

My maternal great-grandfather was born in 1859, and his name was William L. Osborne. He was a well-to-do owner of a grocery and store in Topeka, Kansas. The name of his store was the Will L. Osborne Grocery, and it was located on Topeka Avenue.

His wife, Mary Matilda Piety Osborne, was a concert pianist until the day she married William Osborne. Like many men of his time,

William held a strong conviction about women working outside the home, and he told her, "Now that you are my wife, you will never again give another concert."

Mary and William had five children—Don, Ruth, Edna, Nannie, and Lindsay. Mary never gave another concert, but she taught her daughter Ruth to play the piano. Ruth was my maternal grandmother.

Mary Matilda Piety Osborne (1863-1917) Photo taken in 1883.

Ruth Hazel Osborne in 1899 at the age of ten

My maternal grandfather, Roy Ellis, was born in 1888, and he was left at the Topeka Orphan Home in Kansas. He was most likely brought to this orphanage by the Orphan Train from New York City. In 1894, when Roy was six years old, Jane and Thomas Brandon adopted him. Jane and Thomas emigrated from England in 1861 and Thomas owned a soda pop bottling business in Topeka.

According to my grandfather, when he was twelve years old, he was on a school field trip at a sheet metal factory, and he had a "run-in" with some machinery. He was rushed to the hospital. When he returned home missing parts of four fingers, his adoptive mother said, "Roy, what have you done now?" Roy was a daring and rambunctious boy who was often in trouble with his adoptive mother.

When Roy was nineteen years old, he was ready to go out on his own. On August 8, 1907, he walked into the transportation office for the city of Topeka and asked the boss, Bob Morrison, for a job for the winter. Roy wanted to paint horse-drawn trolleys, and Mr. Morrison hired Roy as an apprentice. Once Roy had a job, he rented a room in the city of Topeka.

Roy Ellis Brandon in 1910

Ruth Hazel Osborne Brandon in 1910

By 1910, Roy was making twenty dollars a week as a carriage painter. In that same year, Roy's life became enchanted when he met Ruth. She was the most stunning beauty he had ever seen. On Sundays, Roy would take a whole day's pay, rent a horse and buggy, and take Ruth for a ride. Afterward, they would sit on Ruth's porch and take turns reading aloud from great literary works. Years later, Ruth remembered every book they had ever read together, but when Roy was asked for the title of even one book, he shrugged his shoulders and smiled.

His white tie matches this white horse. Roy proposed to Ruth on this buggy ride.

Roy had a good job working for the city as a painter, and one Sunday afternoon he proposed to Ruth on a buggy ride. He told her that if she would be his wife, he would make her happy. To Roy's surprise, she accepted. Ruth's family was against the marriage because Roy was missing some fingers, but on December 7, 1910, Ruth married him anyway.

Their son Louis was born on October 25 in 1911. In 1914, they moved to Wichita, Kansas, where Roy bought Ruth a house for one thousand dollars. Their new address was 2045 N. Arkansas Avenue.

World War I came in 1914, and Roy registered for the draft. When he was asked if there was any reason why he could not serve, he said, "No." However, the registrar noted on the Registrar Report, "Four fingers gone from right hand."

Ruth was thankful Roy was missing those fingers because he could stay home from the war and paint streetcars. Their son Thomas was born in 1915, and Roy was now a foreman for the Wichita R.R. Light Co., which would later be named the Wichita Bus Company. At night in their bed, when Ruth worried about her brothers fighting in that horrible war, she snuggled next to Roy who always had his arm around her to keep her from falling out of bed.

Ruth said nothing about not having a piano because her little house, her two children, and Roy's love were more than enough for her. But sadly, in 1921, their second born son Thomas died at the age of six from tonsillitis, and then the baby girl Ruth was carrying was stillborn. This was too much for Ruth. Depression drove her to her bed, and she stayed there.

Unknown to Ruth, Roy had been putting aside money for a piano from every paycheck. Roy had a promise to keep, and with Ruth in bed and Roy a hopeless cook, something had to be done.

Roy wanted to buy Ruth a grand piano, but he couldn't wait to save up any more money. He took all of the cash he had from the cellar strong box, and he and their son Louis took a bus to the piano store in Wichita, Kansas. Roy wanted the best piano he could buy with the money he had. The salesman showed Roy and Louis a grand upright piano with classic lines, mirrored walnut veneer, and brass pedals.

The day arrived when Ruth's piano was placed in the living room, and Roy and Louis sat on the piano bench. Their attempt to play the piano sounded like a cat chasing a mouse on the keyboard, and Ruth, in her nightgown, quickly appeared in the living room. "A piano! Roy, how did you buy this piano?" Louis told her that his dad had been saving for years. Without any sheet music in front of her, Ruth sat down and played her new piano. Roy and Louis ate a tasty supper that night.

Every day, music wafted through Ruth and Roy's home. Ruth gave piano lessons to some of the neighborhood children, and on balmy summer evenings, all of the windows in the neighborhood were thrown open. Ruth played her piano, Roy sang, and the neighbors listened to the melodies of a couple in love. Happiness flowed through their house, and from this happiness came two more children—a girl in 1922 and a boy in 1924.

By now, Roy was a Master Painter, and he was in charge of painting and maintaining the entire fleet of buses for the Wichita Bus Company. DuPont considered Roy an authority on painting public vehicles, and when someone from DuPont had a question, they called Roy.

The Great Depression arrived in 1929. Roy moved his family to a ten-acre farm where he would have plenty of land to grow strawberries, and Ruth could have a garden. The barn sheltered a milking cow, and the large chicken coop housed a brood of hens. Roy had a promise to keep, and empty stomachs would not make Ruth happy.

As a boy, Roy helped his adoptive father grow strawberries, which they used to make soda pop. They would load this homemade pop onto a horse-drawn wagon, and as they drove their wagon through the town, they yelled, "Strawberry pop! Come and get your strawberry pop!" Because Roy had learned all about strawberries from his adoptive father, Roy grew strawberries and made money selling them during the Great Depression. There was food, music, and happiness in their home. When the depression was over, Roy moved his family back into town.

Their daughter was in high school in the 1930s. When her friends came over, the living room rug was rolled up, and Ruth played the latest tunes while everyone danced the swing. The windowpanes shook and the wood floor squeaked. Everyone said they had "a swell time" at the Brandon's house. In May 1941, their daughter was married in that same living room, and Ruth played the wedding march.

December 7, 1941. War again. When Ruth worried about her son LeRoy and her only grandchild, Donald, being away in the war, she played her piano. When the war was over, LeRoy and Donald returned home. In 1946, their daughter brought home her firstborn child.

In 1957, Roy was presented with his first wristwatch at a surprise buffet luncheon at the Wichita Bus Company to celebrate his fiftieth year as a painter at the Wichita Bus Company. At the luncheon for Roy, the president of the company said that, "someone failed to ask Roy for which winter he wanted a job because he never left the company," and he never retired, either. Roy worked a total of fifty-six years for the same company. Roy first painted trolleys, then streetcars, and then buses.

In 1960, Ruth and Roy celebrated their fiftieth wedding anniversary with friends and family. Grandchildren played on my grandmother's piano, and the years passed.

Ruth died in 1963. For Roy, there was silence and loneliness. Within nine months, Roy died in his sleep knowing that he had kept his promise for fifty-three years.

April 10, 1998: Who Wants to Drink His Blood?

Stella came up for an English lesson and asked me about vampires. I like to think I have a good vampire accent, and I went through a whole dialogue speaking to Stella using this accent. Stella especially liked one of the sentences I used. She practiced this vampire expression until her accent was perfect, and she said, "Sharon, please call Martin for me. I must say this to him."

I dialed Martin's phone number, handed the phone to her, and she said, "I vant to d'rink your bl'lud," and hung up the phone. She was quite pleased with herself.

April 11, 1998: Put Her on the Side of the Road

On December 13, 1937, the Japanese Imperialist Army occupied Nanjing, China, and in six weeks this army summarily killed over three hundred thousand Chinese civilians. In Nanjing, there is a memorial hall and museum dedicated to this massacre.

Some of the people at the company wanted to go to Nanjing to see this memorial, and I was invited to go with them. Twenty-four of us caravanned to Nanjing in eight cars.

Barbara, who is a friend of someone who works at the company, is visiting from the States, and she is also invited to go to Nanjing. Someone decided that Barbara should ride with me in Jin's car.

Halfway to Nanjing, we stop to eat and take pictures. Jin and Yang

On the way to Nanjing, Barbara is talking nonstop, and her chattering is getting on my nerves. Why isn't she riding in her friend's car? Every time Jin or I say something to each other, she wants to know what we have said. When a headache threatens to split my brain in two, I say, "Barbara, do you mind if we don't talk. I'm getting a headache." She stops talking for a little while.

Jin looks at me in his rearview mirror and says, *"She talks a lot."*

"Yes, she talks a lot, but you don't have to listen to her."

Jin says, *"Right, right. Jin doesn't understand English."*

I say, *"Jin is a lucky man. I'm getting a bad headache."* Jin looks concerned. He is a problem solver and isn't sure what he can do.

Barbara says, "What are you two talking about?"

I say, "We are making plans for this week."

"Oh? What are you going to be doing?"

Jin says, *"Now what does she want?"*

"She is asking what we said. I told her we are talking about our plans for the week. Now she wants to know what the plans are. Jin, stop the car. Please, stop the car now."

Jin says, *"Why? Why does taitai want Jin to stop the car?"*

"Because," I say, *"I'm going to put her on the side of the road."*

Jin laughs. *"No, no. Taitai, let's not do that. Jin will lose his job."*

Barbara says, "Now what are you two talking about?"

I say, "Human rights."

I take out one of my Chinese books, and Barbara stops talking for the rest of the way to Nanjing. When we are about to enter Nanjing, Jin says, *"Taitai, how is your headache?"*

"I'm fine now. Thanks for asking," and Barbara doesn't ask me what we have said.

When we arrive in Nanjing, Jin wants to stay with the car while Barbara and I go into the memorial hall. Inside the walls of the Nanjing Museum there is an open-air memorial garden. In the middle of a grassy area, there is a dugout covered by a roof. Barbara and I step down into this cellar-like structure where one wall of the dugout is covered with thick glass. Pressed against the glass are human skeletal remains stacked four-feet deep. There are cards and letters posted on the walls by the entrance and exit. The words, left by recent visitors, are written in Chinese. This is hallowed ground, and Barbara and I never speak a word.

The high concrete wall around the memorial garden shows scenes from the massacre in bas-relief. A woman is on her knees as a Japanese soldier points his rifle with a bayonet at her. Children cling to dead mothers. There are scenes where children are being killed. Young and old women are tortured. Unarmed men, young and old, are shot. No mercy is shown in these scenes, and nothing is held back.

This is the first time I have ever heard anything about the Nanjing Massacre. Seeing this museum is a different experience than reading about this massacre in a book. Now I understand why Jin didn't want to see this museum, and I wish I had stayed with him.

When Barbara and I go back to the car, Jin is on his phone talking with Zhu, who is also a driver in the caravan. Jin and Zhu work for the same transportation company. They met when they were both police officers and have been good friends ever since. Zhu, who is Estelle's driver, gives Jin the location of the restaurant where everyone will be having lunch.

Everyone in the caravan meets up at this restaurant at about the same time. The rustic ambiance of this place has been created by nailing wooden planks together to make long tables and benches. I sit across from Jin and Zhu. Barbara sits next to me, and Estelle sits next to Barbara. Everyone else is scattered around the restaurant. Once Jin, Zhu, Barbara, Estelle, and I claim our spots, Estelle and I give money to Jin and Zhu for our meals. Jin knows what I like to eat, which is good because I can't read the menu scrawled in Chinese with chalk on a blackboard. Barbara stands in line to order food behind Jin who helps her to order something to eat.

As Estelle and I sit at the table, she speaks to me in Mandarin when she tells me that she wants to go to Yixing, which is the city where purple clay pots are made. Purple clay is unique to this region, and the Yixing kilns have been firing purple clay ceramic wares, also called Zisha wares, since the Song Dynasty (960–1279). Zisha teapots became famous during the Ming Dynasty (1368–1644) because the method of making tea changed from boiling to brewing tea leaves. Zisha teapots are perfect for this method. As the tea is brewed, some of the fragrance of the leaves stays in the body of the Zisha ware, and as the pot is used, the flavor of the tea is enhanced.

Jin sets my lunch down in front of me, which looks good, although I am not sure what is on my plate. I dig into my lunch, starting with something with a sauce on it. *Jin, this is good. Thank you for getting this lunch for me.*

Jin says, *"Don't be so polite. Taitai, please give me a tissue. They don't have napkins here."* I take out a package of tissues that can be found in many kiosks in China. There is a paper shortage in China, which is ironic since paper was invented in China. In better restaurants, cloth or linen napkins can be found on the table, but not paper napkins. Many restaurants don't offer napkins of any kind, and few bathrooms have toilet paper.

I look at Jin's plate. *"Jin, what are you eating?"* He says he is eating pork, and I nod my head as I say, *"Pork tastes good."*

Barbara seems to be enjoying her lunch although she is having trouble using her chopsticks. The restaurant has no forks. In ten minutes she has managed to put maybe four bites of food in her mouth.

Estelle says, *"Sharon, do you want go to Yixing?"* Because Estelle has spoken in Mandarin, Jin and Zhu know what she has said, and they beam at the thought of going to Yixing.

Barbara says, "What are you talking about?"

Jin looks at me with an unblinking stare—he does that so well—and says, *"Women xian ba ta ren le."* "First we dump her." Jin doesn't want Barbara to go with us because her constant talking might give me a constant headache.

Estelle continues to speak in Mandarin. *"Sharon, what did Jin say?"*

Barbara fumbles with her chopsticks and says, "I have no idea what I'm eating."

I say, "Barbara, we're all eating whatever ran through the kitchen thirty minutes ago."

Barbara stops eating. "Sharon, are you serious?"

I look at Jin and say, *"What's Barbara eating? It isn't rat, cat, or snake? Right?"*

Barbara says, "What are you asking Jin?"

"I'm asking him what he has ordered for you. I'm making sure it isn't rat, snake, or cat."

"Sharon . . . are you kidding?" Barbara sets her chopsticks down.

Jin says, *"I don't know what she said to me. I ordered pork for her. Pork is good for her."*

"Barbara, he says you're eating pork. He is eating pork, too."

Barbara looks at Jin's plate and then at my plate. "What are you eating?"

"Jin," I say, *"what am I eating?"*

"A Buddhist dish."

I point to the food on my plate and say, "This is tofu with vegetables."

Barbara picks up her chopsticks again but continues to struggle with them. I show Barbara how to hold her chopsticks, not that I'm an expert. I also explain to her that food is placed on the middle of the tongue rather than the front of the tongue, and that this is why food keeps falling back out of her mouth.

Because Barbara is between Estelle and me, Estelle leans forward and asks me again what Jin has said to me. I lean over my plate to talk to Estelle and say, *"Ta shou, 'Women xian ba ta ren le.' Ting de dong ma?"* "He says, 'First we dump her.' Do you understand?"

Estelle, continuing in Mandarin, says, *"I don't understand. Jin says we first do what to her?"* Jin takes his napkin, rolls it into a ball, and tosses it into Estelle's empty cup. Estelle stares at the the ball of tissue in her cup . . . and then she begins to laugh with this wonderful contagious laugh. When people hear her laugh, they have to laugh, too, even though they're clueless as to what she is laughing about.

I slap my hands over my face to keep myself from laughing. I don't want Barbara to think we are laughing at her, and oh, please . . . let me not hear anyone belch right now. We aren't laughing at Barbara. She is a friendly and sweet person, and she talks a lot. After I get a grip on my laughter, I take a silent vow to be kind to Barbara no matter what.

Barbara is now in a meditative trance as she focuses on pinching food with her chopsticks and . . . in slow motion . . . ever so carefully . . . moving bits of pork or vegetables into her mouth . . . to the middle of her tongue. She is successful in holding tiny bits of food with her chopsticks about every other try. At this rate, she should finish what is on her plate in about an hour, but then she has a bowl of rice, which might start growing mold before she can eat it.

Having regained my composure, I look across the table at Jin and Zhu and say, *"Do you both want to go to Yixing?"*

Jin and Zhu look at each other. Because Jin is older than Zhu, Jin is the one who makes the decision for the two of them, and he says, *"Sure, sure. We would like to go to Yixing. Monday, Paul's driver can take Martin to work."* Because Martin and Paul go to work at about the same ungodly hour, this should be no problem.

According to Chinese custom, because I am older than Estelle, Jin, and Zhu, I'm the final decision maker for the four of us. Sometimes I like that. As for Barbara, if she wants to go with us, we will get over being annoyed with her constant chatter and endless questions.

"Estelle and Barbara," I say, "would you like to go to Yixing to see the purple clay pots? We won't be back to Shanghai until Monday night." Since this is Estelle's idea, I already know what Estelle is going to say, but Barbara panics and says, "I can't go. I have to go back to Shanghai."

"Barbara, don't worry," I say. "One of the other drivers will take you back to Shanghai with everyone else."

"Jin," I say, *"what driver can take Barbara? She wants to go back to Shanghai today."*

Jin stands up and goes over to another driver. When he returns to our table he says to Barbara, "OK. No problem," as he holds his hand out toward the driver who will take Barbara back to Shanghai. Barbara leaps up and goes to their table with her chopsticks, plate, and bowl of rice.

Jin and Zhu make arrangements for someone to drive Zhu's car back to Shanghai. Now the four of us can travel in one car, and the guys can take turns driving.

Estelle and I take a packed bag with us whenever we travel, and Jin and Zhu do the same. We never know what we might find to do when we are miles away from Shanghai. Did I pack any chocolate candy bars?

After lunch, we say good-bye to everyone, and I glance over at Barbara. Her chopsticks have a death grip on the food she is slowly moving to her mouth. The people around her are watching her with their eyes glazed over.

We arrive in the downtown area of Yixing around four thirty and want to get hotel rooms before we have dinner. Jin drives around Yixing for forty minutes as we all look out the car windows for any building that looks like a hotel. This is such a tiny town there might not be any hotels in Yixing. Not even a two-star hotel.

But then Estelle has a brilliant idea, and she says, "Let's pull the car over, flag down someone riding a motorcycle, and give him ten yuan to escort us to the nearest hotel." Being the oldest person in our group, I explain Estelle's idea to Jin and Zhu. I say that this is a good idea as I give ten yuan to Jin, who then flags down a motorcycle rider. Jin follows him for a couple of miles to a ten-story hotel.

Only Chinese characters are on the façade of this hotel, which is set far back from the road. Estelle and I give Jin and Zhu money to pay for two rooms. While they are in the hotel, we wait in the car because if we go into the hotel, we will have to pay more for the rooms. Foreigners pay more for almost everything. Jin and Zhu book the last two rooms available.

Next on the agenda is dinner, and Jin and Zhu find a Chinese restaurant within walking distance of the hotel. Only Chinese characters are on the façade of this restaurant. We have a late dinner, and then Estelle and I go to our room while Jin and Zhu go out to have a couple of beers and sing karaoke.

April 12, 1998: Purple Pots

This morning we eat breakfast at a restaurant across the street from the hotel, and then Jin volunteers to be the first driver of the day. As we are approaching the center of Yixing, about forty tall smokestacks appear on the horizon. As we get closer to the smokestacks, we realize that these smokestacks are attached to the famous kilns of Yixing.

We stop by a long row of white wood buildings. When we enter one of the buildings, we find a sidewalk running down the middle of the building, and we walk from shop to shop. There are thousands of Zisha wares for sale. All of the clay pots, little cups, and other ceramic items are a reddish chocolate color rather than the deep purple color I was expecting.

I took a few practical ceramics classes when I was a graduate student, and not once did I ever make a ceramic item that was any good. In my ceramics classes, I tried to form ceramic items using an electric wheel as well as using rolled-out slabs of clay and coils of clay. None of these methods worked for me. However, the experience of trying to make bowls, cups, teapots, and other items from clay has given me an appreciation for the work that goes into making ceramic wares.

I find a tiny shop with well-crafted and unusual teapots, and the teapot that speaks to me has a highly detailed Buddha dog painted on both sides. One dog is yellow, and the other dog is green, and their delicate and defining black lines are identical. Colorful ceramic glazes have brought this teapot to life. The Buddha dogs are set against a backdrop of blue and red Chinese symbols that represent heaven. The Wheel of Life on the teapot works tirelessly as it sends out Buddha's message and crushes delusions and superstitions. The spokes of the Wheel of Life symbolize the rays of sacred light emanating from Buddha.

I don't know how many firings have gone into making this Buddha dog teapot. What I do know, however, is that after the bisque firing, or the first firing, good craftsmanship stopped and artistry began when the vivid glazes of light were painted onto this Zisha teapot. The cost to bring this Zisha teapot home with me was one hundred dollars.

April 13, 1998: Psycho and the Shower Curtain

I called my mother after dinner tonight. She asked me if American movies were shown in Shanghai theaters. I said, "You mean like *Psycho?*"

She said, "Don't remind me."

When the movie *Psycho* came to the Chicago area, my mom, being hard up for some family entertainment, decided to take us to see this movie at a local drive-in theater. Being a frugal mother, she brought popcorn and drinks for us from home. Tommy was cleaning up his room while Susann, Marianne, and I were in the backseat of the car munching on popcorn. The salt on the popcorn made me thirsty, and Mom had the drinks up front.

Just as Janet Leigh began taking a shower at the Bates Motel, I had to have something to drink to choke down the popcorn, and I tapped my mother on the shoulder. She screamed so loudly that she scared me, everyone in our car, and all of the cars around us. Then Tony Perkins appeared with the knife. I never received anything to drink, and I believe we went home after that.

For my mother's seventieth birthday, I took her to the National Storytelling Festival in Jonesborough, Tennessee. We met in Knoxville, Tennessee, and we stayed the night in a motel before we drove to Jonesborough. This motel looked exactly like the Bates Motel—it could have been the Bates Motel. As we entered our room, my mother zoomed over to the bathroom and said, "This looks just like the shower in *Psycho*."

I peeked in the bathroom. A terrifying opaque white shower curtain was pulled across the tub. "Mom, could you look behind the curtain?"

My mother held up her hand. "I'm not going to look behind the curtain," and then she put her hand on her hip, but only one hand, and said, "You look behind the curtain."

My mother's phobia and my phobia met for the first time. My mother was too scared to be in the room by herself, so we both went to talk with the manager, who was in the front office, and I said, "Would you please check our room for bodies?"

He looked surprised by my request. "Bodies?" he said.

I rested my elbows on his tall counter and said, "It's a long story. By the way, do any of your relatives go by the name of Bates?"

1998 April 13-14: Shanghai after Dark

Martin is back in the States again. Last night, while I am trying to memorize a list of one hundred measure words, the image of an ice cream bar materializes in my mind. It is around eleven o'clock. I check the freezer. There are no Magnums. I have hardly eaten anything all day.

I study until midnight, the witching hour, when supernatural things happen. I check the freezer again for any errant Magnums that may have wandered into my freezer. Nothing has changed. It is late. I should stay home. An hour later, however, I change my mind. I am not going to call Jin and get him out of bed just so he can walk down one little block with me to the street kiosk where Magnums are sold.

I look out my kitchen window at the street below as it buzzes with life and lights. I tuck enough money in a pocket of my jeans to buy four Magnums, and I go downstairs. I say hello to the guard and expect him to open the heavy glass door for me, but he stands there with his hand pushed against the handle and says, *"Taitai, hello. Where are you going?"*

"I'm going out to buy some Magnum ice cream bars. The woman one block down has some in her street shop."

He looks at his watch. *"Taitai, it's almost two o'clock in the morning. Call Jin. He'll go with you. I would go with you, but I have to stay here."*

"I'll be fine," I say, and I continue to stand in front of the door as he stares at me. Finally, he opens the door, and I say, *"I will be quick, faster than a rabbit."* As I sprint down the steps, I can feel his eyes on me. The Magnum bars are just down the street, and they have my Chinese name on them.

Just a block away, I stop at the kiosk of the woman who has a little freezer in which she keeps Magnums. *"Little Sister, hello,"* I say. *"Do you have Magnums?"*

"Taitai, hello. I am so sorry. I don't have any, but tomorrow I will have some. Go down one block to my friend. She has some. I will tell her that you are coming. Bye-bye." Little Sister calls her friend on her cell phone as I walk down one more block.

I can feel eyes watching me. People on this little street recognize me because of my blond hair. They know where I live, and that I am a student at Fudan University. They also know who Jin is, and that he lives across the street from The Tower. There are no secrets in China. The people who don't know my name refer to me among themselves as the Gold Hair Woman.

Little Sister's friend waves to me as I approach, and she says, *"Taitai, hello. How many Magnums do you want?"*

"Hello. Do you have four?"

"Yes, I have four." Little Sister's friend puts the Magnums in a bag for me. I pay her, say thank you, and wave good-bye.

Walking back home, some of the people on the street wave hello and give me big smiles. I wave and smile back.

April 14, 1998: Uh-Oh

This morning, when Jin comes to pick me up for school, he opens my door for me and then sits behind the wheel. He looks straight ahead and doesn't start the car. He doesn't say anything, either. Uh-oh. And then he pulls on his ear.

One of the guards must have told Jin about my foray at two in the morning. Last night, when I was walking toward my Magnums, I wasn't thinking about the protective instinct men have where women are concerned, and I have stirred up this natural force in him.

Whoever is going to talk first, it isn't going to be me. Finally, he turns around in his seat and says, *"You went out by yourself. Why didn't you call Jin? Taitai should never go out alone at night."* He is boiling mad even though he has just spoken to me in a calm voice.

I know that what I am about to say to him is lame, but I say it anyway. *"Jin was asleep. Jin needs to sleep."* I am now a four-year-old and desperate to avoid a well-deserved scolding.

Jin looks at me with an unblinking stare—he does that so well—and says, *"Jin thinks it doesn't matter, never mind. Two o'clock . . . four o'clock . . . call Jin. OK? It doesn't matter, never mind."*

I know he is right, and I say, *"I shouldn't go out late at night. Jin is right. I'm sorry. I promise you, at night, I won't go out by myself. I won't do that ever again."*

Jin eyes soften a little. He has a tiny smile as he pulls on his left ear a couple of more times, and then he says, *"OK, OK."* He turns back around in his seat and starts the car. Things are pretty much back to normal as Jin begins to drive toward Fudan. I now feel like I am at least fourteen years old.

When Jin stops at a light, I push my luck like any fourteen-year-old would, and I say, *"Jin, because I promise I won't go out again at night, don't tell Martin, OK? . . . OK?"* I extend my hand forward and offer my little finger to him to make a pinkie promise. These promises are taken seriously in China. *"Jin, I will never do that again. You won't tell Martin. OK?"*

Jin and I pinkie promise, and I am now as bound to my promise as Jin is to his, no matter what. Impending death is not an excuse for breaking this promise. (No one ever told Martin, and I never went out by myself at night again.)

April 15, 1998: Room Service

This afternoon, Jin and I went over some English grammar and a few vocabulary words. Jin is helping me with my homework at the dining room table when we hear The Chinese Knock.

Little Sister, who owns the tiny kiosk one block from The Tower, is at the door. *"Little Sister, hello. Please come in."*

"Oh no, no. I'm not coming in. I brought these for you."

I look inside the bag. *"Whaaaaaa! Four Magnums. Thank you."*

"Don't be so polite," she says. *"Call me when you need more Magnums."* She writes her phone number on a piece of paper for me. I pay Little Sister and will not let her give me change.

I put two Magnums in the freezer and unwrap the other two bars. I don't ask Jin what he wants anymore. I take the two Magnums into the dining room and give him his ice cream bar.

As Jin takes a bite from his Magnum bar, I say, *"Jin, there are no secrets in China—unless there is something that Chinese people don't want Martin to know. Then, everyone will know except for Martin. In English, when someone doesn't know what we know, we say, 'He is in the dark.'"*

I take a bite of my ice cream bar, and Jin gives me an impish smile as he says, "Jin is not in the dark."

He continues to munch on his bar as he is thinking about something. He pauses and looks me in the eye as he says, *"Where Jin lives . . . always daytime . . . Jin also keeps his promises."*

April 16, 1998: Snake Blood

When class is over, I am beyond starving. I am so hungry that I feel sick. I don't have any peanut butter or chocolate candy bars in the car, either. As soon as I fasten my seatbelt, I say, *"Jin, I need to eat lunch right now. I'm very hungry. Is there a good Chinese restaurant close to Fudan University?"*

Jin takes us to a restaurant that has parking right by the front door. The sign for this restaurant is all in red Chinese characters, which I can't read. I say, *"Jin, I don't want to eat by myself. We can both eat lunch. OK?"*

Just inside the front door of this restaurant, there are tanks of different kinds of fish and some murky-colored snakes, which are not viperous. The restaurant is busy, and we are seated at a round table. At a table to our right, ten people are celebrating an elderly woman's birthday.

"Jin," I say, *"I need to eat some meat. I haven't eaten meat for some time."*

Jin says, *"Do you need to eat pork?"*

"I don't need to eat pork, but I'm very hungry. Martin isn't here, so I haven't cooked."

I don't bother to look at a menu I can't read. Jin orders for us and speaks to the waitress in Shanghainese. While I understand most of what he says, I only know for sure that he has ordered two vegetable dishes and one meat dish.

Hot green tea is placed in front of us, and Jin says, *"Taitai, drink the tea. I know you don't like tea, but green tea helps the stomach to take food."* A few sips of tea comfort my empty stomach, but the glass is so hot from the tea, I can only hold it for a few seconds before I put it down. The tea is alive with leaves and mysterious green things swirling and floating and settling to the bottom of the glass before bouncing back up. Our lunch arrives quickly.

The people at the birthday table are telling stories and laughing at jokes, and then everyone at the birthday party stops eating to watch two men standing at the kitchen door.

A chef holds a four-foot-long snake by its head and slits its underbelly while another man holds a bowl under the snake to catch the blood as it plinks into a metal pan. The snake is taken away, the blood is poured into a wineglass, and the chef glides into the dining room with the gift. He presents the glass of blood to the guest of honor with congratulations.

Everyone yells, *"Gan bei,"* "Bottoms up," and she drinks the blood down without taking a breath. Everyone at her table applauds.

I prefer making a wish and blowing out candles.

I look at Jin and then look at the meat on my plate that tastes like chicken, and Jin says, *"That isn't snake meat. That is chicken."*

April 17, 1998: A Three-Star Hotel

I want to look at the pearls in Hangzhou, and Jin and I take a train to this city. During the day, we visit a few pearl shops next to some large pearl ponds. All of the pearls are overpriced. Some strands are as much as eight thousand yuan, and for a strand of this same quality, I would pay maybe eight hundred yuan in Suzhou.

In the evening, when the Hangzhou flea market opens, Jin and I again go out to look at pearls. I meet a woman there at the market whose name is Han Wen Qing, and she has beautiful pearls for a reasonable price. Han and her husband agree to bring their pearls to Shanghai. I ask Han to bring necklaces with large pearls, any unusual items made from pearls, and whatever else she would like for me to see. I buy twenty strands of pearls from Han and five strands from another vendor.

I also buy several ceramic boxes. On the underside of the lid, there is a picture of a couple in bed with two pairs of slippers on the floor. These boxes were made before the Cultural Revolution, and no one I ask knows what these boxes are called or their purpose. Some of my Chinese friends think that this kind of box would only have belonged to a prostitute, but they don't know for sure.

Jin and I eat at a restaurant close to the flea market and return to the hotel. Jin walks with me to my room and says, *"So then, you will stay here, right?"* I assure Jin I will be in my room, and Jin goes to his room. At least I thought he went to his room.

Jin doesn't like for me to book rooms at four- and five-star hotels, so for this trip, we stay at a three-star hotel. Three-star hotels are always a mistake. When I try to turn on the television, it doesn't work. I call downstairs and ask to have the television fixed.

Two maintenance men soon come to my room. They tinker with the refrigerator and the television and say, *"You can have the television or the refrigerator. Which do you want?"*

I say, *"I would like the television."* They putter with the television some more and the screen soon blares with *National Geographic* in Mandarin with Chinese subtitles. As they hand me the remote I thank them.

"Don't be so polite," they say as they clank out of the room with their tools strapped to their bodies.

I snuggle in bed and begin searching the channels for something other than documentaries of animals eating animals. The television seems particularly loud. When I put the television on mute, I realize that my room is over the karaoke bar. The song I am most tired of hearing is being sung in English and Chinese. Is there a karaoke singer in China who doesn't know the words to "My Heart Will Go On"? I turn up the television loud enough to hear it and hope the karaoke bar will not be open all night. At midnight, the singing stops, and I go to sleep.

April 18, 1998: My Little Chinese Sister

In the morning, Jin and I meet at the hotel's restaurant at nine o'clock. I peek at the menu the waitress hands to me and set it aside. Jin orders for me, and scrumptious-looking food is soon placed in front of us. We each have two sunny-side-up eggs, freshly squeezed orange juice, and the Chinese version of pancakes.

No one can pick up a runny egg yolk with chopsticks, so Jin holds his plate up to his mouth and sucks up the yolk. That's what I do. How horrified would my mother be if she saw me putting my face in my plate like a dog and sucking up an egg yolk?

Emily Post wrote her famous book, *Etiquette*, in 1922, the year my mother was born. My mother could quote from this 627-page tome. It would be safe to say that my mother would be horrified to the nth degree if she saw my new table manners, but I would just have to explain to her again—Mother, I live in China, and Emily Post is dead.

Since sucking up an egg yolk is an efficient way to eat something so sloppy, this method should work even better on egg whites, right? No. Jin doesn't do that, so I don't do that either, but I want to. Jin and I eat the egg whites and the "pancakes" with chopsticks.

As we are enjoying our breakfast, I say, *"So, Jin, last night, what did you do?"*

Jin considers my question and says, *"Jin drove a little race car outside the hotel, sang karaoke, and drank a couple of beers."* I am pleased Jin has had an enjoyable evening.

Jin puts down his chopsticks, pulls on his ear a couple of times, and says, *"Last night, did you go out?"*

"No, no. I stayed in my room. I watched animals on television. I heard you sing karaoke." Jin gives me a wry smile. He doesn't believe me, and I say, *"You have a beautiful voice."*

Jin says, *"What did you hear Jin sing?"*

"You know . . . that song. 'Every night in my dreams . . . I see you . . . I hear you.'"

Jin looks worried. *"You were downstairs?"*

"No, no. I was in my room all night. Taitai keeps her promises." Jin is no longer worried. Now he is mystified, and he wants an explanation, but I am not going to give him an explanation except to say, *"Where taitai lives . . . always daytime."* Ditto.

Hangzhou is a beautiful city. We stroll around a park and then take a cab to a restaurant close by the station. This restaurant is on the second floor. The wood steps creak under our weight as we walk up to a shadowy room with no electric lights. We sit at a wooden table by a large window, and the light from this window makes up for the lack of electrical lighting in this restaurant.

I look out the window at the scene below, which looks like a movie set from *The Good Earth*. Men pull heavy carts with their shirts off, and old women lug large baskets. People hustle in and out of the train station carrying suitcases made of straw or battered leather. Some people, using both hands, heave cloth bags bulging with possessions. Babies are carried on their mothers' backs, and toddlers clutch at their mothers and want to be picked up. Peddlers park their carts in the middle of the square and sell fruits or vegetables or other wares.

We finish our lunch and walk over to the train station, where there is an alcove in this large waiting hall where every voice and sound echoes. This little out-of-the-way place is quiet, and no one can walk behind me. Jin wants to buy a newspaper and to sit close to the board that has the train station schedule. He soon finds a place about one hundred feet away from me where he can read his newspaper, watch the board, and make sure that I stay where he has put me.

I am seated on a pre-Mao, wooden, church-style bench, and a little girl comes over to me. She puts her hand on the back of my hand and leaves it there as she stares at my eyes.

I say, *"Nihao."* She smiles but doesn't say anything. I see a man across the way, and he is watching her. I say, *"Is he your father?"* She nods affirmatively.

I say, *"Where are you going?"* She answers me, but I have never heard of this town or city. I reach into my purse with my free hand and take out three American coins—a quarter, nickel, and dime. I hold them out to her and say, *"These are for you."*

She looks at her father for permission to take the coins from my hand, and her father nods to let her know she can accept the gift. She picks up the coins from my palm and looks at them, and says, *"American money."*

She runs with the coins to her father and happily opens her hand to show him. Her father smiles as she gives the coins to him. He reaches into his pocket and places some coins in her hand, and she runs back to me and says, *"These are for you."* I thank her, and she says, *"You are beautiful."*

I say, *"You are beautiful."*

She hops up next to me and tries to sit the way I am sitting on the bench, but her legs are too short to reach the floor, so I cross my left leg over my right. She crosses her left leg over her right. I wiggle my left foot three times. She wiggles her left foot three times. She has decided that I am her big sister, and we will wait together for our trains. I open my right hand, and she places her little hand in mine.

April 21, 1998: Electric Eyes at Fudan University

As I walk to my classroom at Fudan, I pass a small building that looks interesting. The door is open, and I look into the room. There are two banks of black-and-white monitors with six monitors on each shelf. When I leave this room, someone closes the door behind me.

May 2, 1998: Palm Writing

Martin and I walk up to the second floor of the Sunday Market, where Martin sees a globe he wants to buy. This clear glass globe looks a lot like Tommy's crystal ball—the one I so enjoyed seeing airborne.

I help Martin to ask a few questions about the globe. After that, Martin is able to bargain on his own, and I walk back to the front of this large room.

A retailer who has seen me many times at the market approaches me and says, *"Hello, may I ask, by what name are you called?"*

I say, *"My name is Wen Li Xia."*

Because there are four different characters for the family name of Wen, she says, *"Please write your name for me."* With my palm in front of her, I write the characters for my Chinese name on my palm using my index finger. I briefly pause between each invisible character, and she says, *"Oh, I see. Your name is Wen Li Xia."* I watch her as she writes my name, 温丽霞, in her palm using her index finger. Perhaps she does this as a memory device.

"Right, right," I say. *"This is my name. By what name are you called?"*

"Cong Mei Li."

I know *Mei Li* means *beautiful,* and I say, *"Cong? This name is like two people walking?"* I write the character, 从, in my palm.

"Yes, Cong. This character. Wen Li Xia, I'm happy to know you."

"Cong Mei Li, I'm happy to know you, too."

She asks me where I learned to speak Mandarin, and then I ask her what she does for a living. As she is explaining her work to me, Martin comes over to us. I introduce Cong to Martin and say to her, *"This is my husband, Martin. He doesn't speak Chinese."*

Cong speaks in Mandarin to Martin anyway and says, *"Martin, I'm happy to meet you. Your wife's Mandarin is excellent."*

Martin looks at me. "What did she say?"

"She said you're handsome."

Martin says, *"Xiexie."* "Thank you."

Cong Mei Li waves good-bye as she says, *"Wen Li Xia, please come and see me the next time you are here. I will look for you."*

I say, *"Cong Mei Li, I will look for you, too. Good-bye."*

June 20, 1998: Joe Bamboozler

Jin and I are in Suzhou, and we go into a pearl shop where I find two hundred strands of pearls I want to buy. The shop owner speaks

English pretty well, and since I have only talked with him in English, he doesn't know I can speak Mandarin.

I agree to purchase the pearls I like if they are strung into necklaces. The shop owner says that Jin and I can come back in the morning to pick up the pearls. Before we leave to find a hotel, the two hundred strands of pearls, along with the clasps to be used to make these necklaces, are weighed. Jin writes down the weight. I have come to call the owner of this pearl shop Joe Bamboozler.

In the morning, Jin doesn't want to take time to eat breakfast, which is always a mistake, and we go directly over to Joe Bamboozler's shop to pick up my order. When we enter the shop, Joe is speaking in Mandarin to one of his buddies, and I hear Joe tell his fellow pearl dealer how he hornswoggled some naïve foreigner and sold him one thousand fake pearl necklaces. Joe and his buddy have a good laugh. When Joe's friend leaves the shop, Joe goes to his backroom to get my pearls.

Joe Bamboozler makes a big show of putting the pearls on the scale. The weight of the finished pearl necklaces is slightly more than the original weight because twice as much string has been used to make knots between the pearls. I take two strands off the scale and hand one strand to Jin. I test the pearls to see if they are real or faux. They're real. I take a few more strands over to the window to look at the pearls in good light, and Jin follows me.

I hold the necklaces to the light and whisper to Jin, *"Are these the same pearls? What do you think?"* The exact weight of the pearls is secondary to whether or not I am buying the same pearls that I saw yesterday. After inspecting them in the light, Jin and I think they are the same. I pay for the necklaces and tell Jin I want to go to Xia's pearl shop. I won't have any worries with Xia, and I trust her. Joe Bamboozler will never see me again.

While I'm looking at some large peach pearls at Xia's, I realize that I am famished, and I say, *"Jin, I need to go to a restaurant to eat lunch. Then I can finish looking at pearls."* Jin wants me to finish looking at pearls first, and Xia and Jin have a quiet conversation.

This is Xue Cai Xia. She is my favorite pearl vendor in Suzhou.

When they finish talking, Xia opens the back door of the shop and goes outside. I hear the clucking and screeching of chickens with a temper. When Xia comes back inside, she holds two eggs in her hands and says to me, *Jin says you will eat eggs, right? He can fix these for you, OK?"*

"Oh, thank you," I say. *"This will be good."* Jin takes the eggs to a room next to the back door, which is a small kitchen. I look at more pearls until Jin puts the eggs in front of me and hands chopsticks to me. The eggs are delicious. After I purchase several strands of pearls, Jin and I head for home.

There is something endearing about Xia. I know when she is going to show me something amazing because she stands close to me with pearls in her hands and says *Whaaaaaa!* as she gently sets the pearls in front of me. I love that.

Among all of these dealers, I trust Xia the most. From now on, I will only go to her pearl shop when I am in Suzhou.

June 21, 1998: Friends Will Take You by the Hand

It is a sunny day. Martin is away on business for a few days, and I want to buy enough food to eat for two days from my favorite Chinese restaurant. This restaurant, however, at 555 Lao Shan Lu, is *across* the street from The Tower. How can I safely get to this restaurant without disturbing Jin's Sunday by asking him to walk me across the street? I have a plan.

I say, *"Nihao,"* to the guard who opens the door for me.

The guard says, *"Nihao."* He looks out toward the front of the building and expects to see Jin.

To save him the trouble of figuring out where I am going, I say, *"I'm going across the street to buy take-out at Wu Wu Wu Lao Shan Lu."*

The guard says, *"OK, OK. See you later."*

As I walk down the steps, I see a Chinese woman walking with an elderly man who I assume is her father. She is a woman who has, by her age, safely crossed many Shanghai streets. When I get to the bottom of the steps, she is only a couple of feet away from me, and I say, *"Little Sister, hello. May I bother you to help me cross the road? I'm afraid to cross the street by myself."*

She says, *"I would be happy to help you. Just a minute."* She turns to her father and tells him in Shanghainese that she will be right back.

She takes my hand, and we walk to the curb where we stand for thirty seconds or more. When we step off the curb to jaywalk across the street, I close my eyes as her steady and confident hand guides me.

When I am on the other side, I say, *"Thank you for helping me. You're very kind."*

She says, *"No problem. Don't be so polite."* We say good-bye, and she goes back to her father who looks bewildered as he stands where his daughter has left him.

When I enter the restaurant, some of the employees wave to me while others say, *"Wen Li Xia, nihao."* At the front counter, I take out a piece of paper. This is the list of my favorite dishes written in Chinese. Every time I eat something I like at this restaurant, I write down the name of this dish. I now have a collection of six entrees. I order one of each for take-out. These dishes will be my meals for the next two days.

The woman who takes my order is named Di, and she asks me to sit down on a chair near the counter. She places hot green tea on a table in front of me to drink while I wait. I thank her and drink the tea to show my appreciation for her thoughtfulness. My six meals are soon ready and placed in two plastic bags. As I pay for my food, I say, *"Di, may I bother you to help me cross the street? I'm afraid to cross the road by myself."*

"Yes, yes. I can help you," she says. Di takes one of the plastic bags while I hold the other. When she is ready to take me across the road, she gently takes my hand as we safely jaywalk across Lao Shan Lu. I thank her, and she says, *"No problem. Don't be so polite."*

When I enter The Tower with my plastic bags from the restaurant, the guard is relieved to see that I have made it across the dangerous road and back. All is right with the world, and nothing will be reported to Jin.

July 25, 1998: I Don't Speak Chinese

The company hired a Chinese tutor to teach Martin some basic Chinese phrases, but the lessons didn't last long because Martin had no time to study. Martin did, however, learn about asking questions in Mandarin. He knows that when he hears the sound of *ma* at the end of a sentence, he is being asked a question. Also, if Martin hears words like *shenma*, which means *what*, or *nali*, which means *where*, or *jiyou*, which means *how many*, he knows that these are question words.

Martin returned from the Philippines this evening and took a cab from the airport to give Jin a Saturday night off. When he walks in the door, I say, "Marty, it's good to have you home again. How was your trip?"

Martin looks tired and says, "All the way home, this taxi driver kept asking me questions."

I say, "What questions do you think he asked?"

"He most likely asked me where I flew in from . . . If I'm an American . . . Where I work . . . If I live in Shanghai . . . How many kids I have . . . How many wives I have. You know . . . the usual questions."

I sit down on the couch in our living room. "What did you say to this driver?"

Martin flops in a plush chair by the couch and says, "I kept telling this guy that I don't speak Chinese."

I say, "Marty, how did you tell him that you don't speak Chinese?"

Martin says, "I kept telling this guy, *'Wo bu zhidao.'*"

Uh-oh. Martin is not going to like this. "So, Marty . . . if this driver asked you where you worked, you said, *'Wo bu zhidao.'* If he asked you how many wives you have, you told him, *'Wo bu zhidao.'*"

Martin nods as he says, "That's right."

"Marty, if this driver asked you how many children you have or how many wives you have, you told him that you didn't know because *wo bu zhidao* means *I don't know.*"

Martin jumps up from his chair and says, "I'm never speaking Chinese again."

I am thinking that this is a good idea.

July 28, 1998: I Will See You Again

Jin takes me to Shu Cheng, a four-story bookstore on Fu Zhou Lu. Jin can't find a parking spot, so he drops me off in front of the bookstore.

I want to buy an electronic English-Chinese dictionary. If I can find such a dictionary, I won't have to write my new words on bits of paper and then stuff them in my purse. I can just whip out my electronic dictionary to find the word I need.

On the fourth floor of the bookstore, there are many electronic dictionaries, but all of the directions for these dictionaries are written in Chinese, which means that the dictionaries are for Chinese speakers learning English.

I go back downstairs to the sidewalk to wait where Jin said he would look for me as he circles around the block. Most of the cars in Shanghai are black, so it isn't easy for me to pick out Jin's black car. He will have to watch for me.

As I stand facing this bustling street, something over my right shoulder catches my eye. A tall Chinese man holds a little boy's hand as they walk down the sidewalk. As they pass behind me, I turn away from the street to watch this cute little guy as he takes quick steps to keep up with his father's long strides, and then this child looks at me and tugs at his father's sleeve.

The father leans over as the boy cups his hand to his father's ear to whisper to him. The man looks at me and says something to the little boy who lets go of his father's hand. The child turns toward me, presses his tiny hands together, and bows to me. I put my hands together likewise and bow to the little boy.

The young child takes his father's hand once again. As they start to walk away, the little boy turns his head back toward me and gives me a cheerful smile. He waves *zaijian*, "I will see you again." I smile and wave back.

July 30, 1998: A No-Good Painting

Jin and I are at my favorite framing shop in Pudong. I have come to pick up some paintings that I have had framed. I pay for my paintings, and as we are leaving the shop, I see an abstract watercolor painting. The name of the artist is Lee. This work has been inspired by a green bowl of brilliant and lively flowers in sprays of gold, blue, and red. I want to buy this painting, but Jin says, *"Don't buy that. There are better paintings to buy."* Because I have a rule about not arguing with a Chinese person, I drop the subject of the painting.

August 11, 1998: The Bra Shop at the Zipper Factory

An American woman I met at a Shanghai Expatriate Association meeting wants to go to a mini-department store called the Zipper Factory. This department store is a collection of little shops selling household items, clothing, and tourist kitsch. It is called the Zipper Factory because zippers used to be manufactured in this building. Monique, not her real name, knows the location of this building, and as Jin drives, I interpret Monique's directions for him.

I would describe Monique as exotic. She is tall, blond, buxom-to-the-extreme, and blessed with more beauty than Helen of Troy. A while back, Monique and I went pearl shopping in Suzhou. When we returned to Shanghai in the evening, we were at Monique's apartment when her husband, Mark, came home for dinner, which he fixed for himself. Mark has a great sense of humor. He is a happy guy, the envy of many men, and so smitten with Monique I don't think he could take a breath if she were not in his life.

Monique purchased about five hundred dollars' worth of pearls in Suzhou, which I helped her to pick out and to price for sale in the States. A week after our Suzhou trip, Monique returned to Minnesota to take care of some financial matters.

On the way to the Zipper Factory today, Monique told me that while she was back in the States, Mark called her one evening. He was laughing as he said, "Monique baby, sweetheart, what are ya doing? Hooking? I just balanced our checkbook. You haven't taken any money out of our account for two weeks." He was teasing her, of course.

Monique said she brought the Suzhou pearls back home to Minnesota and kept them in her purse. One afternoon, she went to a bar to have a drink, and as she was sitting on a bar stool, guys kept coming up to her and hitting on her. As each guy would come up to her she would say, "Would you like to buy some real pearls for your wife?"

Only one guy was hesitant about buying a necklace for two hundred and fifty dollars cash. Monique told him that she would leave his two hundred and fifty dollars on the bar while he took the necklace to the jeweler down the street. If the jeweler said that the pearls were fakes or not worth at least five hundred dollars, then she would give him his money back.

Thirty minutes later, the guy came back and said, "Lady, I don't know where you got these pearls, but that jeweler said these are worth at least one thousand dollars. These pearls will keep me outta the dog house for the next six months." Monique said in that one hour at the bar, she made over three thousand dollars—cash.

At the Zipper Factory, people stare as Monique and I walk around the collection of shops. I buy some wrapping paper that illustrates a boy with a bone on top of his head. This paper is a literal translation of the word "bonehead" and makes me laugh.

Monique and I pass by a shop that sells bras, and the three women who work there look gobsmacked when they see us, although I am sure it isn't because of me. One of the women says something in Chinese to us and holds out two crossed fingers as if she has just sighted two vampires. This hand signal means, "Don't come any closer."

When we are out of hearing distance of the bra shop, Monique asks me what the Chinese woman said. I tell her that she said, "Not have . . . not have your size." Monique turns around, stomps back to the shop, throws them the bird, and yells, "—you!"

Oops. Not only is Monique gorgeous, she is strong, too. She could have taken those three tiny women down at the same time and still had energy to burn.

August 16, 1998: Dino-the-Houdini

Jin took me to see the bird market where not only birds are sold but other pets as well. I told Jin that we once had a pet parakeet, and that his name was Dino-the-Houdini.

Dino was Heather's parakeet, and he often escaped from his cage. One day, Dino escaped again and flew into a large sliding glass door.

Wolfgang, our black cocker spaniel, was a bird dog by nature, and when Dino slammed into the glass and dive-bombed to the floor, Wolfgang's instincts went on red alert. Impulses inside his bird-dog brain flashed: THE BIRD IS DOWN . . . GET THE BIRD . . . THE BIRD IS DOWN . . . GET THE BIRD.

Martin was home by himself, and he saw Dino go down, too. Wolfgang raced over to Dino and quickly had him in his mouth. Martin chased Wolfgang around our four-bedroom house yelling, "Wolfgang, drop it! Drop it!" As a proud working dog, Wolfgang trotted around the house with his tiny trophy. Wolfgang finally dropped Dino, and when Martin picked him up, his little body was limp.

Martin didn't want Heather to come home from school and find Dino-the-Houdini dead. So he put Dino in his birdcage, placed the cage on the front seat of his truck, and tore off toward the veterinarian's office. Maybe something could be done to help Dino, but if not, then Martin would buy another bird just like Dino. Heather would never know what happened.

As Martin was speeding toward the doctor's office, he heard, "Peep . . . peep . . . peep." When Martin looked over at the birdcage, Dino-the-Houdini was sitting on his swing. Not only could Dino-the-Houdini escape from his cage, he could escape death, too. Jin liked that story.

August 21, 1998: Sometimes I Get My Way

I want to see the Shanghai Museum, and I ask Jin to drive me there. Jin pictures me going into the museum by myself while he waits in the parking lot. No, no. That isn't going to happen. I will be buying two passes into the museum.

When Jin is parked in the museum parking lot, I say, *"OK, OK. Let's see the museum."*

"Taitai can see the museum," Jin says. *"It's too expensive for two people."*

I say, *"Jin, mei guanxi."* "It doesn't matter, never mind." I take off my seat belt, get comfortable in the backseat, and say, *"If Jin won't go with me, I won't go."*

Jin is silent for a few moments before he says, *"So, if Jin won't go, then taitai won't go?"*

I look out the car window at the museum and say, *"Exactly."*

"But it's too expensive," Jin says.

I say nothing because I am not going to argue with him. I am either going to get my way or not.

Jin pulls on his left ear a few times and says, *"So, if Jin won't go, then taitai won't go?"*

"Exactly," I say. This is not an argument. I am insisting on getting my way, which is not the same thing as being argumentative.

Finally, Jin says, *"OK, OK. Jin will go with taitai."*

I put my hand on his shoulder and say, *"Jin, thank you. Let's go."*

August 30, 1998: Love Me, Love My Paintings

This afternoon, Martin is downstairs watching *CNN,* and I am upstairs when I hear The Chinese Knock. Martin answers the door and yells upstairs, "Honey, Jin's here." I scuffle in my bunny slippers down the stairs. Jin and Martin are standing by the front door, which is still open.

"Happy birthday!" Jin says, and he steps back into the hallway where he picks up something. He holds up a framed watercolor painting. It is the painting I admired by an artist named Lee. Jin says, *"I know taitai likes flowers and paintings. At the framing shop, taitai admires this painting. Jin thinks, 'Taitai will like this.'"*

I thought I would never see Lee's painting again after I left the framing shop. *"Jin, this painting is beautiful. Thank you. The gold frame you chose for this painting is perfect, too. You are very thoughtful. Jin, you know, I wanted this painting."* Jin nods in agreement. *"Jin . . . thank you, thank you."*

Martin says, "Oh, my honey. More paintings?"

The last time I counted, I had fifty-one paintings on the walls of our apartment. I also have about a hundred paintings rolled up in art boxes, stashed in the cubbyhole under the stairs. Martin doesn't know about those.

Jin says, *"What did Martin say?"*

"Martin says this is a beautiful painting. Thank you for my birthday gift. I will put this painting right by the door. I will see it every time I come home." I point to a spot on the wall next to the door.

After Jin leaves, I sit down on the couch next to Martin and pick up one of my Chinese books. As I begin looking for the page where I left off, Martin puts his arm around me and says, "How are we going to get all this stuff home?"

I say, "In a big box."

"That is going to be a huge box," he says. Martin hugs my shoulder and says, "I know what you're thinking . . . love me, love my paintings."

"Actually, Marty, I'm thinking love me, love my paintings, love my books, love George, and you should know that you have more to love than you know. I have a hundred paintings in the cubbyhole under the stairs. Would you like to see them?"

September 12, 1998: Emily the Hairy Crab

Jin, Zhu, Estelle, and I want to see Tea Island and the famous caves close to Hangzhou. We all ride in Jin's car, and the guys take turns driving.

Jin is safeguarding my purse.

Pickpockets and purse-snatchers are everywhere. Jin carries my purse for me when we are in places where I am easily distracted by shopping or sight-seeing.

The caves have sculptures and bas-reliefs of Buddhas and Bodhisattvas that have taken Buddhist monks four hundred years to complete. I especially like the large reposing Buddha inside this cave. Jin and Estelle take the same pose in front of this statue. The pose of this Buddha is called the Lucky Repose and is a reference to a story about a giant who wants to see Buddha, but this giant does not want to bow to anyone. The giant, after all, is a giant of a man—a great one. The giant says, "Why should I bow to Buddha?"

When the giant comes to see Buddha, the giant enters Buddha's room, and Buddha is lying down. He has his left hand on his left leg while his right hand supports his head. This is the Lucky Repose which demonstrates Buddha's humility. When the giant sees Buddha in the Lucky Repose, he realizes that Buddha is greater than he is. The giant is the small one because he is without humility, and he bows to Buddha.

Jin is taking the Lucky Repose of an enlightened one.

Zhu, Sharon, and Jin

In the caves, there is also a seat between two Buddhas. Perhaps the idea is that whoever sits in the middle of the Buddhas will be, for the moment, in a place of enlightenment—being neither to the right nor the left—the perfect place. A Dzogchen Buddhist would call this place the "self-perfected state."

A seat between two Buddhas—The Perfect Place

We have lunch at an outdoor restaurant by West Lake and then take a boat ride on the lake. The man who takes us on the boat ride tells Estelle that her necklace is made of fake pearls. A lot of people in China think they are an authority on pearls. Estelle's pearls aren't faux pearls, but none of us corrects him.

When we are ready to have dinner, we find a restaurant close to our hotel, walk up to the second floor, and are seated in a private dining room. Because I am the oldest person in the group, I can order for us from a menu I can't read or I can delegate this responsibility to someone else. Delegation seems like the smart thing to do. I ask Jin to order, and because we will be walking back to the hotel from this restaurant, Jin and Zhu can drink beer with their dinners. Jin orders, among other things, hairy crabs.

Shortly after our order is taken, the manager of the restaurant brings a female crab to our table and says, *"Is this the kind of crab you want to eat?"* She isn't moving, so I think she is dead until she winks at me. With that blink of her eye, I know she is not only alive, but she has a personality and a name. She is Emily. Suddenly, Emily begins to desperately move her legs in all directions. Yes. We are going to eat Emily and three of her cousins. Jin tells the manager that this is the kind of crab we want to eat.

Four dead hairy crabs soon arrive at our table, and as the oldest member of our group, I have the first pick of the crabs. I take a male crab. I have never met him and don't know his name. I don't look to see who is eating Emily with the personality as Jin opens my crab for me.

Throughout dinner, Jin says to Zhu, *"Gan bei,"* "Bottoms up," and Zhu and Jin guzzle a very small glass of beer. Almost as soon as the bottom of the glass hits the table, the woman who is serving us our dinner fills up the little glasses with beer again. Jin is doing fine, but Zhu begins to look a little green.

Finally Zhu says, *"I'll be back,"* and he leaves the table. When he returns, he says he feels better.

After dinner, the guys want to continue their evening, but Estelle and I want to get some sleep. Jin and Zhu walk us to our room, and Jin returns my purse to me at the door.

October 3, 1998: Prayers for Dad

I have known for a while that my stepfather has cancer. Around two o'clock this morning, Shanghai time, Mom calls, and she is crying. Dad is in the hospital and not expected to live. I say, "Mom, do you want me to come back?"

"Could you?" she says.

Last week, when I talked with Dad, he said he was doing all right.

Martin puts my luggage in the trunk of Jin's car, and Jin helps me to get a plane ticket at a travel agency.

On the way to the airport, Martin holds my hand as we sit in the backseat. When Jin stops at a stoplight, I give him two hundred yuan and ask him if he could take his mother to the temple for me. I would like for her to have my stepfather's name written in The Book. With his name in The Book, the monks will pray for him to have a wonderful next life, and they will pray for him every day for one year. One hundred yuan is for the monks, and the other one hundred yuan is for Jin to give to his mother for any expenses she might incur by going to the temple for me. I write my stepfather's name on a piece of paper that I give to Jin.

October 4, 1998: The Last Word I Heard Was My Name

When I arrive at the airport in Texas, Mom is waiting for me, and she takes me straight to the hospital. When I am at my stepfather's side, I say, "Hi, Dad, I'm here from Shanghai to see you."

His eyes are closed as he says, "Sharon." This is the last word I ever heard him say.

He died a few days later. After his memorial service, I stayed with my mother for a week.

October 20, 1998: A Blonde Joke

On the flight from Houston to San Francisco, I fly first class. At an en route stop, I am told that I can deplane as long as I return to my seat in two hours with my ticket stub, which shows my seat number as 3B. No problem.

Most people have heard the joke about the blonde who buys a ticket in economy but sits in an empty seat in first class. The flight attendant repeatedly asks her to return to her seat in economy, and she refuses.

Finally, the pilot comes out to save the day, and he steps up to the blonde. "Where are you going?" he says.

With a squeaky voice the blonde says, "I'm going to San Francisco," as she giggles and bats her eyelashes at the handsome pilot.

"Well," says the dashing pilot as he puts both hands on his hips, "everyone in first class is going to Los Angeles." The blonde jumps up from her seat and runs back to economy.

I deplane to eat lunch at the airport, return to the gate, and amble down the ramp. When I arrive at 3B, however, a brunette is sitting in my seat. "Excuse me," I say. "I think you're sitting in my seat." All of the first-class passengers train their eyes on us.

The brunette looks perplexed and says, "Let me see your ticket."

I show her my ticket stub, and she produces hers, which is also stamped 3B. She says, "Where are you going?"

I say, "I'm going to San Francisco."

The brunette snorts as she laughs, and she says, "We're going to Los Angeles."

Everyone in first class bursts out laughing. Heads in economy lean into the aisle to see what is so funny.

I can't leave the plane fast enough. As I turn left to deplane, a handsome pilot sticks his head out the cockpit door and says, "Hey, what's the joke? I like a good joke."

1998 October 22: Who is SOL?

It is good to be back in Shanghai. Last night, Jin picked me up at the airport and gave me a prayer mala of yellow beads, the color of royalty. Jin said, *"Your stepfather's name is in The Book. My mother bought this mala for you at the temple."*

This morning, before Martin leaves for work, he asks me to buy a comb for him because he lost his, and when Jin and I check Lotus Super Center for combs, there are none. There are, however, a lot of hairbrushes. Then we go to Babaiban. No combs. We check a few street kiosks. No combs. Then we go to City Supermarket where they have Magnum ice cream bars, which I buy, but no combs. Where do Chinese people buy combs? Plastic combs are made in China. Is there a comb shortage?

On the way home from City Supermarket, I thought it would be fun for Jin to know some American slang, and I say, *"Jin, because we can't find a comb for Martin, tonight you can say to him in English,* 'Martin, you are SOL.'"

Jin repeats this English sentence after me, and his pronunciation is good. Jin says, *"What is the meaning?"*

"If I say, for example, 'You are SOL,' *this means you have bad luck."* I take out a piece of paper and write "You are SOL" in English and Chinese characters, 你运气不好, and pass the piece of paper to him when he is at a stoplight. I don't tell him that SOL means, "Shit out of Luck." How could I explain that?

I also teach Jin the present verb tenses for this expression, and he practices them several times by saying, "I am SOL. You are SOL. He is SOL. She is SOL. We are SOL. You are all SOL. They are SOL."

"So, Jin, when you pick up Martin tonight, you can say in English, 'Martin . . . your comb. You are SOL.' *OK?"*

I look at Jin's eyes in his rearview mirror, and his eyes sparkle as he says, *"Sure, sure. Jin will say this to Martin. Every time Jin speaks to Martin in English, Martin says, 'Jin, very good.' Then Martin gives me a thumbs-up."*

As I walk up the stairs to The Tower, Jin says, "Bye-bye. See you."

"OK. See you later," I say.

Jin says, "No, no. Not later. See you tomorrow."

Not only does Jin correct my Mandarin, he corrects my English, too. As I wave good-bye to Jin, I say, *"Jin's English is good. See you tomorrow."*

When Martin comes home, he says, "Jin said I was SOL. I wonder who taught him some bad English." The answer is that my Rascal is the one who decided to teach Jin some . . . interesting English. On some days, my Rascal is just not sleepy. That's not my fault, is it?

Martin says, "Since you're his English teacher, it must have been you. You know, he might teach the other drivers to say, 'You are SOL.' He might even teach his daughter, and she'll repeat that to her English teacher at school or, even worse, his daughter will teach the other kids at school."

"Oops, I didn't think about that."

"Honey, you better hope Jin has a bad memory."

I walk over to Martin and sit next to him on the couch. "Marty, Jin keeps a mental log of every Chinese word I have ever said. The other day, I use a Chinese verb I never used before, and when Jin uses the same word, I tell him that I don't know that verb, and he says, 'How can you not know this word? You used it yesterday.'

"Jin also remembers every English word I have ever taught him." I don't tell Martin about the tapes Jin has of every English lesson I have ever taught him. Martin puts his arm around me. I say, "Tomorrow, I was going to teach Jin to say, 'What a bonehead.'"

Martin looks at me and says nothing.

"OK, OK," I say. "I won't teach Jin any more American slang. I wouldn't want him to be SOL."

October 23, 1998: A Big Laugh

"Jin, what did Martin say when you told him he was SOL?"

Jin says, *"Martin gave me a big laugh."*

October 26, 1998: Who Is Sick?

The other day, Jin's English lesson was on how to use regular verbs in the present tense along with some useful adjectives. As usual, I gave him a recording of his lesson.

This morning, as I'm putting on my seat belt in the backseat, Jin says in English, "I am sick."

I say, *"Oh, this is not good. If you're sick, you shouldn't drive."*

Jin says, "No, no. I am sick, you are sick, he is sick, she is sick, we are sick, you all are sick, they are sick."

"Jin, your English is excellent. You are speaking with my accent, too."

Jin says, "Taitai is a good teacher."

"I'm not a good teacher. Jin is smart. Jin studies hard, too," I say.

Jin takes me to the three-story silk fabric store, which is called the Shang Hai Zhen Si Shang She You Xian Gong Si and is located on Tian Ping Lu in Shanghai. The translation of this long name is the Shanghai Silk Commercial Building Company Limited. Mrs. Wang will be making two blouses for me, and I want to pick out the fabric.

In front of the silk shop, Jin squeezes the car into a parking spot by a post. We go upstairs to the third floor where there are many bolts of silk fabric, and I find some teal and maroon silk for blouses. Someone cuts the fabric off the bolt, I pay for the fabric, and we leave the store.

Jin gets behind the wheel, turns on the ignition, backs the car out of the tight parking space, and hits the post. We get out of the car to inspect the damage, and there is a large dent in the back fender of his car. As we are looking at the dent, Jin says in English, "This is bad. Jin is SOL."

The parking situation in Shanghai is horrible, but Jin's English is good.

October 30, 1998: Someone Is SOL

About two months ago, I attended a Shanghai Expatriate Association meeting where I met Marcia, a former teacher like myself, and we hit it off. She is funny and likes to laugh. At that meeting, we planned a luncheon for over a hundred women to be held at the

Garden Hotel. Marcia asked me if I would pick her up on the day of the luncheon, so that we could go together.

Today is the luncheon, and Jin drives over to Marcia's building to pick her up. Once Marcia is in the car with me, I introduce Marcia to Jin. Marcia speaks no Chinese.

The traffic is slow, and as Marcia and I are talking in the backseat, we notice two construction men who are wearing hard hats and pushing on an all-glass phone booth. The glass panels of the booth are at least two inches thick. One young man stops pushing to pick his nose while the other young man continues to push on the glass. While we are at a standstill in the middle of traffic, the phone booth topples over and splatters glass shards all over the sidewalk and street. Jin glances over his shoulder at Marcia and says, "He is SOL."

Marcia looks at me and says, "Did he say what I think he said?"

I'm not admitting to anything.

"Sharon," Marcia says, "you have created a monster."

I shrug my shoulders and say, "Marcia, I'm taking the Fifth even if we are in China."

Lunch was good. Chicken was supposed to be on our plates. At least it tasted like chicken. However, there was neither a head nor a foot on our plates. So I wasn't sure what we were eating. We used knives and forks, and there were no chopsticks in sight.

November 9, 1998: The Eyes of Buddha

My favorite furniture shop in Shanghai is Ann Ly's Antique Warehouse. The first time I met Ann Ly, I stepped into the doorway of her office and spoke to her in Mandarin. Like most Chinese people, she was surprised to hear me speak Chinese.

As I walk through her showroom today, high up on a shelf, I see a red wooden box, and I want to see it up close. This is the first red Chinese box I have ever seen.

I knock on Ann Ly's open office door. *"Ann Ly, nihao. You have a large red box. Would you give me a look at this box?"*

"Wen Li Xia, nihao. I would be most happy to give you a look."

We walk into her gigantic showroom, and as we step down one walkway, I see a large Buddha on top of a gigantic cabinet. This Buddha has a red scarf tied around his eyes. *"Ann Ly, what is the meaning of the red scarf wrapped around Buddha's eyes?"*

"Shh, don't let Buddha hear you," she says. *"The red scarf covers his eyes. I don't want him to see that I have not been praying."*

I start to laugh but quickly cover my mouth. I don't want Buddha to hear me. I put my arm around Ann Ly and whisper, *"Do you sell red scarves too? I need one of those scarves. I didn't know you could do that."*

1998 November 10: I Am SOL

I almost have dinner ready, and I call Jin on his cell phone. *"Jin, hello. Tonight I would like Martin to be home by five thirty for dinner. Please tell Martin, 'No McDonald's.'"*

After a moment of silence, he says, "Taitai . . . you are SOL."

November 13, 1998: A Pearl Bra

Han and her husband, who live in Hangzhou, brought pearls for me to see today. The most unusual item they brought was a bra made of pearls.

I bought quite a few strands of pearls from them as well as some men's ties made with pearls. I also bought a necklace of large pearls to give to my daughter to wear on her wedding day.

December 13–25, 1998: A Shiver of Sharks in the Maldives

Martin's employer is paying for us to vacation anywhere in Asia, and someone has suggested that a vacation in the Maldive Islands would be wonderful. The Republic of the Maldives is an archipelago of about twelve hundred islands in the Indian Ocean. Many of these islands are vacation resorts. Because this country is near the equator and slightly southwest of India, we packed swimsuits, cotton clothing, and books, and left for our vacation on December 13.

We arrive in the middle of the night at the Ibrahim Nasir International Airport, located on the largest island in the Maldives. This is the tiniest airport I have ever seen. I quickly name this the Barbie and Ken Airport. We board a speedboat that will take us to our island resort, and this boat throws us around as it hits waves head on. Martin holds on to me to keep me from being tossed overboard.

After forty minutes of terror, we arrive at our resort where only men are employed, and I feel out of place. Muslim women are not allowed on these resort islands. The brochure failed to mention that the Maldives is a country of Sunni Muslims. When we check in at the front desk, we are told that nudity is not allowed on the beach, which is fine with us.

We are taken to a bungalow with a linoleum floor from the 1950s. When we see the beds, we realize that we forgot to ask about the sleeping accommodations when we booked this vacation. Our room has twin beds and is not the room pictured in the brochure.

In Shanghai, Martin and I sleep in a king-sized bed, and if my feet get cold, I put them on Martin to warm them up. What am I going to do about cold feet here? I didn't pack any socks, either. The air conditioner is blasting freezing air into our room, and we hear the constant sound of dripping water coming from our air conditioner. In a day or two, I expect to see stalactites forming on this air conditioner. The sink in our bathroom is constantly dripping water, also.

Martin and I collapse onto our separate beds in the same clothes we wore on the airplane. I take the bed farthest away from the door because if anyone comes into our room during the night, Martin is the first line of defense. It is his duty as a man.

On the following morning, we decide to unpack and change our clothes, but I can't unlock my suitcase, which I recently purchased in Beijing. The suitcase has a built-in lock by the handle, and with the jostling on the airplane, the combination has retumbled. I have no patience for this. Martin takes over and soon has my luggage unlocked. I won't be traveling with this suitcase again.

Just as Martin opens my luggage, and I am going to change my clothes, we hear three light knocks on our door. Then we hear a key jiggle in the lock. A man walks in with a broom. With no bolt lock on our door, anyone with a key can come into our room at any time. Mr. Interloper says hello and starts sweeping up the sand that has come in under the door during the night. (This happens several times during our stay.)

On our first morning on the island, we have breakfast in a dining room where Martin and I are the only Americans. Everyone else in the dining room is from Europe. I know this because of their graceful walk. When Americans walk, we galumph and thump around to get where we want to go as fast as we can because we have places to go, people to see, and things to do, and everyone else needs to get out of our way.

Also, only Martin and I are speaking English. Obviously, the Maldives is a popular vacation spot for Europeans. The distance between the Maldives and Germany, for example, is a little less than five thousand miles. The distance between the States and the Maldives is almost ten thousand miles. (We never see any other Americans on this island while we are there.)

The customary European late-evening mealtime is practiced on this island. In Shanghai, Martin and I eat dinner around six o'clock, but in this country, with the European custom of late evening meals, dinner is at nine o'clock Shanghai-tummy-time. There are three restaurants on this island, and none of them is open when we want to eat. After breakfast, on our way back to our room, we step into a gift shop, and behold—imported from America—chocolate with caramel candy bars. I buy three of them.

The beds are the first hint that this is going to be a so-so vacation. But when Mr. Interloper and the twilight dinners are added to the mix as well as the small supply of American candy bars—along with no department store where I can buy socks—this vacation is on a level so far below a so-so vacation that we don't even know what this level is. We only have one question: How soon can we get off this island?!

Trying to make the best of things, Martin signs up for a scuba diving lesson. I have a fear of drowning, so scuba diving is not something I would ever do for fun. While I don't want Martin to go scuba diving, I remind myself that I'm his wife, not his mother, and I say nothing, even though I fear that his scuba diving lesson will end his life.

The next day, Martin and I take a tour on a glass-bottom boat to see the coral reef, which we can't see because of the cloudy water. Add this to the growing list of reasons to exclude the Maldive Islands as a vacation spot. The only way to see the coral reef is by scuba diving, which Martin might enjoy if he survives it. Martin and I do, however, see a shiver of grey reef sharks. These three sharks are about four feet long. This is a shark species that has been known to attack humans if provoked or threatened.

For the beach, Martin and I are each given a plastic lawn chair that can be purchased at Walmart for seven dollars. For the greater part of each day, we sit on these chairs in the shade. One day I see a hermit crab next to my lawn chair, and I watch him until he is out of sight. Wandering hermit crabs are the island's version of a zoo.

The average temperature during the middle of the day is eighty-four degrees Fahrenheit. The air is humid and muggy. Sometimes it rains too, which makes the humidity and mugginess oppressive. Water droplets loiter in the air, wait for me, and glom onto me as I walk by them.

At least once a day, I go out for a quick swim in the ocean while Martin sits in his plastic chair and reads. One day I swim out as far as I can until I come to a barricade made of boulders and heavy-gauge fencing. When I come back from my swim, I say, "Marty, I saw quite a few little fish out there by the boulders."

Since we have arrived, Martin has only gone into the water up to his knees even though he is a powerful swimmer. He splashes water over himself to cool off. Martin stops reading and says, "What are those boulders for?"

"That's a shark barricade," I say. "Only little fish and shark puppies can squeeze through. There's also heavy-gauge fencing attached to those boulders. When I was next to the fencing, I didn't see any sharks trying to get through the barricade. If an adult shark wants to get in here, it would have to jump over the boulders." Martin shifts uncomfortably in his lawn chair before turning back to his reading.

Other than the glass-bottom boat trip, meals right before bedtime, some water splashing, raiding the gift shop for candy bars, and the zoo, Martin and I read books. By the seventh day, I have finished reading my twelve books, and I am well into reading Martin's books. I am getting a fierce tan even though I sit in the shade. (My tan lasted eighteen months.)

Every day after lunch, we go out to the wharf and look at the tropical fish swimming inches from the surface of the water. People throw bits of bread to the fish, which they gobble up.

One time, all of the tropical fish swiftly swam away when a shiver of sharks showed up. None of the grey reef sharks ate any of the bread. Martin gazed at the shiver of sharks as they flipped their tails in unison. I said, "Marty, I wonder if sharks hunt in packs like wolves."

We take an excursion to the island of Malé, the capital of the Maldives, which is the center for trade, government, and education. This island is also the location of the Barbie and Ken airport. Before we leave for the capital, I am told to cover my arms and legs because the modesty of women is important in this Islamic country. This requirement is something else not mentioned in the brochure. I say, "Marty, who suggested we vacation in the Maldives?" He doesn't remember. This is probably a good thing.

This slow boat, thank you very much, to Malé putters along as it makes its way to the capital, and we see some islands about the size of an eight-car garage. On one of these tiniest of islands, there is a tiny hut. A glum-looking dog sits with slumped shoulders as he watches a man hang shirts on a clothesline. If I could have, I would have told this dog, "I know how you feel. There's not much to do around here."

Before we arrive at the capital, we are told that we cannot wander around Malé unaccompanied and must hire a tour guide—also not mentioned in the brochure. When we step off the boat, tour guides clamor on the dock to be picked as tour guides for this miniature capital. We choose a guide who charges us twelve dollars for a tour of Malé, and we follow him as he walks to the center of the city, which doesn't take long.

Our guide points out the attractions, although I don't remember what they are now. He frequently stops in front of a street shop and says, "Do you want to buy anything here?" We go up to a second-floor shop that has black coral for sale, which is on the endangered species list. I buy a colorful wrap skirt and two towel hooks with turtles painted on them. There are no socks for sale. They have no American candy bars, either.

The few women I see on this capital island are Islamic women. Their heads are covered with black scarves or hijabs, and they wear black robes called abayas. They don't look at anyone as they walk.

Malé is one of the smallest urban capitals in the world. Including all of the islands, the Republic of Maldives has a little over three hundred square kilometers of land, which is a little less than two times the area of Washington DC, and only ten percent of this land is arable. The population of the entire archipelago is slightly more than 290,000. Why did we go to the Maldives for a *vacation*? Someone, please remind me. When the tour is over, our guide asks if we have any questions. "I have a question," I say. "Is there a hospital on Malé?"

"Oh, yes," he says. "We have a modern hospital. We even have a decompression chamber." Our guide looks toward the Indian Ocean. "You know, the Maldives is famous for its scuba diving, and a decompression chamber is important for this type of thing." The day after our Malé visit, Martin cancels his scuba diving lesson, and my feet do a happy dance.

By the last day of our vacation, Martin is finished reading his books and is making good headway through my books. I am almost finished reading his books, and I have eaten every American candy bar on the island.

As we board the tiny aircraft at the Barbie and Ken Airport, we congratulate ourselves on having muddled through the twilight meals, lack of privacy, separate beds, an inadequate supply of American candy bars, and sand on the floor of our room, as well as no department store, no socks, and my cold feet. We vow to never return to the Maldives.

When our jet lands in Shanghai, we are delighted to be home again where . . . once again . . . I can warm up my feet at night.

February 1, 1999: Some Cars Drink Beer

When I don't feel like looking up a word in my Chinese dictionary, I make up a Chinese word or use a Chinese word in a different way. Jin and I call this *Wen Jin Hua*. My Chinese last name is *Wen*, Jin's family name is *Jin*, and *hua* means *language*, so that *Wen Jin Hua* means *Sharon* [and] *Jin's Language.*

Jin says something about stopping at the transportation office to get something for his car. I assume he needs to get gasoline, but I don't want to look up the word for gasoline, even though my colossal dictionary of sixty thousand Chinese words is next to me in the backseat. I used to have a small dictionary in the car, but I gave that dictionary to Martin.

"*Jin,*" I say, "*does your car need beer?*" Jin looks baffled. I say, "*This is Wen Jin Hua.*"

"*Right, right,*" Jin says. "*The car needs beer.*"

So now, whenever Jin needs to get gas for his car, he says, "*The car needs beer.*"

This is one less word that I need to know, and I still haven't looked up the word for gasoline.

February 4, 1999: The Chief and the Smoke Alarm

At The Tower there is a head fix-it guy. I call him The Chief. The smoke alarm is still going off when it shouldn't and not going off when it should. The time has come for The Chief to fix this pesky thing.

I call The Chief on the phone, and when he answers, I say, "*Sir, please fix the smoke alarm. It must not go off anymore. When there is no smoke, the smoke alarm goes off. When there is smoke, the alarm doesn't make any noise. Please fix the smoke alarm today.*" For almost two years, the smoke alarm has been going off a couple of times a week.

I soon hear The Chinese Knock, and when I open the door, The Chief comes in followed by four other maintenance men. The Chief and his warriors take off their shoes, and we crowd into my narrow kitchen. I stand next to the window.

The Chief hops up onto the countertop and opens the door to the cabinet where the smoke detector lives. As he examines the naughty alarm, his warriors take turns making suggestions until, finally, a decision is made, and The Chief summarily pulls the plug on the smoke alarm.

The four warriors walk out of the kitchen as The Chief closes the door to the smoke alarm's home, hops back down to the floor, and says, "*Now be careful.*" The Chief and his warriors put their shoes back on and file out the door.

When I shut the door after them, I think, The Chief has done what I asked him to do, which is to make the smoke alarm not go off anymore. The alarm has never worked right in the first place, and now it doesn't work at all. Isn't that the same thing? I sum up my thoughts with the frequently heard words of *mei guanxi*, "It doesn't matter, never mind."

When Martin walks through the door this evening, I am getting dinner ready, and I say, "Guess what, Marty. The Chief fixed the smoke alarm."

Martin stands by the door to the kitchen. "Really? What did he do?"

"He unplugged it."

"He unplugged it? What do you think of that?"

I say, *"Mei guanxi."*

Martin looks puzzled. "What does that mean?"

"It doesn't matter."

Martin puts his briefcase down. "No, no. I'm asking you, what does that mean?"

"I told you, Marty, it doesn't matter."

"Honey, I'm going to ask you one more time. What . . . does . . . that mean?"

"Marty, I told you. It . . . doesn't . . . matter."

Martin lets out a weary sigh and says, "Never mind."

"Exactly," I say. "That's what I've been trying to tell you."

February 19, 1999: Soybeans

Stella and I go to a restaurant for dinner, and among the dishes she orders is a green pod vegetable dish. I am back to not eating meat. Having never seen this vegetable before, I don't know what it is. Not knowing what I am eating, however, is nothing new to me. Our waitress is standing close by our table.

I pick up one of the pods with my chopsticks and put it in my mouth. This vegetable is impossible to chew, and the waitress and Stella start to giggle. I have to take this leathery thing out of my mouth, and I say, "Stella, what is this?"

"That is soybean," she says. *"You only eat the beans inside."*

February 20, 1999: Aunt Misery

Tonight was our final English Night Party. Dinner was catered by my favorite restaurant, and we ordered a cake from the Chinese bakery down the street.

Before dinner, I entertained our guests with an American Jack Tale. I dressed up as my storytelling character, Aunt Misery, who has red hair and a prosthetic nose that looks like it belongs to a witch. This nose was made for me by a prosthetic artist and fits over my nose perfectly. It looks like a real nose, too. When I finished telling my story, some of the guys tried on Aunt Misery's nose and red wig. The guys looked better in the nose and wig than Aunt Misery.

Sharon Winters as Aunt Misery

I told stories at a private party one time as Aunt Misery. A plastic surgeon came up to me after I finished telling my stories, gave me his card, and said, "I can help you."

March 20, 1999: Farewell My Good Friends

As a farewell dinner, Jin and his family take Martin and me to a Chinese restaurant where Jin orders beer for everyone except his daughter. When the beer arrives, I say, *"Gan bei."* "Bottoms up."

Jin laughs and says, *"No, no. No gan bei."* Jin lifts his glass and says, *"To the friendship between our families . . . To a safe journey back to the States for taitai and Martin."*

Glasses click around the table, and I take a sip of my beer. Martin drinks about a third of his beer. In the nineteen years since I have known Martin, this is the first time I have ever seen him drink beer.

Jin's daughter is studying English in school, but she is shy and only speaks to me in Chinese. Jin's wife looks lovely as usual.

After dinner, we go to Jin's home, where he sings for us. He has a beautiful voice. I will miss Jin and my Chinese friends who have made China a place where I lived rather than a place where I stayed.

March 22, 1999: The Shanghai Museum Curator

A museum curator came to our apartment today, and two other men came with him. Before Martin and I can take our antique furniture and Chinese artifacts back to the States, everything I have purchased in China must be inspected by the curator of the Shanghai Museum.

Any item the curator considers to be both an antique and permissible for exportation, he stamps with hot wax. Antiques without a wax stamp are not allowed to be taken out of the country. Exportable artifacts are items that the curator believes to be in adequate supply in Chinese museums and collections. The aim of this inspection is to ensure the preservation of China's art history. The curator stamps all of the antiques I have purchased with dark red wax.

March 29, 1999: A Final Gift

This is one of the last days I will see Jin, and he is driving me around Shanghai to run a few last errands. I want to buy a mah-jongg set to take back to the States.

Jin turns down an alleyway I have never seen before and stops in the middle of a little street with no traffic, aside from a few bicycles. With the car in park, he rummages in the passenger seat and then passes something gold and the size of a baseball card to me. He says, *"Taitai, I want to give this to you. This is from the Buddhist temple."*

I take the engraved card, which is made of gold metal. At the bottom it says 24K. The shiny card feels heavy in my hand. A picture of Guanyin, the goddess of mercy, is etched on the front of the card along with four Chinese characters, 一生平安, *yi sheng ping an*. These characters mean *have a life of peace*. This peaceful life is also a safe life because the last character, 安, means *safe*. This is a pictograph of a woman with a roof over her head—a roof that will keep her safe and protected. Jin will no longer be with me every day to keep me safe, so this card will have to do that job for him.

Prayers for my happiness, prosperity, and good health are on the back of this card. At the bottom is the Wheel of Life that will spin tirelessly as it sends these prayers to the heavens where all of the Buddhas who have ever come to earth now live. The wheel represents the sacred light that emanates from the head of Buddha, a light that goes out to infinity. As the light of Buddha passes over these prayers, the prayers are transported and presented to all Buddhas who will acknowledge these prayers for me and watch over me.

Dye cut from each corner of the card is a heart, and along the edges of the card is the symbol of Buddha's heart and mind. This card is Jin's way of telling me that he wants me to always be happy, healthy, prosperous, and safe. I wish no less for him. *"Jin, I like this card. Because you have given this card to me, this card will always be special. I will keep this with me wherever I go. You have been good to me. Every single day I will miss you, but now I won't get lost because I have this card."*

Jin laughs. *"Taitai will get lost, but call Jin. I will help you."*

"Jin . . . you always help me. Thank you. Thank you for the card. Thank you for being my friend."

In perfect English, Jin says, "You are welcome."

Epilogue

I have been back in the States for a few days. I think in Chinese, dream in Chinese, and every morning I wake up with a heavy feeling of missing my Shanghai and Beijing friends.

Everyone talks too fast here. Sometimes I only catch snippets of what people are saying. I have forgotten some English words, and even worse, occasionally, when I'm speaking English, I switch the sound of the letter "L" with "R" or vice versa. Chinese speakers also transpose "L" with "R" when speaking English, and I have no explanation as to why this happens. Class becomes crass, blast becomes brass, cricket becomes click it, and crowd becomes cloud. The list is endless. Native Chinese speakers cannot say, "Red leather, yellow leather" really fast, three times.

Martin spoke English at work and at home, but he learned to slow down the speed at which he spoke English and to use common English words because his days were mostly spent around nonnative English speakers. The same was true for me, except that during my day, I seldom spoke English except with Martin and Stella. I noticed that even the women at the Shanghai Expatriate Association slowed down their speech after living in Shanghai for a few months because if they didn't, women would respond to whatever someone was saying with, "What?"

After being back in the States for a few days, my friend Sharon Wilson invited me to have lunch with her, which meant that we would each be paying for our own meal. Once we were at the restaurant, I asked Sharon to speak slowly. At the restaurant, I didn't want to look at the menu because my brain was tired. I told myself that I didn't have to read any English unless it was a traffic sign or a label on a can at the grocery store. I was in reverse culture shock, or whatever it's called.

The waitress at this restaurant had no idea about the challenge I was having with English, and she rattled off the specials like a Gatling gun. Even though I only understood a few words that she said, I told her, "I'll have the second thing you said." I was too embarrassed to ask her to speak slowly. Even though I didn't know what I ordered, I was pretty sure she didn't mention pig feet, pig brains, or chicken feet. How bad could it be? I was back in the States.

Minutes later, an appetizing corn beef sandwich was placed in front of me. This was the first sandwich I have eaten since I left for Shanghai two years ago. I excused myself to go wash my hands in the "wash hands room."

The sandwich was good, but it felt odd to be touching my food with my hands. There was an uncivilized feeling about it. I stabbed some lettuce on my plate with a fork. I wanted chopsticks. Forks were quite inefficient, and this lettuce would have been much easier to pick up with chopsticks.

I first met Sharon at Illinois State University when we were both teenagers, and she was a psychologist now. I was only half kidding when I told her, "I need a shrink." I knew I would be OK, but at that moment, I didn't feel OK. I wanted to be beamed back to Shanghai right that minute even though I was enjoying being with Sharon, and I had missed her.

After I had lunch with Sharon, I went to a department store to buy towels. When I walked up to a salesperson to ask her where the towels were, I couldn't remember the word for towels. The word came back to me when I was driving home.

Martin and I have carried over a habit of speech we picked up in Shanghai. This is a linguistic pattern I call Double Words. In Shanghai, everyone uses Double Words, and when these words are spoken, they can have any one of several meanings, such as, "I want to reassure you . . .

I am paying attention to what you are saying . . . I really mean what I am telling you . . . I understand what you want me to do . . . Thank you for your thoughtfulness . . . Everything will be fine." The meaning depends on the Double Words that are used and the context of these words. Examples of Double Words are, "Right, right . . . Yes, yes . . . Sure, sure . . . OK, OK . . . No, no . . . Good, good."

Martin and I often catch ourselves answering people with Double Words. So far, it seems like no one has even noticed. However, when someone says "yes" only once to us, we aren't sure that they are paying attention to what we have said.

Another thing I keep doing is adding Mandarin sentence-final particles to the ends of my sentences in English. I do this with Spanish, too. When the particle of *ma* comes at the end of a sentence in Mandarin, this means, "I asked you a question and would like a yes or no answer." Using *ma* at the end of a sentence is a handy convention I wish we had in English.

Another particle I keep putting at the end of English sentences is *ba*, which means, "What I have said is a suggestion. I respect you. I am not bossing you around." The particle *a* means, "Sure, sure, why not."

Martin has been spared this embarrassment. His problem is that no one will get in his truck with him because he has only driven a vehicle fifty miles in two years.

Today, I noticed that our backyard needs to be mowed. I look up lawn services in the phonebook and call a few places. I say, "How much do you charge to cut glass?" Everyone I call says, "We're a lawn service, lady," and they hang up on me.

When Martin comes home from work, I am close to tears, and he says, "Why are you upset?"

"Marty, I want to go back to Shanghai right now. I called three places to come out and cut the glass, and everyone hung up on me."

"What's wrong with the glass?"

I take him to the patio door and point to the backyard as I say, "Look how tall the glass is *ba*."

Martin puts his arms around me. "Don't worry, honey. This weekend I'll cut the glass. You'll be OK. Everything is all right."

I say, "You're right." Martin is still holding me as I say, *"Mei guanxi."*

He says, "What does that mean?"

"It doesn't matter."

Martin steps back and says, "No, no. We don't want to go through that again."

APPENDIX

I wrote "The Rules of China" to give to my friends in the Shanghai Expatriate Association.

1. If you think you understand a Chinese person, it is certain that you don't.

2. Never eat alone in a Chinese restaurant. People will feel sorry for you and think that you are friendless.

3. If a foreign woman wants to buy clothes off the rack in China, she had better wear a size zero to six. A woman of any size who wants to buy a half-slip or a full slip in China is SOL. Purses are a good bet.

4. To keep insects from raising families in your locally purchased flour, place your flour in the freezer for forty-eight hours. This will stop insects from raising families in your flour.

5. The Chinese love to bargain. This is Chinese theater. Never be without your calculator to use while shopping. Punch in your offer and pass the calculator to the merchant. This saves time.

6. Whenever you are a passenger in a vehicle, never look out the front window to view oncoming traffic unless you have low blood pressure. Look only out the side windows or put your nose in a book. If you choose the book method, you will leave Shanghai well read.

7. Never get into an argument with a Chinese person. You will not win.

8. On your arrival in Shanghai, purchase several bonsai trees. When culture shock is getting the better of you, sit in front of your Bonsai

tree and watch it grow. When your butt gets numb, move to the next tree. Repeat until your mind is calm. To buy your Bonsai trees, see rule number five.

9. Don't expect a restaurant to have a menu in English, and if there is a menu in English, don't expect the menu to make sense to anyone who can read English. Intuition and guesswork needs to be applied and then hope for the best. If you are fastidious about your food, life will be difficult for you in China.

10. Kentucky Fried Chicken restaurants can be found everywhere in China, but KFC doesn't have a menu in English or English-speaking employees. The menu does, however, have little flames shooting from spicy-hot items. These flames are warning signs. Learn to say, I don't want spicy-hot, by saying, *"Wǒ bú yào là,"* and hope you don't get a look that says, I don't understand a word you're saying. In the alternative, learn to love spicy food. It is everywhere.

11. As an alternative to avoiding restaurants without menus in English, carry pictures of a chicken, cow, fish, and pig. Have photographs of vegetables and fruits, too. As you point to your picture say, *"Nǐ yǒu ma?"* "Do you have?" They will shake their head yes or no.

12. If you like to laugh at yourself and the dumb things you do, you will have opportunities to laugh every day. Laugh wrinkles are prettier than worry wrinkles.

13. Taxi drivers who speak English? Not just no, but hell no.

14. During the rainy season in Shanghai, it is so muggy that you will pray for the rain to stop. When the rain stops, it is so hot and muggy, you will pray for rain. After a few months of living in Shanghai, wisdom will be gained, and you will no longer waste prayers. Learn how to be miserable without looking like you are insane.

15. If you want rain in Shanghai, leave your umbrella at home and take your sunglasses. From the heavens over Shanghai, rain will fall like white sheets from a clothesline in the sky.

16. If you need an ambulance, don't bother. A taxi is faster. If you are bleeding, only bleed on the floor of the taxi because if you bleed on the seat covers, there is an extra charge.

17. Two inches of rain water on the floor of a taxi is acceptable, but slapping your feet in the puddle and getting everyone else wetter is not. On the other hand, this might be fun.

18. Never, ever, at any time, look into the kitchen of a Chinese restaurant. If you do, you will only do this once.

19. With bicycles, trucks, cars, and pedestrians, there is not always a clear right-of-way. Whoever occupies the space first gets it—maybe. It helps to feel lucky when crossing a street.

20. If your driver sees you give the bird or hears you cuss, he or she will pick up on this faster than a two-year-old.

21. When your Chinese driver rolls down his car window to yell at a bicyclist who has bumped into his car, he might have something to say to the bicyclist about his mother. He is not inquiring about her health. Never repeat these phrases.

22. Taxi drivers always think they know where they're going, and if you don't know where *you are going,* your taxi driver will take the long way to your destination. Think of this as a scenic tour.

23. Most importantly, if you keep your sense of humor with you wherever you go, you will find that everything is an adventure. But if you lose your sense of humor, do everything you can to find it. Your survival and happiness in Shanghai depends on it. Step out, have fun, be silly, and you will light up the city of Shanghai for everyone. Shanghai is a city with billions of lights. Be one of them.

24. Finally, here is the most useful expression in the Mandarin language. Use it often. It will serve you well.

没关系

Méi guānxi

[máy gwān-sea]

It doesn't matter, never mind.

25760231R00156

Made in the USA
Charleston, SC
10 January 2014